*A tradition is only as old as when it was first invented,
and innovation is only as new as what we have forgotten.*
—Marcus Katz

We have here a detailed and exhaustive method by which the cards may be read. The beginner may feel somewhat alarmed at the mass of explanatory matter there is for him to study, but once the information has been acquired, the would-be cartomancer will find he possesses a sense of power and comprehension, that will give both confidence and dexterity to his attempts to unravel the thread of destiny.
—Professor P. R. S. Foli, *Fortune-Telling by Playing Cards*, 1903

LEARNING
Lenormand

Marcus Katz

Marcus Katz is a professional tarot teacher at the Far Away Centre, a contemporary training centre in the Lake District of England. As the Codirector of Tarot Professionals, the world's largest professional tarot organization, he has studied and taught tarot for thirty years and has delivered more than ten thousand face-to-face readings. His first book, *Tarosophy*, has been termed a "major contribution" to tarot by leading teachers. Marcus is also the cocreator of *Tarot-Town*, the social network for tarot, with more than ten thousand people worldwide sharing innovative tarot development.

Tali Goodwin

Tali Goodwin is the Marketing Director and Cofounder of Tarot Professionals, the largest professional tarot organization in the world. She has coauthored innovative teaching books such as *Tarot Flip*, which is regularly in the top ten best-selling tarot books on Kindle. Tali is a skilled researcher and is credited with bringing the long-hidden Waite-Trinick Tarot to publication in *Abiding in the Sanctuary: The Waite-Trinick Tarot*. She also coedited the leading tarot magazine, *Tarosophist International*, in 2010–2011.

To Write to the Authors

If you wish to contact the authors or would like more information about this book, please write to the authors in care of Llewellyn Worldwide, Ltd. and we will forward your request. The authors and publisher appreciate hearing from you and learning of your enjoyment of this book and how it has helped you. Llewellyn Worldwide, Ltd. cannot guarantee that every letter written to the authors can be answered, but all will be forwarded. Please write to:

Marcus Katz and Tali Goodwin
⅓ Llewellyn Worldwide
2143 Wooddale Drive
Woodbury, MN 55125-2989

Please enclose a self-addressed stamped envelope for reply,
or $1.00 to cover costs. If outside the USA, enclose
an international postal reply coupon.

LEARNING Lenormand

TRADITIONAL FORTUNE TELLING FOR MODERN LIFE

26. The Book - secrecy and knowledge

33. The Key - opportunity, unlocking a situation

34. The Fish - money and good fortune

MARCUS KATZ & TALI GOODWIN

Llewellyn Publications
Woodbury, Minnesota

Learning Lenormand: Traditional Fortune Telling for Modern Life © 2013 by Marcus Katz and Tali Goodwin. All rights reserved. No part of this book may be used or reproduced in any manner whatsoever, including Internet usage, without written permission from Llewellyn Publications, except in the case of brief quotations embodied in critical articles and reviews.

First Edition
Fourth Printing, 2021

Author photos © www.derwentphotography.co.uk
Book design by Bob Gaul
Cover background image © iStockphoto.com/benz190
Cover design by Kevin R. Brown
Editing by Laura Graves
Interior card art © See art credit list on pg. 279

Llewellyn Publications is a registered trademark of Llewellyn Worldwide Ltd.

Library of Congress Cataloging-in-Publication Data (Pending)
978-0-7387-3647-1

Llewellyn Worldwide Ltd. does not participate in, endorse, or have any authority or responsibility concerning private business transactions between our authors and the public.

All mail addressed to the author is forwarded, but the publisher cannot, unless specifically instructed by the author, give out an address or phone number.

Any Internet references contained in this work are current at publication time, but the publisher cannot guarantee that a specific location will continue to be maintained. Please refer to the publisher's website for links to authors' websites and other sources.

Llewellyn Publications
A Division of Llewellyn Worldwide Ltd.
2143 Wooddale Drive
Woodbury, MN 55125-2989
www.llewellyn.com

Printed in the United States of America

To Marie Anne Adelaide Lenormand and Johann Kaspar Hechtel.

"It's a bit green."

Acknowledgments

We would like to thank the staff at the British Museum's Prints and Drawings department for again kindly extending their time to assist us during the research for this book. The staff at the National Library of Scotland were excellent in taking time to set up microfiche rolls for us. We would like to acknowledge the Wellcome Trust collection and the Royal Society (London) for providing invaluable research material on the development of early game and fortune books, not all of which made it to this final publication but will be made available in our Lenormand courses. We would particularly like to acknowledge the Royal Society, which made such delicate works carefully available for our viewing and study.

We would also like to acknowledge Steph Myriel Es-Tragon for further research and translation work, and Andi Graf for providing another rare deck of early fortune-telling cards. Stella Luna also assisted us in locating versions of Partridge & Flamstead in the Australian National Library. The researchers at trionfi.com assisted in the correspondence of coffee-grounds reading meanings to the interpretations of the Lenormand, which we mention herein and cover more in our online courses.

Ciro Marchetti generously offered his expert design skills in the production of the Original Lenormand, which illustrate the card-by-card descriptions here and are now available as a deck.

We have been delighted to have received contemporary Lenormand images from Ciro Marchetti, Andi (Rootweaver) Graf, Robyn Tisch Hollister, Gidget London, Anna Simonova, and Carrie Paris, which grace this book. The links to their decks in development or for purchase can be located in the resources section of this book.

And to the New Lenormandists and Cartomanciens, we remain your *tres obeisant et humble* servants.

—Tali Goodwin and Marcus Katz

Five Notes Before We Begin

A Note for Absolute Beginners

This book was written to introduce you quickly and easily to a wonderful way of reading Lenormand cards for fortune-telling and divination. We have tested the methods in this book with hundreds of students to ensure that you will soon be reading the cards confidently. You do *not* need to have used tarot cards or any other divination method previously. In fact, if this is your first experience of card reading, you will be starting your journey in one of its most traditional and elegant courtyards.

A Note to Tarot Readers

You will discover that the Lenormand cards are not the same as the tarot in structure nor in their method of reading. In fact, we tend to refer to two different spaces when discussing the two systems: "T-space" and "L-space." They both have different landscapes and require different navigation. The Lenormand cards make excellent companions to tarot readings and are suited to direct readings for practical matters.

If you are a tarot reader already, you may like to consider jumping ahead first to our afterword, which sets out the significant differences in the decks and methods between Lenormand and tarot.

A Note to Lenormand Readers

For those who have been reading Lenormand cards for some time, we have endeavoured to ensure this book introduces newcomers easily to the cards in general and encourages them to discover more about traditional methods beyond this work. We hope it serves as a springboard for students to encounter Lenormand decks, perhaps for the first time, and then jump off into deeper pools or trace original sources. Where possible, we have made clear our own unique tweaks to the methods from our practice, which occur increasingly as the book progresses.

A Note on Lenormand Cards

You will need a Lenormand deck to accompany this book, or alternatively you can create a simple set of thirty-six playing cards numbered 1 through 36, or use collage, magazine clips, photography, or your own artwork to create the cards. We would recommend you purchase the Original Lenormand (Game of Hope) cards, which are a reproduction of the first images that became the Lenormand deck. These are available at www.originallenormand.com. A list of many other decks is given in the resources section of this book.

A Note on Research

Tali would like to say that all research is only as valid as the day it was written and stands to be corrected, overturned, and refined. Please check her website at www.newlenormand.com and her Tarot Speakeasy blog at www.tarotspeakeasy.com for revisions and updates.

Contents

Introduction 1

One: A Tale of Two Cities 3

Two: Getting Started 21

Three: The Cards 49

Four: Reading the Cards in Context 101

Five: The Grand Tableau 125

Six: The Houses 143

Seven: Knighting, Counting, and Diagonals 181

Eight: Zones and Shadows 193

Nine: Card Layouts and Sample Readings 221

Afterword: Lenormand for Tarot Readers 243

Appendix One: The Game of Hope 249

Appendix Two: The Game of Picket (Piquet)   255

Further Resources   261

Glossary   269

Bibliography   273

Endnotes   275

Art Credit List   279

Introduction

> There was an anchor, an hourglass surmounted by a skull, a bull, a beehive…
> Thirty-six altogether, and she couldn't even guess what they meant.[1]
> –Philip Pullman, *Northern Lights*

In the His Dark Materials trilogy, a device is used called the Alethiometer, a "golden compass." This device has upon its surface thirty-six mysterious symbols, which Lyra, the heroine of the books, uses to divine truth throughout her adventures.[2] As Pullman says in the books, the device originates from the seventeenth century, when "buildings and pictures were designed to be read like books. Everything stood for something else; if you had the right dictionary you could read Nature itself."[3]

In this book, you are going to encounter thirty-six similar symbols on cards arising from the same tradition from which the Golden Compass was designed, and learn to read their simple and literal images as a dictionary of life—your life, and the lives of those around you. You will quickly learn a new way of looking at cards and your circumstances as you get a grip on this new language.

Unlike tarot or other systems, in the Lenormand cards you will not be overcome with *symbolitis*, having to learn complex correspondences of arcane lore. You do not need to understand Kabbalah, astrology, or complex numerology. You will see instead simple domestic objects such as a dog, a house, a child… it is like a children's book, because in fact it was designed as a simple parlour game for the whole family. It really is child's play.

We will take you through a series of simple exercises to learn the literal language of the Lenormand cards. Again, unlike tarot, here we require more cards to build up our reading, and it gets easier the more cards you use, whether for fortunetelling or self-discovery. In fact, we will quickly progress to learn the Grand Tableau method of reading all thirty-six cards. This will give you one simple layout of all the cards from which you can read for any aspect of life, be it romance, career, money, travel, education, or spiritual matters—all from one spread.

The Lenormand method is very straightforward and domestic. As Lenormand reader Stella Waldvogel remarked, "The tarot will tell you that he has projected his anxiety about his mother onto you and that is why he has walked off; the Lenormand will tell you that he is down at the bar with his beer buddies, and it's your money he's spending." One can make a decision from either perspective.

We will take simple steps, and you may notice a gentle reprogramming of your brain; imagine being an explorer, standing in front of a door carved with two hieroglyphs, a yellow honeybee and an oak leaf. You are trying to work out what is behind the door before you venture within. You suspect perhaps a storage vault of honey, or maybe even an orchard. You may even think that behind the door is a treasure that will give you "sweet strength" because the honeybee symbolises sweetness and the oak is a symbol of strength.

However, the answer is staring you more literally in your face—you just need to stand back and read the images literally, out loud: "bee leaf"—"belief." The door leads to a church or temple…and has nothing to do with bees or leaves. This is the sort of reprogramming you are about to experience with the Lenormand cards, and we trust it will open many new doors for you in your life.

We'll begin at the beginning and discover that the Lenormand cards had very little to do with Mlle. Lenormand herself (correcting a thousand websites in the process) and discover what we owe a brass factory family from Nuremberg, and in particular, one man who died at the same time his little deck of cards was published.

ONE

A Tale of Two Cities

....

Je prends un jeu de piquet, composé de trente-deux cartes. Je les coupe trois fois et les pose huit par huit, ayant soin d'examiner les extremites de mon tableau. Et apres les avoir relevees de droite et de gauche, j'apercois, sur la seconde ligne, le valet de carreau et le sept de pic renverse; l'as de pic se trouvoit, avec son neuf, en face du roi de trefle et de la dame de coeur avec le huit de pic; ce qui sembloit lui annoncer des larmes. Je dis a cette consultante: Vos craintes ne sont point chimeriques; car le pere et le fils sont en presence. Tous les deux sont blesses; maise le jeunne homme l'est tres-grievement. Ah! Courez promptement a leur secours.

I take a Piquet, composed of thirty-two cards. I cut three times and place them eight by eight, taking care to examine the ends of my table. And after having noted to both right and left, I perceive, on the second line, the Jack of Diamonds and Seven of Spades (Reversed); in the Ace of Spades I find the Consultant, with his Nine, opposite the King of Clubs and the Queen of Hearts with the Eight of Spades, which seemed to move him to tears. I say this to my consultant: Your fears are not *chimerical*, for your father and son are here seen present. Both are wounded; but the younger man, very seriously. Ah! Run quickly to their assistance.

—Marie Anne Adelaide Lenormand,
Les oracles sibyllins ou la suite des souvenirs prophétiques (1817)

....

What Are the "Lenormand" Cards?

The Lenormand cards, technically the Petit Lenormand of thirty-six images ranging from the Rider to the Cross, are a deck of cards originally designed as a parlour game but now used for divination and fortunetelling. You may be surprised, but as far as we know, this particular type of deck was not actually used by the famous fortuneteller Mlle. Marie Anne Adelaide Lenormand, whose name was only associated with the deck after her death.

Unlike the tarot, which originated in Italy, the Lenormand cards are a European and cosmopolitan child of Paris, France, and Nuremberg, Germany. The name of the cards derives from Mlle. Lenormand (1772–1843), a notable fortuneteller of Paris, and the images and deck derive—totally separately—from a card game designed by J. K. Hechtel (1771–1799) in Nuremberg, published in 1800. They became a "love child" in the first "Petit Lenormand" decks published from around 1850 onwards in Germany, capitalizing on the death and name of Mlle. Lenormand.

If it were today, it would be as if we took the game of Monopoly (itself originally called "The Landlords Game"), turned it into a divination system with forty cards (twenty-two street cards, four station cards, two utility cards, and the remaining cards, including a jail card) and then called it "the Fortune-Telling Cards of Aleister Crowley." We would choose his name because he is well-known, was connected with magick, and has died, and if we had done this before the rise of mass and instant communication, no one would know he had never played Monopoly.

More than two centuries later, most people would then assume these were indeed the cards the legendary Great Beast used in his rituals and divinations. There might even come a time when arguments would rage about the "true" Kabbalistic correspondences of the twenty-two street cards!

Furthermore, two centuries later, we might suddenly see a renaissance of our Thelemopoly deck with new variants being created, such as in Monopoly, where we now see Totopoly based on horse-racing, a Dallasopoly, and even a Dinosauropoly. It may not be too long, then, until we see a Dinosaurnormand.

The set of images commonly called "Lenormand" is also a little like a genome, a piece of genetic information that has been dropped into the wider evolutionary stream of cartomancy and tarot. It has been mutated several times, most notably into the Gypsy Fortune-Telling decks and the Black Cat fortunetelling game published by Parker Brothers in 1897, with feline cards for "Danger" and "Love Matters." These variant decks often have similar cards to the Lenormand although they vary widely. It is not uncommon to see decks with a Train card or a Spider, for example, which do not occur in the generally accepted Lenormand cards.

Here are two examples of very early Lenormand-type decks, the first of which contains a Butterfly card and the second the more common pattern of images, in this case an early deck published by Dondorf.

Figure 1. Antique Lenormand Cards

Figure 2. Antique Dondorf Lenormand

The most comprehensive and reliable study to date in English on the development of the Lenormand cards and the life of Mlle. Lenormand is to be found in Decker, Depaulis, and Dummett's *A Wicked Pack of Cards*.[4] In German, the exhibition catalogue *Wahrsagekarten* (Fortunetelling Cards) by Hoffman and Kroppenstedt collects together many examples of Lenormand and variants, such as the "Sibylle des Salons" (Sybil of the Salons) and "Livre du Destin" (Book of Destiny) decks.[5] It was also the first publication, now more than thirty years ago, to point out that what are now commonly known as "Lenormand" cards were not used by Mlle. Lenormand but rather created from the Hechtel "Game of Hope" deck.

So, whilst the Lenormand cards are named after Mlle. Lenormand, she did not use these types of cards, and they actually arose after her death. It is somewhat uncertain, even by her own voluminous writing, exactly what type of cards and methods the Parisian fortuneteller used, although we do have some general ideas. It is perhaps possible she had a "Game of Hope" deck in her possession, if it had travelled from Nuremberg to Paris during her life, but this was likely not the deck she was using for cartomancy.

Left to right: Figure 3. A Portrait of Mlle. Lenormand
Figure 4. A Consultation with Mlle. Lenormand

Her story is best told in *A Wicked Pack of Cards* (1996), which covers the historical references in some detail. Her work *Les souvenirs prophétiques d'une sibylle sur les causes secrétes de son arrestation* (1814) is typical of her output, being a sort of scandal sheet of its time. We cannot help but think of her as being a sort of Paris Hilton of her time, constantly in the broadsheets, writing up her escapades and alleged involvement with celebrities of the time, at length, for further self-promotion.

Figure 5. Mlle. Lenormand prophesying for the Duchess of Berry, Princess Caroline

Which cards she actually used as part of her involvement in the growing movement of *tireurs de cartes* (fortunetellers of cards) is somewhat vague. There are references to Thoth and "strange figures" on the cards; in her own words, she speaks about using a "blazing mirror," the "thirty-three Greek sticks," and a variety of grimoires, wands, and talismans. There is no specific mention of tarot as we would know it today.

It is in her 1817 work, *Les Oracles Sibyllins*, where we learn more about her apparent methodology and meanings; she appears to use a Piquet pack (thirty-two cards), which was commonly used for gaming and derives such meanings as "the King of Spades, together with the 8 of Diamonds, means that a skilful man has made trials to stop, if it is possible, the progression of illness."[6] We have provided the original rules of Picket (as it was called in English) as an appendix so you can play this game if you wish. She also appears to refer to the "78 tharot cards," including the Fool, Devil, and Death.

However she worked, others followed after her death, including Mme. Clément, who wrote *The Bleeding Raven*, a book on fortunetelling that was actually based on Etteilla's earlier work and cards. It was Etteilla (1738–1791) who seemed to inspire Mlle. Lenormand, as he was widely regarded as the first true teacher of tarot, however she conspicuously does not mention him at all in her many writings.

It was not until two years after her death that a "Grand Jeu de Mlle Lenormand" was first published, based on a fifty-four-card pack, with astrological, mythical, and symbolic layers on every card. This is the deck still published by Grimaud. This was followed by a German fifty-five-card version, "Wahrsage-Karten der berühmten Mlle Le Normand" in about 1850. It appears that as the designer of the "Game of Hope," J. K. Hechtel, died shortly before or immediately after its publication, this later publisher was not concerned about using a recently deceased woman's name and a dead man's deck for a new type of fortunetelling publication.

These were followed by many miniature decks, particularly in Germany, of thirty-six cards, called Petit Lenormand. The further irony is that not only do these have nothing to do with Lenormand herself, the Lenormand decks were not at all popular in France, but in Germany, and thence to Holland—even as far as Brazil and Russia.

What has been lesser-known and described by Decker, Dummett, and dePaulis is that this Petit Lenormand deck is actually based on a "race game" pack of cards, from around 1800, called Das Spiel der Hofnung, "The Game of Hope." This prototype was discovered by Detlef Hoffmann in 1976, and clearly shows the symbols and numbers we see in the Petit Lenormand. The game is played with all thirty-six cards laid out, and one die. It is suggested in the accompanying booklet that the cards may also be used as a simple question-and-answer fortunetelling system, which is what we will do. We also give the first English translation of the booklet from the game in this book as an appendix so you can read how the cards were used and may have been interpreted as part of a fortunetelling game in the salon.

It is probable that the reason there are thirty-six cards (rather than, say, the lesser number of thirty-two found in some Piquet games or the seventy-eight of a tarot deck) is because of the game design involving two six-sided dice, i.e., 6 x 6 = 36. Laying out the Game of Hope cards and noting which ones are negative, positive, and neutral reveals a standard game design (such as could be found in Snakes & Ladders) rather than any deeper significance.

Figure 6. Portrait of J. K. Hechtel

Following that lead to the work of Detlef Hoffmann led to more discoveries, including the actual prototype of the Lenormand deck, Das Spiel der Hofnung, created by Johann Kaspar Hechtel, published circa 1800. A copy exists in the British Museum, and we commissioned photography so you can now see it online; the cards are used here to illustrate their descriptions for reading.[7]

Hechtel was part of a large family that owned several of the brass mills in the area of Nuremberg, and whilst we have not finished research, there is evidence that his family took over a mill in 1776 and worked in the trade until 1845. As well as brass-making, which was often used to supply musical instrument manufacturers, an important industry in the city was, appropriately, card-making and toy-making. Hechtel also designed other diversions, including two morality-teaching games and a parlour game called Pandora.[8] Whilst there was a Rosicrucian (and Alchemical) society in Nuremberg at the time called the "Society of Buccinators," we have no evidence of any esoteric involvement by Hechtel.

We have also published a thirty-six-card deck to accompany this book, the Original Lenormand, which is a reproduction under license from the Trustees of the British Museum of Das Spiel der Hofnung.[9]

In the appendix, we reproduce the first English translation of the original game instructions in order to perhaps appreciate how players of the time would have divined fortunes. If we return to our Monopoly analogy, the "Go to Jail" card would obviously be read from our experience of the game as a negative card of imprisonment, whilst one would have to understand the culture of the time to appreciate what the difference might be between the "Baltic Avenue" and "Atlantic Avenue" cards ("Old Kent Road" and "Leicester Square" in England).

Across Europe there were also many types of card decks and games, including Trappola (c. 1550),[10] and Tarocchi, of course. The number of cards would vary, as would designs; the suits for example could be acorns, leaves, fruit, even bells.

Sometimes cards would feature German or Latin verses upon them, which we see in some Lenormand cards with a piece of poetry to give the card meaning. Often the cards would be fully illustrated, as we see in the Two of Vases and Three of Vases from a deck designed by Jost Ammon (c. 1570). This deck was actually designed, like many, to be an instructive deck, here teaching the virtues of book-making over drinking. A lesson for us all.

There are also Piquet packs, with the usual three court cards of Valet, Queen, and King, and even decks that were satirical of current situations; one deck in 1720 was based on the South Sea and Mississippi Companies stock crash, with the verse on the Ace of Hearts saying, "The Southern Mermaid I tried to catch in vain, she took the money and left me the empty book." It seems like these cards would be just as relevant today.

Morality Cards

In 1718 we find morality cards being used as an equivalent of the modern practice of choosing a card of the day. The deck was called Geistliche Karten, published in Ausberg as "a motto for the day," each card containing a spiritual musing that promoted virtuous behaviour for the day.[11]

The text on each card of the day begins with *Heut*, in English, "Today." It continues with a homily to guide the reader toward the moral lesson for that day in order to prepare for judgement. As an example, one card (Hertz 8) contains the verse:

> *Today imagine death, you have to die, death is certain and will come soon, do not know today or tomorrow or whether he waits longer. Prepare soon, take the ladder of Christ and climb up to virtue. To achieve this mercy say a Lord's Prayer and an Ave Maria for the soul that does not regard death and doesn't prepare enough for it.*

It is in this climate of moral teaching that the use of playing cards as instruction advice—even in gaming form—arose. The Game of Hope is only one of many such games popular over two centuries throughout Europe, played with cards, dice, and often a board.

Games of Morality and Education

The Wellcome Trust in London is in possession of some very special old games that really do bear mentioning here.[12] These board games are testaments of the "how we used to live" sort and go some way to helping us understand the original groundwork for the Lenormand's conception. It helps us understand what inspired such devices. It would seem from this evidence that historical beliefs and concerns really did help to shape what we know today as the Lenormand.

The fact that these were what you would call "race games" is significant; they derive from a game called "the Game of Goose," an Italian game of Middle Eastern origin using the roll of a die to move the players around the board in a circuit. This game was also called the "Newe and Most Pleasant Game of the Goose." It was first translated into English by John Wolfe in 1597. It was this game that was seen as the "big daddy" of educational morality games. The oldest in the collection is one called Le Iev Desnations, published in the seventeenth century, an educational game. The game teaches "morals, fashions, and customs" of the "other nations" worldwide.

There is also evidence of similar images being used in "lotto" games of the time, such as we see in this lotto sheet from Nuremberg, where the Game of Hope was devised.

The two games that are of particular significance to the Lenormand are the morality games of the collection. One of these two games, "Laurie's Instructive and Entertaining Game of the Mansion of Happiness," is very similar to the Game of Hope from which Lenormand cards were created. The tagline for the game does not mince its words: "virtue rewarded and vice punished." The traits of "audacity, immodesty, or ingratitude" are frowned upon. This behaviour will not be rewarded; the players are not to expect to "even think of happiness, much less partake in it." There are many forfeits in the game that punish bad criminal behaviour, one of such being "whoever becomes a PERJURER must be put in the pillory and pay a Fine of one." Punishment by stock or whipping posts is mentioned. The fashion in games had far shifted from the past of rewards being given for being sociable with drinking and gambling, such as in the Game of Chance, to these morally educational games.

The Game of Hope (which has become the modern Lenormand) was based on this thinking—that cards showed a variety of favourable and unfavourable moral aspects of life, and one's task was to navigate through them, making the right choices. In fact, in the Game of Hope, the goal was to win by reaching the penultimate card, the Anchor—a traditional symbol of hope and faith—and not the final card, the Cross, which meant you had overshot and had to return backwards! Here the Cross was the most negative card of trial and suffering, not an interpretation of faith, which belonged to the symbol of the anchor.

Figure 7. Nuremberg Lottery Sheet

Similarly, if the cards are laid out in a six-by-six grid as was given in the original instructions, we might detect an ascent narrative of morals and virtues being displayed to the player. In the first line, we have symbols of being at home and being away, of travel and opportunity. We then move to mortality, time, and work. The Child in the third row heralds the animal kingdom, leading to the Tower in the next row, from which follow ways, places, food, and the heart. The penultimate row shows communications: the Ring, the Book, the Letter, followed by the Gentleman, the Lady, and the Lily—an allusion to sexuality. The final line shows us the stellar symbols of the Sun and Moon, followed by the religious iconography of Key, Fish, Anchor, and Cross.

In appreciating this background, we can come better to understand some of the sources for the eventual meanings of the cards, even the manner in which they are read—using gaming-like directions, unlike tarot. The cards also remain closer to their roots as playing cards, many decks having "inserts" showing playing cards. Whilst we do not look into this in this introductory book, we can look briefly at how cards were originally read for fortunetelling to appreciate our later methods presented here.

Casanova and Cartomancy

We have quite a considerable amount of evidence of how cartomancy was used in Europe—in this case Italy and Paris. In the life of Casanova, we find mention of reading gambling cards for fortunetelling, to his detriment, it appears.

Giacomo Girolamo Casanova de Seingalt (1725–1798) was an adventurer and author, born in Venice and died in Bohemia; his name is popularly associated with seduction and womanising. His memoirs—which are part autobiography—detail his life and loves across the eighteenth century.

The first mention of cartomancy is when he is talking about his new mistress, Zaira, who was "purchased" from a local farm:

> She was only fourteen, so her breast was not yet developed, and she bore about her few traces of puberty. Her skin was as white as snow, and her ebony tresses covered the whole of her body, save in a few places where the dazzling whiteness of her skin shone through. Her eyebrows were perfectly shaped, and her eyes, though they

might have been larger, could not have been more brilliant or more expressive. If it had not been for her furious jealousy and her blind confidence in fortunetelling by cards, which she consulted every day, Zaira would have been a paragon among women, and I should never have left her.

We can see here that there is a mention of "fortunetelling by cards" but of course, given Casanova's often-detailed accounts of card-playing over this period, these would have been a regular deck of playing cards, certainly nothing associated with tarot or Lenormand as we see it now.

The text continues later with the "reading" itself, following Casanova's return from a night of his usual escapades:

I got home, and, fortunately for myself, escaped the bottle which Zaira flung at my head, and which would infallibly have killed me if it had hit me. She threw herself on to the ground, and began to strike it with her forehead. I thought she had gone mad, and wondered whether I had better call for assistance; but she became quiet enough to call me assassin and traitor, with all the other abusive epithets that she could remember. To convict me of my crime she showed me twenty-five cards, placed in order, and on them she displayed the various enormities of which I had been guilty.

I let her go on till her rage was somewhat exhausted, and then, having thrown her divining apparatus into the fire, I looked at her in pity and anger, and said that we must part the next day, as she had narrowly escaped killing me.

What follows is the original French, followed by a closer look at its translation:

Pour me convaincre de mon crime (of the night before), elle me montre un carré de vingt-cinq cartes où elle me fait lire toutes les débauches qui m'avaient tenu dehors toute la nuit. Elle me montre la garce, le lit, les combats et jusqu'à mes égarements contre nature. Je ne voyais rien du tout mais elle s'imaginait de voir tout.

Après lui avoir laissé dire, sans l'interrompre, tout ce qui pouvait servir à soulager sa jalousie et sa rage, je pris son grimoire que je jetai au feu.

Which translates in more detail as:

To convince me of my crime (of the night before), she shows me a square of twenty-five cards which she makes me read all the debauchery that had kept me out all night. She shows me the bitch, the bed, fighting, and even my wanderings against nature. I saw nothing at all but she imagined seeing everything.

After having been told, without interruption, everything that could be used to relieve her jealousy and rage, I took her spellbook that I threw into the fire.

That is to suggest that she laid out twenty-five playing cards in a square and then read through them the "bitch," "bed," "fighting," and so forth. We will come to see how these matrix layouts are common in Lenormand reading, particularly 3 x 3 squares, 4 x 4 squares, and the Grand Tableau using all thirty-six cards.

Artwork of the time shows many other layouts, usually a matrix layout, horseshoe, or pyramid. We will provide a selection of these layouts for you try at the conclusion of this book as well as sample readings to assist your own interpretations.

A Cartomantic Revelation

....

The rolling dice, in whom your luck does stand,
(With whose unhappy chance ye be so wroth)
Ye know yourself came never in my hand.
Lo, in this pond be fish and frogs both.
Cast in your net; but be you leve or loath,
Hold you content as Fortune liste assign
[For] it is your own fishing, and not mine.
—Thomas More, *Fortune Verses* (c. 1504)

....

Before we start our practical lessons, we wanted to tell you something really important about cartomancy, and the history of Lenormand and tarot. It may totally change the way you think about cards and is very simple. **Originally, the cards themselves did not have meanings.**

We'll say that again: the cards never had meanings. To historians, this is an obvious thing; however, for many of us card readers it is perhaps a little hard to wrap our heads around the idea, having spent our lives learning the meanings of the cards. So, let's take another look at this revelation and see how it affects not only the way we think about our cards—and how the Lenormand and other cards fit into the tradition—but also how we read them.

A Bit More History

Long before Lenormand and tarot, there was a craze (a little like the Lenormand, which is now having a second renaissance in English, like a key opening a rose) for things called fortune books. These oracular books contained a variety of verses, giving both questions and answers for all likely predicaments. They were consulted with a range of means: by casting dice, pulling threads fastened to various pages, turning a paper wheel embedded in the book, counting the number of letters in one's name, and of course, by drawing cards.

One would then consult an appropriate portion of text that would often lead (a bit like a contemporary "choose your own adventure" book) to branching avenues of verse and oracle, based on some further combination of your dice or decision.

These books were so popular that even the famous Thomas More and William Lilly translated one such book from the Italian, in about 1500. This was the *Libro delle Sorti* (1474) of Lorenzo Spiriti.

There is a similar fortunetelling book in the library of the Royal Society in London, which Marcus visited to view last year. This is the *Triompho di fortuna* (the Triumph of Fortune) by Sigismondo Fanti, published in Venice in 1527.

The book is full of incredible woodcut drawings, some of which have a coincidental similarity to tarot card images.

As these books became popular, English equivalents eventually started to appear from the early 1700s onwards. One such original book we went to look at last year had questions such as whether children would be dutiful or whether you would die rich or poor. Other questions perhaps are more suited to the time, such as "In what kind of cattle, beasts, or poultry is it best to deal?" It is interesting that these books often chose the question as well as the answer, making it more of a parlour game.[13]

As time went on, often these questions, verses, and answers were depicted **next to** the playing cards that might have been chosen for that particular route. So it was only a matter of time for people to simplify the whole method (who wanted to buy a big book when you only needed cards?) by writing down a simplified form of the verses on a pack of cards. Also, perhaps it became even more obvious to have a small vignette (picture) on the playing card, to help with the interpretation!

So over time, the cards became stuck with one meaning, one image, one set of interpretations. But this was not how they started—they started as **keys** to unlock a separate book of meanings, map of routes, and set of oracles. So when we are reading playing cards, they have no meanings, they just point us to possible verses and meanings. When we read tarot, they have "traditional" meanings.

The Lenormand stands as a bridge between these two phases—the cards only have meanings when considered with the whole tableau, and at the same time have some limited and fixed meanings, such as the anchor being hope or faith. In our Lenormand reading, then, we must recall: **The cards are the keys, not the doors.**

Now let us go ahead and take those keys…and unlock the doors.

TWO

Getting Started

....

L'Art de Tirer les Cartes (The Method of Using the Cards)
Donnant la maniere infallible de connaitre le passé, le present et l'avenir, tant pour soi-meme, que pour autrui, d'aprese lese plus celebres cartomanciens tells que la Mlle. Lenormand.

Giving the infallible way of knowing the past, present and future, both for oneself, for others, in the manner of most famous cartomancers such as Mlle. Lenormand.

....

Choosing a Lenormand Deck

There is a growing range of Lenormand-style decks—actually "Petit Lenormands," with thirty-six cards—from which to choose. These have been less available outside of Germany, the Netherlands, and Russia, though a revival has widened the choice; new decks are being increasingly brought to the market.

We have published The Original Lenormand, a reproduction under license from the British Museum, carefully and painstakingly worked upon by the award-winning artist Ciro Marchetti to provide an authentic Lenormand for use with this book.[14]

Marcus uses the Mertz-style deck for its most simplistic images. You can also buy the French Cartomancy deck, which is actually based on a German design but is very traditional.

We also particularly like the Blue Owl version, although we also have a soft spot for the Piatnik deck from Vienna.

Originally created in 1942, the Piatnik deck has a chintzy yet stylish design and the cards reflect the time period. Warner Brothers movies especially spring to mind; we look at the Ship card and see how it conjures up an image of *Now Voyager* (1942) with Joan Crawford, where the downtrodden character Charlotte Vale escapes on a cruise ship and returns dramatically transformed. If you have not come across this old movie, check it out, and see how the themes of journey, transformation and rites of passage assist your understanding of the Ship card. The movie puts us in the mood for reading in this style, and this is what makes the Lenormand very special—it has one voice but many different accents.

If you are looking for a contemporary deck, you can try the Mystical Lenormand by Urban Trosch, published by US Games Systems, although it does add more symbols to the starker original images. There are now many new decks being produced, including the Gilded Reverie Lenormand deck by Ciro Marchetti, the Minute Lenormand by Robyn Tisch Hollister, Anna Simonova's Lilac Twilight Lenormand, and Andi (Rootweaver) Graf's Vintage Lenormand. Gidget London has also produced a stick-figure deck, harking back to the original cards, which would have been hand-coloured, mixed with a mischievous pixie twist.[15]

It is possible that more new Lenormand decks will be produced in 2012–2013 than in the entire previous century.

Left to right: Figure 8. The Woman card; Figure 9. The Snake card; Figure 10. The Ship card; Figure 11. The Messenger card

A new Lenormand by Carrie Paris and Roz Foster, the Lenormand Revolution, also known as "the Game of Change," Le Jeu De Change, based on the French and American revolutions, is to be produced both as a deck and as an iPad app, bringing the Lenormand totally up to date.[16]

We have provided a list of decks in the appendices to get you started in discovering the Lenormand for yourself.

Learning the Lenormand Language

As the Lenormand cards have proven popular in Germany and across Europe, little of the material is written in English. In fact, this book is only the third comprehensive introduction to be published, and the first by a major publisher. We expect that many other titles will follow should the interest continue, and we look forward to the widening interest in this and many other forms of cartomancy.

Figure 12. The Tree card

Luckily, as the namesake of the cards was French, we have many words that mean the same in both French and English (we'll leave German for the moment) and some stolen words that we will be using to good effect in our lessons later, such as *Liaison*, a meaning of the Rider/Messenger card.

Incidentally, it is "Mademoiselle" and not "Madame" for the lady herself, as she never married, and generally "Le Normand" or "Le-Normand"—not "Lenormand," and it is pronounced "luh-nor-ma" with a nasal vowel at the end and a silent "d." We use "Lenormand" throughout for simplicity.

A few other terms will help put us in the Lenormand-style space, which we would encourage you to start using instead of their tarot equivalents:

- Salon or boudoir: not "office" or "reading space"
- Sitter: not "querent"
- Sibyl: not "reader"
- Tableau: not "spread"
- Vignette: not "layout"

You may find other words come more to mind when reading Lenormand, as it has its own particular voice. We can't wait for you to discover its unique spirit as it talks to you, no matter the accent.

The Two Towers

When we first approach the Lenormand cards, one of the first confusions for students is that there are alternative keywords given for each of the thirty-six cards. There then becomes a scramble to somehow find the "true" keywords or a "valid" traditional set. This becomes further confused by different authors then presenting different versions—in one or several cards—of key concepts whilst all belonging to a particular school or tradition.

We will present one set of keywords in the following chapter and then elaborate on these in the third chapter, whilst encouraging you to experiment with different traditions. Every reader has developed their own particular style, and you will eventually find your own version based on tradition. We will first look at one particular card in detail to discover how these meanings vary, and in this particular case, to the tarot, where the card has an equivalent.

It is of note that the only cards immediately comparable between the regularly recognised tarot structure and the majority of decks known as the Lenormand are the astral principles of the Star, the Moon, and the Sun, and the more manifest Tower. We will briefly outline how we can use the Tower as an illustration of the divergence between the two deck types: tarot and the Lenormand. You will also discover how meaning has been ascribed to the cards as a whole and understand that originally the cards had no meaning at all.

As we have mentioned, in the original Game of Hope, instructions were given for most of the cards to indicate their nature in the game—a nature that would have been carried across to their interpretative meaning. We'll take a look at the Tower in the game and how it can be developed into this interpretative meaning.

The Lenormand Tower

Here is the instruction for a player landing on the Tower: "19: To enjoy the pleasant vista from the Tower, one pays 2 marks."

The Lenormand Tower is specific in that it is a **Watchtower** in an interpretative sense, it is very much about being alert and prepared for something that has not yet happened—in order, when it does, to stop it in its tracks or to premeditate a more pleasant outcome. The Watchtower is more enabling and less intimidating. It is very much about keeping control of the physical state of being, and it has more promise of the material.

You could describe the Lenormand Watchtower as a promoter of autonomy (from ancient Greek, meaning "one who gives oneself one's own law"), which fits in with the original intentions of the Game of Hope, that it would be a tool for didactic learning. The game presents thirty-six cards of moral lessons and how one deals with the "Vice and Virtue" each presents along the way. It tells us "you too can have a pleasant life if you look ahead and plan your life carefully and make the appropriate choices."

The tarot's Tower, by contrast, is almost saying "all is now lost to those who enter here." The Lenormand offers more hope, in a way. The Lenormand Tower would not be out of place in a tourist guide book, and it does not elicit a gasp or a shock as the tarot Tower usually does.

The image of the Tower in the Game of Hope is clearly an observatory form rather than a defensive emplacement or a "House of God." There is a balcony at the top providing a clear view of the surroundings to the distant horizons. A flag is raised to full mast and is caught in a full breeze, perhaps signifying that the sky is clear. There are no obstructions around it, and it is slightly raised upon a grassy mound emphasising its elevation. It is functional and unadorned, merely a watchtower—suspiciously identical to the eighteenth-century watchtower in Nuremberg where the game was devised and produced. A tourist in the Nuremberg of 1800 would no doubt discover many of the cards—garden, house, etc.—in plain sight throughout the town.

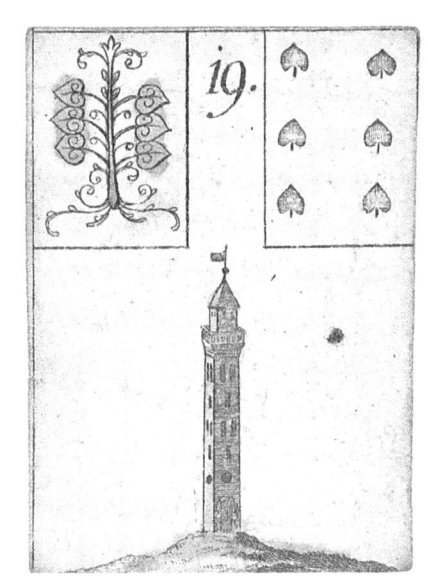

Left to right: Figure 13. The original Tower card;
Figure 14. Nuremberg Tower, Germany

Traditional and Contemporary Meanings

When we look at various schools of thought with regard to the Lenormand deck, we discover a variety of meanings for each card, some similar, some variant. We have used the original French and German books in our collection for these meanings; they are listed in the bibliography.

Halina Kamm (54) gives the Tower as rigidity and inflexibility, might, power, and egotism, whilst at the same time equating it with magic and occultism—perhaps as a watchtower within the inner world. There are often conflicts of meaning with the card as representing authority—is it self-mastery and wisdom, educational authority, or military might? At heart, the essence of the card to us is "vision"—the clear-sightedness the watcher in the watchtower brings, whether used for learning a lesson, martial victory, or inner knowledge.

Mertz (48–9) concentrates on the Tower as the house of wisdom, saying it depicts the place where wise men and women might live in the winter, suggesting interpretations of quiet success and isolation, to some extent. Kienle (2001) depicts the card more literally as a "school," "education," or "place of work."

Dee (128), writing in English, stresses the "castle" nature of the card, suggesting that if it is surrounded by more negative cards, it could be that the sitter feels "under siege" or could be suffering from a debilitating illness.

Treppner concentrates on the "authority" aspects of the Tower (62–3), and Steinbach (85) extends the Tower symbolism to cover governmental institutions, the "power and hierarchy of the corporate pyramid system." Whilst adding it covers colleges and other learning establishments of education, she also adds that it symbolises "the ego, someone's ambitions and belief systems."

In the Brazilian version, Dos Ventos (73) combines meanings of isolation and independence with similar meanings of "government offices and even foreign countries." If the card comes up close to issues of employment, it signifies a "complete change of job," possibly even "relocation."

AndyBC on his "Journal of a Cartomante" site—shows that whilst the Tower may signify loneliness, it also separates out the cards to either side of it, which we think is an important placeholder function in the overall tone of a Grand Tableau reading in particular. It shows how cards can have functional effects in a layout, rather than purely symbolic ones, something that is not considered as much in tarot, where every card is read as an entity of itself.

The Tarot Tower

The Tower symbol in the tarot is very much about sudden catastrophic collapse and the end of an era. There is not much scope to be able to make amends or take action; it is more how we deal with the effect of an inevitable upheaval and how we come to terms with reacting to that loss and change. We have as much control over it as the figures usually falling from the Tower itself.

The first reference to the card that would become the Tower of the tarot was in a late fifteenth-century Italian manuscript, *Sermons de Ludo Cum Aliis* where it was called La Saggita (the Arrow). The oldest example of the card was in the Gringonneur deck of approximately 1475.[17] The whole section of Farley's piece on it in "Tower: Absent or Lost?" is of interest in tracing the history of this specific card.

In tarot, the Tower then starts to get extended in symbolic and interpretative meaning. If we look at Crowley's take on the Tower and the inclusion of references to doctrines of yoga and the Eye of Horus (Eye of Shiva), Crowley says of this "that on the opening of which, according to the legend of this cult, the Universe is destroyed." It is the card of "annihilation," "to make of nothing," which Crowley explains is the end goal, to become broken as the figures that fall from the garrison—lost but transformed into "mere geometrical expressions" without human form.

Here we are going mystical and spiritual, far away from the watchtower of the Lenormand. According to Crowley, this is the sought-after state to be in, a state of non-attachment to the physical realm and intellectual ego. This is partly why Tali uses the "essence word" of "vision" in her own Lenormand readings, as it does allow some overlap into tarot in this way.

In his appraisal of the Tower, Waite is very much of the same consensus of Crowley and the doctrines of yoga, in that he says, "I agree with Grand Orient (himself, writing under an earlier pseudonym!) that it is the ruin of the House of Life, when evil has prevailed therein, and above all it is the rending of a House of Doctrine. I understand that the reference is, however, to a House of Falsehood."[18] This would be the pride that goeth before the fall, the sin of Lucifer, the Devil (the card before the Tower).

So in tarot we have come a long way from the literal watchtower to the sin of pride. However that may be, the vice and virtue of each card, image, and symbol can be read according to its own nature—we read the cards. On that note, we will briefly look at the cartomantic reading of the Six of Spades, which is associated with the Lenormand Tower card.

The Six of Spades

In the earliest attributions of the playing cards to cartomantic divination, we find verses that dictate how the card is read depending on the gender of the sitter. These simple couplets, easily learnt, would have been a wonderful parlour game. We recently visited a library in Edinburgh to view a copy of Flamstead and Partridge's *Fortune Book* from 1750. This is a very useful resource for those of you looking to read fortunes by the appearance of moles on the body! Be that as it may, here is the original reading for the Six of Spades, the first couplet applying to a gentleman, the second pair to a lady:

This six fortells that when you do wed
You will have a cracked maidenhead,
But the girl this number draws
She'll wed one with great applause

It is interesting that by the time this gets to Dee (2004) the meaning has been slightly modified to avoid the "cracked maidenhead" allusion:

The six fortells whene'er wed
You'll find expectations fled;
But if a maid the number own
She'll wed a man of high renown.[19]

Again, this is a far cry from our "watchtower" or "fall of man" interpretations of Lenormand or tarot, although perhaps there is a common theme of surveying the landscape before you leap—into the unknown, yourself, or marriage alike.

Arranging the Lenormand cards into the order of the suits or other similar arrangements and patterns does not appear to show anything other than a relatively random attribution of suits, numbers, and cards to the inserts, however we are still investigating.

In presenting these parallel tracks of Lenormand, cartomancy, and tarot interpretations, it is perhaps important to remember that their coming together was often for marketing purposes, later brought into the service of divination. The playing card inserts were put into decks such as the Game of Hope simply to ensure they could be used for playing other card games, such as Piquet, and not limited to a niche market or singular usage. Similarly, when cards were originally used for divination along with dice, they were simply keys to look up interpretations in fortune books, not given any particular meaning in themselves.

We often wonder if it is likely that years ago, some marketing person thought, "Why not produce a little white book with a deck, or put the meanings onto the deck in verse, and then we can sell the deck without the big book?" and then went and undercut all those publishers selling expensive fortune books, particularly the Italian ones.

However that may be, we are now in a situation where people can read the Lenormand cards without any particular reference to the fact that they were never used by Lenormand, they came from a family card game, and their meaning is subject to drift and reinterpretation.

We will next list two suggested keywords for the cards, both Tali's essence words and selected traditional meanings. We will then expand on each card before looking at how we read the Lenormand. If you are already working with a particular tradition, style, author, or course, you may substitute these lists with your own.

TABLE ONE: ESSENCE WORDS

1. The Rider/Messenger: Communications (Liaison)
2. The Clover: Luck (Good fortune)
3. The Ship: Adventure (Travel)
4. The House: Security (Home)
5. The Tree: Longevity (Health)
6. The Clouds: Transition (Change)
7. The Snake: Stealth (Suddenness)
8. The Coffin: Initiation (Immediate health)
9. The Bouquet: Appreciation (Gift)
10. The Scythe: Clearing (Harvesting)
11. The Rod/Whip: Service (Disagreement)
12. The Birds/Owls: Divination (Discussion)
13. The Child/Little Girl: Innocence (Youth)
14. The Fox: Cunning (Planning)
15. The Bear: Headstrong (Power)
16. The Stars: Creation (Navigation)

17. The Stork: Deliverance (Delivery)

18. The Dog: Codependency (Loyalty)

19. The Tower: Vision (Authority)

20. The Garden: Communing (Society)

21. The Mountain: Durability (Obstacle)

22. The Ways: Choice (Decision)

23. The Mice: Productivity (Losses)

24. The Heart: Courage (Love)

25. The Ring: Continuity (Commitment)

26. The Book: Knowledge (Learning)

27. The Letter: Sentiment (Written word)

28. The Gentleman: Analytical (Man)

29. The Lady: Intuitive (Woman)

30. The Lily: Purity (Sex)

31. The Sun: Success (Will)

32. The Moon: Dreams (Fame)

33. The Key: Access (Discovery)

34. The Fish: Resources (Business)

35. The Anchor: Standstill (Stability)

36. The Cross: Burdens (Faith)

Here is a typical traditional set of keywords:

Table Two: Traditional Words

1. The Rider: News
2. The Clover: Luck
3. The Ship: Travel
4. The House: Home
5. The Tree: Long-term health
6. The Clouds: Confusion and trouble (lack of foresight)
7. The Snake: Someone who means harm, a liar, competitor
8. The Coffin: Immediate health
9. The Bouquet: Gift
10. The Scythe: A sudden cutting or planned harvesting
11. The Rod, Birch, Whip: Argument, troubled communication
12. The Birds: Communication, mass communication (gossip)
13. The Child: A young person, innocent and new
14. The Fox: Cunning, both bad and good (deceit and cleverness)
15. The Bear: Power and a powerful (influential) person
16. The Stars: Hopes
17. The Stork: Delivery (often of change)
18. The Dog: Loyalty and close friends and companion(ship)
19. The Tower: Solitude, borders (politics, law, education)
20. The Garden: Society and meetings with others
21. The Mountain: Blocks and obstacles, requiring detour

22. The Ways: Choices and decisions

23. The Mice: Gradual loss

24. The Heart: Love and romance

25. The Ring: Commitment and contracts

26. The Book: Knowledge (or secrets)

27. The Letter: Messages (but not necessarily 1: news, nor 12: gossip)

28. The Gentleman: A man

29. The Lady: A woman

30. The Lily: Sex

31. The Sun: Best/Big luck

32. The Moon: Dreams (in some traditions, work; *see* Alternate Traditions)

33. The Key: Certainty (locking or unlocking, security or insecurity, dependent on context)

34. The Fish: Resources and money (as in netting a good catch)

35. The Anchor: Stability (in some traditions, work)

36. The Cross: Struggle (as in "cross to bear")

We have already seen that some cards will have different meanings in different traditions, and with authors and teachers within those schools. Some cards are similar but have subtle differences. Here we will list the cards that have similarity of image or meaning, but contain subtle differences:

The Letter and the Rider: In the first card, we have specific written or formal communication, perhaps a confirmation of something already decided or known (a contract, particularly with the Ring close by in a layout), and in the second case we have something new—news, information, a newcomer, or a visitor from afar. They may bring a letter, but they are themselves the new delivery in the reading.

The Fox and the Bear: The Fox as employment would be more connected with self-employment, or individual cunning in continuing one's career. It could also be someone plotting against you in career matters, but not at a corporate level. The Bear may represent persons of power and long-term employment, perhaps more in a large, powerful organisation. If it were close to the Tower, for example, representing a border-post, this would be authority and hence a bigger institution for work prospects.

The Whip and the Scythe: These two implements, like the mice and the birds, may appear similar in some regards, but the birch/rod is a symbol of domestic servitude and trouble—the sound of the whip (hate speech, for example) causing pain and hurt. The Scythe is an agricultural tool belonging to the outdoors and references a more clear cutting away, even a harvesting and reaping. This depends too on the card closest to the point of the Scythe in the image (see "Facing Cards" below).

To some extent too, the Mice and the Birds both have multiple animals, but in the first case we have potential teamwork or long-term nibbling away of something (hence, loss), and in the second case we have individual birds flocking together and perhaps gossiping which comes to no good—the opposite of teamwork.

Facing Cards

Some cards may dictate—depending on the deck and the image—a direction of interpretation depending on which way they are facing. If your deck does not clearly depict a facing for these cards, you are not able to use this aspect of Lenormand reading.

In the original Game of Hope from which the first Lenormand deck derived, the Gentleman and Lady cards are drawn very clearly as a matching pair, set next to each other as cards 28 and 29, the Ace of Hearts and the Ace of Spades. They adopt matching and complementary poses, both dressed in formal attire—the Gentleman holding a walking stick in his right hand and the Lady a fan in her left. They are looking into each other's eyes, both with similar expression.

It has been suggested to us that the positions of the Heart, Gentleman, and Lady cards and their particular racing rules (see appendix) are part of the "love game" embedded in the whole game, and that the deck is thus stacked in favour of the Lady players winning.

When the Gentleman and Lady are used in cartomancy, their respective poses allow us to have them facing each other or to fall into a layout with their backs to each other. This often is used to signify their relationship. Where other cards have been designed to have them both facing in the same direction, this allows for one to be looking at the back of another, signifying that one is looking to another who is disinterested. If both cards have been designed to be facing the viewer, we cannot tell the direction of their regard.

In the Mertz deck, the Gentleman looks face on and the Woman looks to the right.

It is best to experiment with different decks to determine which works best for you, particularly when also choosing to use the method of right/left of the charged card to determine past/future rather than the regard of the Gentleman/Lady cards.

A Brief Note on Same-Sex Relationship Readings

Where both partners are male or female, there are a number of solutions to the traditional Lady and Gentleman cards. You can purchase two packs of a deck and have two Gentleman or Lady cards (clearly marking one as the significator/charged card to be used as representing the sitter). A number of contemporary decks actually supply two of each of these cards. Alternatively, you can ask the sitter to select any of the other cards as their partner (or potential partner), although this does remove that card from being used as its traditional meaning.

The Main Facing Cards Are:

The Lady and the Gentleman: Their facing across a layout can be used to determine their attitude toward each other. If the man is facing the woman and they are positioned closely with positive cards between them, this bodes well. If our male sitter has a layout in which the Gentleman is looking toward the Lady, who has her back to him with a great distance and negative cards between them, it does not immediately bode well.

The Scythe: The point of the Scythe shows what is being cut away, cleared, or harvested. It can also indicate which direction and cards determine what can be reaped from the situation in the rest of the layout.

The Clouds: The edges of the clouds are sometimes depicted as having a brighter and darker lighting, one side and the other. If so, the darker side—if closer to the charged card/

significator—brings trouble and lack of clarity, whereas the bright side being close indicates that such turbulence is quickly passing.

The Stork: The Stork is often seen as a delivery card with no other connotation, although of course with the Child card close at hand, we would be hard-pressed not to interpret this as a pregnancy. However, we can look at the two sides of the Stork and see the card before the Stork (either visually, the card "behind" the direction in which the Stork looks or flies) as what has come before the delivery or change, and the card after the Stork to see into what circumstances we are being taken.

The Ship: The direction in which the ship is sailing may be taken to denote where we are being taken—either literally or figuratively. The Ship followed by the Rider bordered by negative cards might indicate we are literally being "taken for a ride." Look for that snake!

The Book can also be read as a facing card, if the image shows which side the book is opening toward. This can be read as from where (or whom) the information/knowledge is coming.

Different Names for Cards

Some of the Lenormand cards have variations in their names. This rarely affects the reading; however, you may describe a single bird on card 12 called "the Owl" as "wisdom" more easily than the identical card being called "the Birds" and featuring a picture of many birds on it, which would tend to be interpreted more as "gossip."

Other cards that have variant names include:

- 1: Rider, Messenger, Cavalier

- 9: Bouquet, Flowers

- 11: Rod(s), Birch, Whip(s), Broom (this is possibly a mistaken drawing of the original, as it leads to more domestic interpretations other than the original implied by a birch)

- 22: The Ways, Paths, Crossroads

Different Meanings than Tarot

Several Lenormand cards hold different meanings than they would do in tarot, psychological symbolism, or other systems. It is best to change one's mindset to enter L-space first, rather than trying to shoe-horn the L-meanings into one's existing symbolism. This is one of the big stretches for those readers who are already used to dream symbolism, Jungian interpretation, Gestalt, tarot, astrology, etc., where such meanings will have already been internalised.

The most variant meanings might be considered to be the Cross, the Tower, and the Lily, with perhaps the Moon also carrying different connotations than its tarot equivalent.

- The Moon as Work/Fame
- The Cross as Pain and Grief
- The Lily as Sex
- The Tower as Authority

Whilst we can read all the cards literally—and we'll learn methods to do so later—in order to free up our interpretative ability to combine cards, we'll present here our first exercise, taken from our tarot work, but even more useful for Lenormand: the keyword kaleidoscope.[20]

Exercise: The Keyword Kaleidoscope

When we read Lenormand, we often put sequences or sets of cards together—far more than with tarot. The way in which we make meaning out of multiple images is quite spectacular and mostly unconscious. It is equal turns and inspirational. Sometimes it is as obvious as reading a list of standard meanings as a beginner and the interpretation applies accurately to the situation.

Here we are going to give you a practice method to install the unconscious pattern into your own brain—like training wheels that strengthen a particular process in your head. It is the pattern from experienced card readers, only taken out of their heads, polished, and given back to you.

We will start with two cards and move to three, from which the possibilities are endless. You'll be surprised how this works for you.

The Method

1. Shuffle your Lenormand deck and take out any two cards, turning them face up.
2. Write down their two keywords from the list above or your own references.
3. Look at both of them and say them both out loud or clearly in your head. Move from one to another.
4. See or hear what sensation arises from merging both words.
5. Give that new sensation one word.

It is most important to come up with one word, although you may note down other phrases, concepts, feelings, snippets of meaning, etc. The one word is important to install and provoke the unconscious pattern into your head. You have to sort a lot of associative connections and meanings to produce the one word, and your unconscious is geared to do this automatically, far better than you can do consciously. We trick the conscious mind into keeping itself busy producing the one word whilst the unconscious does all the work—easily.

For example, we choose two cards, Bouquet (9) and Book (26).

Figure 15. The Bouquet and the Book cards

We look up the keywords: "appreciation" and "knowledge."

We think about these two words and get "certificate." We first thought about "teacher," then "school," but then "certificate" came to mind very clearly. On further reflection, we can also picture "libraries and learning," or the awarding of a degree and similar ideas, all about the appreciation of knowledge.

Try it with two cards. You can repeat this exercise as often as you like.

6. Now we move on to using this simple skill, in which we have combined meaning from two symbols (and you'll realise this is what we do with a single tarot card, which is a metaphor, or constellation of symbols), to do something rather special. This is a skill that multiplies in such a way that you need nothing more than this in order to read a Grand Tableau of all thirty-six cards, as we will cover later in this book. If you can do two cards, you can do the rest.

Take three cards and lay them out in a triangle.

Repeat the exercise of combining two keywords for each of the three pairings that are possible. Make a note or write on a slip of paper between the cards the one word which arises out of each pairing.

In the example that follows, we have Tree (5), Mouse (23), and Moon (32). The choices of keywords for those cards are longevity, productivity, and dreams. So, we firstly consider Tree and Mouse, longevity and productivity. What comes into our mind are ideas of acorns becoming oaks, small things (mice) building up over a long period of time (tree), and suddenly we get the word "accumulation." We write this word down between the two cards.

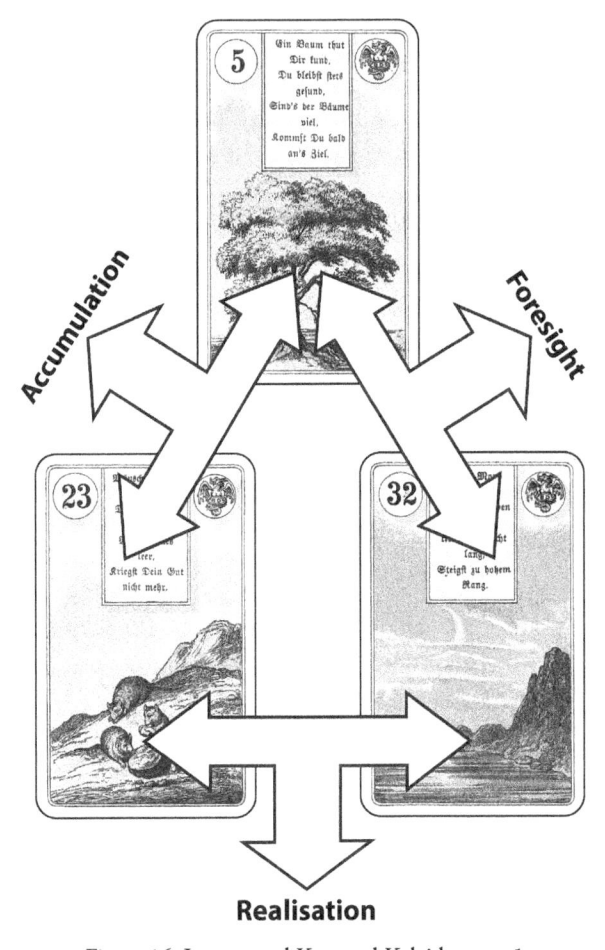

Figure 16. Lenormand Keyword Kaleidoscope 1

We then consider Tree and Moon, longevity and dreams. Don't forget that you can use your own keywords from anywhere you like, be it from other books or simply the images (if you feel like going totally intuitive). We use this method for tarot and Lenormand to answer that old question, "Why do the books have different meanings? What is the meaning of that card?" or to work into our minds new words and meanings presented by a book.

When we think of Tree and Moon, longevity and dreams, we somehow get the image of forestry, then factories, like sawmills. We guess this is somewhat inspired by the image on the Moon card. We keep considering, and get "foresight," like planning, long-term vision, that sort of thing. The song "Telegraph Road" by Dire Straits comes to mind. You can do this with songs too.

We write this word down between those two cards. You can sketch them out in your journal when you do this exercise, or do it on one large piece of paper.

Finally we have our third pair, Mice and Moon, productivity and dreams. We mull over these two words (although we quite like "Mice and Moon"—perhaps it is made of cheese after all!) and get ideas like "following a calling" when you work productively because you are working on making your own dream real … then the word "realisation" comes to us very clearly, so we write that one down.

Now we have three new words: **accumulation, foresight, and realisation.** Don't forget too, these are our words; you'll find your own unique voice. We like to teach in a "clean language" fashion so you can use your own words, ideas, and voice, draw on your own experience, and simply plug those into these teaching methods to discover your own style.

We now come to the trick, and it really is magic. We can now "kaleidoscope" the words together, backwards and forwards (remember the last time you held a kaleidoscope tube to your eye and turned the thing one way and another?) to come up with more meanings. Simply take the new words and write them on a new triangle, and repeat the process.

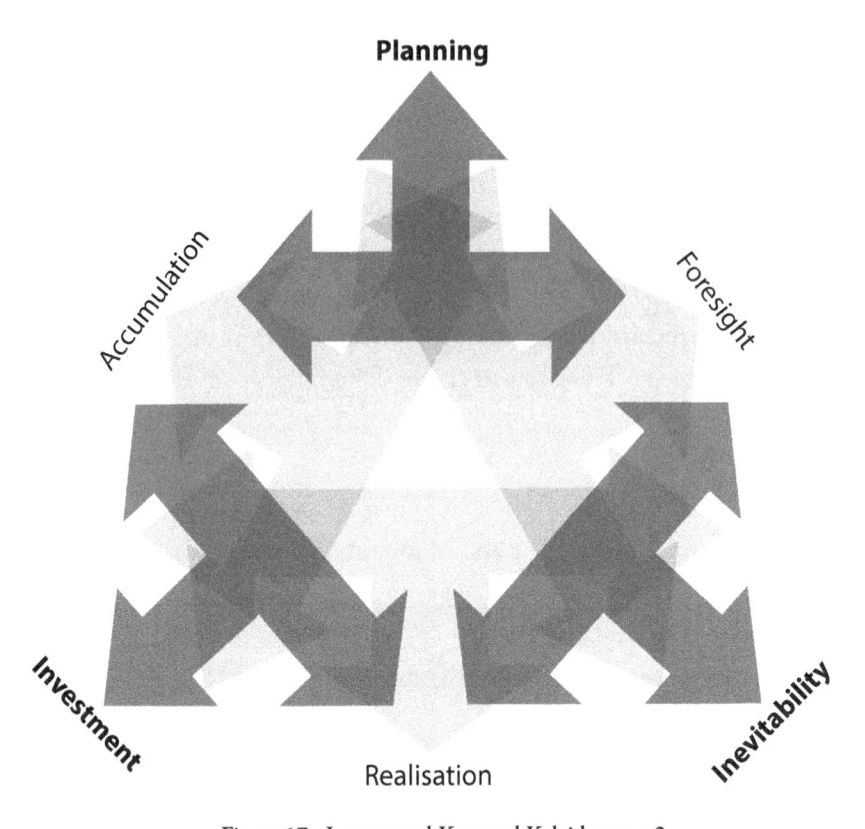

Figure 17. Lenormand Keyword Kaleidoscope 2

So we take accumulation and realisation, and out of that we get the idea of "investment" ("savings" also came to mind, but investment seemed a stronger idea). We mix realisation and foresight, and get the sense of "inevitability"—someone who can realise their plans, making them inevitable. Finally we kaleidoscope accumulation and foresight and out pops "planning."

We now have three new words that have "kaleidoscoped" out of the others. You can keep repeating this as much as you like.

Optional Exercise: You can also collapse the three words inwards, to see if you can come up with one word that arises out of all three. You can do this with the first three actual keywords that we gave the cards, or the next layer of three words that you generate, or any combination. This is what goes on unconsciously in the mind of very experienced readers. You'll also recognise it as a fractal if you've ever seen those types of diagrams—it's a range of meanings approaching a never-ending vanishing point of what the card "actually" means. We can now (or at any level) turn this into a more useful exercise by simply making a sentence or story using the three new words. So if I were to take my three new words—investment, inevitability, and planning—I might say: **With the right planning and investment, the outcome is inevitable.** And that is a possible reading of the Tree, Mouse, and Moon cards.

Of course, the Mice in many traditions indicate loss—even theft, and the Moon is recognition or fame. So whilst the kaleidoscope exercise shows the advice, underneath is the message that (if it were a business question) our business health (tree) would only accumulate recognition slowly—hence the advice.

Interestingly enough, our single collapsed word for all three generated words was "reward." So if these three cards were drawn for a business venture, given that advice above—get investment and plan, don't rush into it, and long-term success is inevitable—the reward of the venture would likely be considerable and assured. We just have to watch those Mice nibbling away at our marketing (Moon).

Try it and see what happens for you. Practice with as many variations of three cards together, or go back to practising with just two for a while until you get the hang of it and then return to the kaleidoscope.

By the way, if you are ever thinking of designing a Lenormand or tarot deck, or want to work in a new book of meanings into your own readings, the kaleidoscope will work wonders to put all that apparently different information together, leading to unique insights. In effect, you are also short-cutting years of actual readings by this method. We like it when we can get a head-start on our readings before we even begin!

How Not To Learn Lenormand

....
The Fox is work...
The Secrets of the Lenormand Oracle, Sylvie Steinbach, 63
*To say 'John is' anything, incidentally, always opens the door to spooks
and metaphysical debate. The historic logic of Aristotelian philosophy as embedded
in Standard English always carries an association of stasis with every 'is,'
unless the speaker or writer remembers to include a date...*
–Quantum Psychology, Robert Anton Wilson, 102
....

The Word Is

When I (Marcus) read sentences in which one thing "is" equated with another in an almost absolute manner, I physically flinch. This is probably because it was one of the logical fallacies that was beaten out of me over many months as a young neophyte in my occult training. My teacher would yell, "Correspondence! Correspondence! Not 'is'!" In this section we will show (without physical torment) how that lesson has helped us not learn Lenormand (or any other system) in a limiting fashion. We'll look at something called e-prime and the differences between tarot and Lenormand as simile and metaphor.

In *Quantum Psychology*, Robert Anton Wilson introduces the idea of e-prime from the work of Alfred Korzybski, who developed the field of General Semantics. The idea can be considered as straightforward as removing "is" from language. As an example, I could have said, "the idea is straightforward," but I said "the idea can be considered ..." thus giving some room for your own decision as to whether it could be seen as straightforward or not.

As another example, let's say I said to you, "John is the good-looking guy over there." You look across the room and see John. Well, you see a good-looking guy next to three other guys. You may be able to see where this is going, particularly when you end up spending the evening talking to Clive by mistake. That word "is" can lead us astray when we take it as fact.

The notion of "is-ness" I believe might be seen as the bane of lazy writing in occultism and any system that relies on symbolism and correspondence. When we read "Mars **is** anger" or "the Hanged Man **is** Neptune in astrology" we create a totally invalid equation between a planet, an emotion, an image, and another planet. They are not each other, they are not the same. They are not fixed in anything; the mind creates a fictional equation.

Lenormand as Simile and Tarot as Metaphor

We like to use the symbol of a triangle above a straight line instead of two straight lines, which determine equivalency rather than equals. It is the same with metaphor or simile. A metaphor is defined as a group of symbols creating a mapping to another situation, and a simile might be something like "it is as easy as falling off a log." When we say "life is a journey" (or a Fool's journey) we are creating a metaphorical mapping, which has many correspondences between attributes of both parts, but they are still not identical.

So a card—in this case Lenormand—is more of a simile than a metaphor, as might be a tarot image. The image of a fox is a simile for certain attributes of a fox—as we will see—but not a complex metaphor such as the story of the Tower of Babel for the Tower card in tarot. These similes work together in a Lenormand reading to provide a tableau—a living set of relationships which then map to the sitters' real lives.

The fox has no direct mapping—another difference from tarot; it is only in its relationship, context, and position to other cards the mapping is provided.

In a moment, we'll see how this works and why I suggest it is important to learn bare keywords and raw concepts for each card before building them up into "meaning." First we will take a look at the fox itself and look at how it functions as an analogy marker in a reading. We'll examine one example in a Lenormand tradition and see how this symbol's meaning has travelled over time since its first use in fortunetelling and cartomancy.

The Tale of the Fox

Halina Kamm (44) gives the fox as a false partner in any regard such as a tricky business partner or even a false prophet. Dos Ventos (58) picks up on this by concentrating on the aspects of betrayal and "sneakiness," whilst suggesting it can show that it is the client who is secretive when positioned "in the back" of the sitter's card.

Mertz (38) also depicts the fox as a cunning predator, ears flat, about to pounce on his unsuspecting prey. The card is hence a mixed card of being fixed on a goal, alert and sensitive, yet also being cunning—so it must be determined if one is the fox or the hen. This is as

Kienle (14) who gives keywords such as "cleverness" and "intelligence" for the positive aspect of the card, and "falseness" and even "theft" for the negative.

Dee (136) provides a means of using distance in a reading with the Fox, in that whilst it symbolises deceit, its proximity to the sitter's card (the Gentleman or Lady) indicates the likelihood of that deceit in the sitter's immediate social circle. A Fox close to hand is troublesome; one far away shows that one can rely on close friends.

Steinbach (63) presents the fox as "work in general, like our daily job, career, employment." She differentiates between the fox as "job" and the fish as "business." However, she goes on to discuss the nature of the fox as disloyal friends.

AndyBC in his "Journal of a Cartomante" site demonstrates a number of factors that can influence how the Fox card applies in a reading depending on its order, and whether it is above or below a sitter's card (he gives keywords such as "wrong," "manipulation," etc. for his language-based construct method of reading/teaching the cards). He also points out that the Fox is a symbol in itself and should not be dressed up with other symbolism or correspondences, such as the mirror in the Mystical Lenormand deck, or an association with Neptune. He also notes that there is far more similarity between traditions, i.e., French and German, than differences.

Reynard, the Original Fox

In the original Game of Hope from 1800, we see that the Fox was perceived as a negative card, one that would result in the player having to change course and take refuge. The little white book that came with the cards explains: "The cunning Fox leads the player astray…"

At about this time, in fact six years prior to the publication of the deck, Johann Wolfgang von Goethe had written his free translation of *Reynard the Fox*, so the tales of the cunning fox would have needed no introduction to the participants in the game. The story had been available in Germany (in Latin) as early as 1498, as *Reinke de Vos*. Reynard is the archetypal bestial trickster-cum-preacher, and these satires were part of the social fabric. The Fox then would have almost certainly been interpreted in divinatory terms as **a trickster**—one who spread a false gospel even, and was not to be trusted.

Other similar tales that give context to the original cards include the fable of the stork and the frog king. We see in the original Game of Hope that the Stork has a frog in its mouth. This is perhaps an allusion to the common European fable of the frogs who each plotted in the depths to rise to the surface and become king over all the others. They struggled with each other, and one eventually fought his way to the lily pad on the surface of the pond to declare his mastery and kingship over his peers—whence he was promptly swallowed whole by a waiting stork.

Furthermore, the association of the serpent (snake) card with a temptress or "other woman" hardly needs pointing out its biblical context.

Learning the Lenormand

When learning the elements of Lenormand, the language of L-space, consider that the terms of reference are like unlit bulbs—they may be coloured differently, like the Fox is not the Tower, however, they have no intrinsic light until they are plugged into the mains.

The Fox is a simile for trickery, the ability to hunt with cunning, and for single-minded determination. These mappings have no absolute meaning; the Fox is no more "workplace" than it is "intelligence"; it is no more a "false gospel" than it is "a cheating lover." It is pointless arguing over interpretation at that secondary level. The important thing should be to learn the alphabet of the symbols in a consistent manner, then test them out in practice and, like any language, we will get corrected in our precise pronunciation along the way.

When "plugged in" to the other cards in combination (and in a Grand Tableau in particular), the circuit becomes connected and the individual bulbs are lit up. However, they also reflect the glare of the images around them, and the circuit transforms as it makes connections across different combinations of resistance and flow. Thus the Fox bulb might be totally shadowed in one corner of the tableau and of no import whatsoever at the oracular moment of reading. It may, however, be sneaking up right behind us, lit balefully by the Snake, the Bear, and the Tower, showing a prism of possibility that someone is indeed building up a strong position from which to leap upon us. The simile of the Fox is now *constellated* by the other images and forms in that relationship alone, an oracular mapping to our life. When it is removed from that relationship, it is merely a picture of a fox and a simple simile.

Let us now look at each of the cards in more detail before considering the far more important points of reading them in combinations and layouts. Unlike the tarot, Lenormand cards are quite simple in themselves. Many books give them individual meanings, but the real trick is reading them together.

THREE

The Cards

....

*Their new-invented method of knowing one's Fortune from a Pack of Cards;
there being fifty-two Questions (and their several Answers) corresponding with
each of the fifty-two cards; each Question being governed by its proper card;
adapted to every Age and Sex; and to Persons of all Degrees and Stations in Life;
Wherein there is Diversion for the Melancholick, Wit for the Ingeneous,
Pleasantry for the Humourous, and Laughter for the Serious.*
–Dr. Flamstead's and Mr. Partridge's New Fortune-Book, 1710

....

Before we look at individual cards in order, let us first try a little experiment with literal reading of the Lenormand. Shuffle your deck and remove two cards, placing them next to each other.

EXERCISE: READING LITERAL LENORMAND
Say out loud, "[Name of card 1] finds itself next to [name of card 2]."

As an example, we might pull the Lady (29) and the Snake (7) cards. I would say, "The Lady finds herself next to the Snake." Now that will immediately conjure up a particular image and feeling—she should get away from that snake, as it probably means her no good. She may not even see it, because it is so close to her.

Or we could pull the Dog (18) and the Anchor (35) cards. This sounds immediately like the name of an English pub, "The Dog and Anchor."[21] So we say, "The Dog finds itself next to the Anchor." What does this bring to mind? We get the idea that the dog is standing by the anchor, perhaps waiting for a ship. Perhaps the dog is guarding it. What do you think it might mean?

You can repeat this exercise for two or more cards. With three cards, you can say out loud, "(Card 2) finds itself between (card 1) and (card 3)." Really stick to the literal image of the cards before going into the meanings below. We have all been in a situation that could be described as "the Child finds itself between the House and the Garden." It is wonderful how literal and direct the Lenormand cards will be if you allow them to speak clearly and simply.

Once you have mastered a few horizontal arrangements of two or more cards, you can work on vertical arrangements.

Lay out two cards, the second below the first, and say, "[Card 2] is below [card 1]." This might be as simple as "the Dog is below the Whip," which would need hardly any interpretation, or slightly more obscure such as "the Sun is below the Tower." In this latter case, perhaps we might sense that the day is late for the situation, and whatever authority or power the Tower had is now diminished. Try saying it the other way around: "The Tower is above the Sun." What sense might that make?

A Note on the Clover

The Clover troubles us deeply. The concept of luck in the cards seems to be at odds with the actual practice of fortunetelling. There is a far deeper meaning to the symbol of the clover both in theory and practice we would like to consider at more length. Whilst it relates to the Trinity (it is a trefoil), the actual illustration is often of the white buds or flowers of the plant—which had a different significance to those who would be using the cards at the time. In the playing game from which the Lenormand cards developed, this card is the one to which one has to return if you land on the Thundercloud, the original description of card 6, the Clouds. To us, this means in symbolic interpretation that when we encounter turbulent change and bad conditions, we return to ourselves for transformation and recuperation.

The white buds of clover in the language of flowers signify "think of me" or "will you be mine?" Again, notions of self-reference and identity. The early German verses on this Lenormand card sometimes allude to celibacy (being by oneself) and the joy that can be found in friendship—certainly romantic notions rather than merely luck. There is almost a sense of the Hermit tarot card here, particularly with the druidic associations of the clover, although that is pushing our associations very far indeed.

When compared with the associated playing card on its earliest design, the Six of Diamonds, the earliest meanings of that card (1750) include the verse:

> He that draws the number six
> Will have sly and cunning tricks.
> But if a woman draw the same,
> It doth show them free from blame.

Whilst we understand that the earliest connection of playing cards with this game was mainly an economic/marketing necessity rather than a divinatory one—i.e., placing the images of playing cards, both French and German, on the Lenormand decks made them available as playing cards for many other games—it is not to say that an oracular connection cannot be constructed or conjured.

In practice, we have always found this card to relate to "integrity" and "authenticity," particularly with regard to one's own purpose or sense of identity. This is similar to how we saw in our beginner's tarot book, *Tarot Flip,* that the unconscious "meaning" of the Magician card, for example, was "success."[22] This is implied but not obvious from the usually given meanings of "elements, channelling, willpower, resources, magic" etc. In actual practice, when we reverse-engineered readers' interpretation of the card for readings, it turned out that most were talking about "success" in context of real questions.

This is actually also the keyword of the Clover card in Laura Tuan's *French Cartomancy* book—so perhaps the tarot Magician and the Clover have something in common in this correspondence. Steinbach seems to associate it with "luck" and its more trickster element such as in gambling—again, we would see this as a divorce or split from one's sense of self, often the root of many gambling or obsessive behaviours and compulsive patterns. The Clover tells us to be close to our own roots.

Whilst Dee suggests the Six of Diamonds as a card of optimism, we feel he goes deeper when he suggests that there will be a change in the sitter's fortunes, and "after this transformation has taken place, the questioner will find that his mind is clearer and that he has **a better vision of where he wants to be**" [emphasis ours] (54). This accords with our view of the card signifying a strong self-identity and knowledge, from which all opportunities and optimism flow.

Treppner (28) also provides the meaning of "luck" for the Clover card, saying that it means some profit will be found in the day, even if not a large casino win. Other European writers extend the meaning to concepts including "time and space travel" as the magical properties of the clover (Kamm, 21). Bartschi adds the concept of endurance and vitality, known homeopathic associations with the clover, which we might add can be connected with the treatment of gambling and the state of clarity—treating a problem with the symbol of its essence, "luck." (18)

Overall, when considered as luck, the card is only "small luck" (Kienle, 10)—to us, it is the essence of where luck arises (making one's own luck in life)—and the Sun, card 31, is more the "big luck" card (Dos Ventos, 22). We give the Sun card the meaning of "will/purpose," the natural extension of self-identity. The Clover grows in the Sun, the Sun places its energies into the plants, which act as resources for work and transformation (cattle and butterflies).

This deeper practical unconscious keyword is the same with the Clover card—whilst it may be taken as luck, this is a state of being, a subjective notion, and also a potentially disempowering one—if your reading involves a card signifying luck that the sitter sees as out of their hands, then what use is a reading?

In practice, we find "luck" arises from one's sense of identity and relationship to the world—and hence we associate these with the Clover card. Those who are whole in themselves (their trefoil or trinity is unified) tend toward luck in that they become satisfied with their being in the world. As a result, rather magically (hence maybe the connection back to the Magician in the tarot), the universe seems to become a welcoming and supporting place for them.

So this card is in its *essence* about one's relationship to oneself and the world; "think of me" in its most spiritual sense. The simplest keyword for this is "identity."

And don't forget too that the clover (shamrock) is very much part of the identity of Ireland, as is the flower eidelweiss for Austria. The daffodil is the flower of national identity for Wales. The national flower for Scotland is the thistle. There are many precedents for having a simple flower represent the essence of your identity.

Finally, it is interesting to note that in Cirlot's *Dictionary of Symbols*, the clover leaf is combined with the symbol of the mountain (another Lenormand card image, quite coincidentally), where it can signify the discovery and journeying toward spiritual identity, as "when clover is located upon a mountain it comes to signify knowledge of the divine essence gained by hard endeavour" (50–1).

We will now look at individual meanings of the cards whilst remembering that they are components of a bigger language, best read together.

Figure 18. The Rider

1. The Cavalier/Messenger/Rider

We begin at the beginning with the Rider; he is the carrier of news, the messenger, who can herald change in your life. This card can be indicative of an actual person of influence coming into your life. The Rider card traditionally brings good news; something of importance you have been anticipating and waiting on will come about. The positive influence of the Rider can be negated by the cards around it; for example, the Rider followed by the dark shadow edge of the Cloud is the ominous delivery of bad news. It is a warning of bad influence entering the sitter's life. Literally speaking, this is saying, "The Rider brings dark clouds." All is not doom and gloom in the Lenormand; this combination can have some light thrown on it by the appearance of the Sun card. Take a look at how the following can foretell "sun after rain":

- The Rider + The Clouds + The Sun
  Literal reading: The Rider brings dark clouds, followed by the sun.

If this card is all about you, there is an emotional imperative that you are not acting upon, where action needs to be taken. You need to express how you feel and stop dragging your heels; you can only do this by moving onward. However, it is important to keep your poise and centre or you could be easily thrown off your course. As a general interpretation, this could involve receiving a visitor who has some good news to impart.

2. The Clover

The card of luck, as seen traditionally, and as discussed earlier in this chapter. We take it as being fortunate, as being given a "little luck," and a positive card in a reading. It is an encouragement to try something new, or to receive (particularly when combined with the Bouquet/Flowers) an offer of assistance.

In financial situations, it is a card of lucky returns or a good investment, depending on the surrounding cards. The obvious and literal meaning of a House card, a Clover card, and a Heart card needs no explanation! If you add the Gentleman and the Ring, and present the Lady card, no doubt you would expect the Child card to follow!

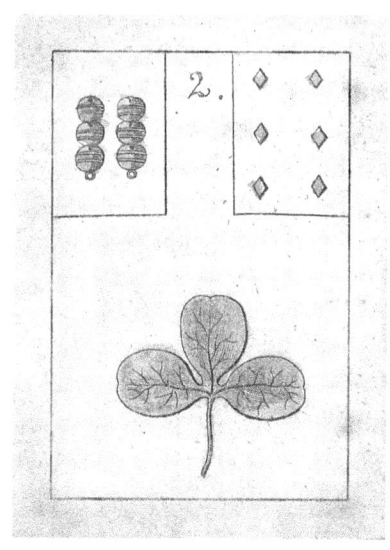

Figure 19. The Clover

This card is a reassurance that all is well, and that the situation you are in is secure and will bring peace of mind. You can relax and spend time enjoying this security. Treat yourself and be kind to yourself—you deserve the best.

This card says for you to keep positive; you are in for some good luck and great abundance.

3. The Ship

The Ship is a signifier of travel and movement. This card can signify potential and opportunities out there. If there is a situation or project you have been wary of acting upon, now is the time to set sail and embrace the change and progress that will be yours. Have you found yourself settling into a mundane routine? If so, you need to make changes, think about where you see yourself in the future. It is never too late to do the things we have been putting off!

Moving on, the conditions are perfect and the timing is right to move forward. The journey will require a certain amount of skill as you navigate onward, plotting through difficult conditions to ensure a safe passage. Harness the power of natural resources; the wind brings change and movement—do not shy from making the changes. A new life could be yours!

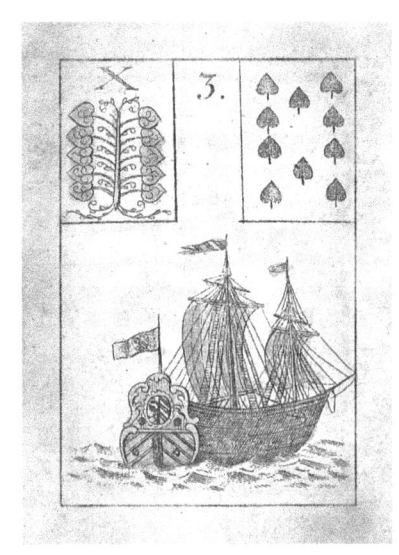

Figure 20. The Ship

We would also like to extend the meaning of this card in a way that can be repeated for all cards in the Lenormand: look at the original gaming meaning, and interpret it in five levels, starting with the literal, then moving through a simple, symbolic, extended, and secret interpretation.

> *No. 3: The one, who throws 3 pips and thus gets to the Ship, will be happily taken by this ship to the Canary Islands, where the well-known beautiful birds are at home, no. 12.*[*]

In the original game, we see that the dice may take one to position 3, the Ship. Here we are instructed that we can move our marker all the way to position 12, the card of the Birds. This is a very fortunate card, which brings far faster progress by luck alone—we are carried by the ship farther than we could go alone.

It is a very favourable card and takes us to a good place.

---

[*] This quote is taken from the English translation of the Game of Hope instructions, available with deck at: http://www.originallenormand.com.

4. The House

The House in the Lenormand is sanctuary, security, and most of all "home, sweet home," which gives it a very positive context. It is shelter from the turmoil of the outside world and signifies familiarity. However, as with all the Lenormand cards, its positive aspect can be influenced negatively by the following combinations.

- The Whip + House = Strife in home
- The Fish + Whip + House = Money-related strife in home
- The Anchor + House + Key + Snake = Stable home open to threat

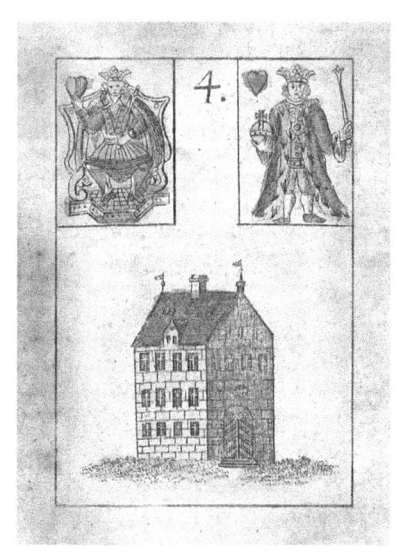

Figure 21. The House

This last combination is a warning to beware of snakes at your door. Take care not to invite anyone into your inner sanctum you cannot trust.

Consider the saying "home is where the heart is." This card is one of stability and strength, an indicator of a good life, the perfect combination of family contentment and emotional well-being accompanying it. If this card appears in relation to a query on making a commitment to a relationship that has come into your life, the card is optimistic that there is healthy compatibility.

5. The Tree

This card is all about tradition, lineage, and ancestor wisdom, the wisdom of the ages that stands the test of time. Think of the enormous life span of a tree, such as the Methuselah Tree, which is thousands of years old, and has stood solid and strong through many changes that have brought famine, war, and turmoil. It has seen all around it alter for good and bad, man has encroached upon its sacred space, but still it maintains its dignity. It has staying power; this card is advising you too to have staying power. The Methuselah Tree is known to have a survival strategy that has enabled it to do this; it "spreads its roots and expands its crown," and to make the most of the resources it absorbs to survive.

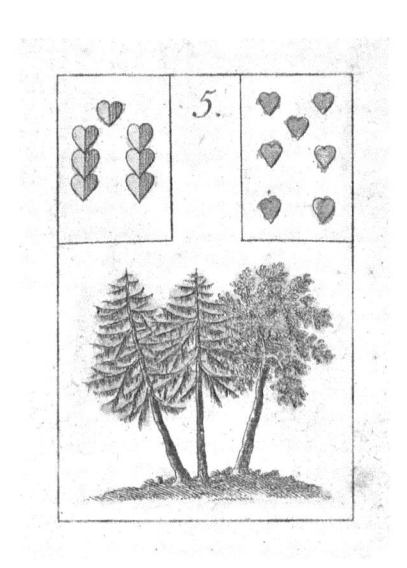

Figure 22. The Tree

Take a leaf from this old tree, and do not bend and give up when all around you is out of control; reconnect to the wisdom that is within you, the wisdom that has been passed down through your own family tree from your ancestors. Honour them and they will honour you.

6. The Clouds

The Clouds card in the Lenormand is traditionally a harbinger of uncertainty. It could also indicate a state of confusion, of thoughts and emotions, air and water. We all have heard of someone who walks around "with their heads in the clouds"—they are in a state of mental and emotional detachment that makes them unable to see what is really going on in a situation. The confusion of the Clouds cards could be lent some clarity, if it was placed in close proximity to the Sun card, especially directly above it. The sun would burn the clouds away.

The shading around the edge of the cloud card can also point out if the uncertainty is moving towards the sitter or away from them.

Figure 23. The Clouds

A cloudy sky can portend good or bad weather. When we see dark and angry clouds in the sky, we are made aware of bad weather coming our way, and we prepare our day accordingly. This card then is very much about being aware of what is going on in our environment and reading and acting upon the signs that we see. The image on the card usually depicts cumulus clouds, dark and light. This could say there will be change ahead, good and bad equally. This card can then imply that the time is right for issues that have been brewing to be brought out into the open, dissipating the pressure that has built up.

7. The Snake

The Snake card stands for a significant other person in the sitter's life, usually a woman, and usually up to no good. This is in part due to the biblical association of the snake with Eve's temptation. There is certainly cause for concern if the Snake card is found lying (literally) underneath the sitter's card.

"Take care where you step." The Snake is strong but silent, stealthy, and ready to strike when least expected. It warns us to be ready for the unexpected. If this card makes itself known with regards to relationships, it could signify that somebody may find themselves drawn into a highly sexual and magnetic entanglement.

Figure 24. The Snake

On a more abstract level, this is a card that favours regenerative healing. If it turns up in response to health, things bode well. Be strong and discreet, cautious, and especially take care to respect the confidentiality of others.

There is no other way to begin the interpretation of the Snake card than with a pantomimed hiss, and there is no getting away from the fact that the Snake is seen as trouble. When used as a person card in the Lenormand, the Snake expresses negative character traits, such as being manipulative and slippery by nature. Traditionally it could signify the presence of a jealous woman, a rival in love in the equation. There is betrayal here.

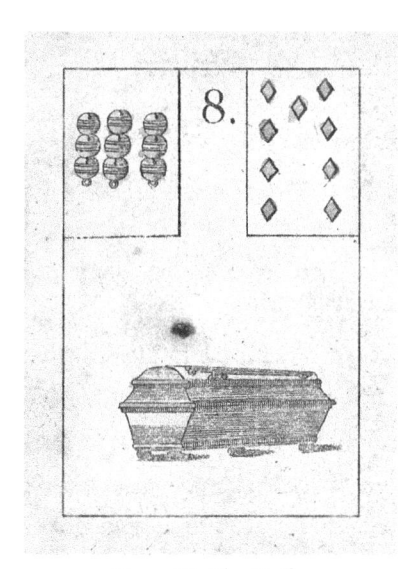

Figure 25. The Coffin

8. The Coffin

Traditionally the Coffin is symbolic of loss through ill health and death. However, one must remember that when the cards were first devised, illness and death played a brutal hand. You would be considered fortunate to live to the age of forty. Women frequently died in childbirth and infant mortality was high. The attitude to illness and death was one of reconciliation; it was something people of the time were quite understandably very preoccupied about.

So what does the Coffin really mean? It can literally be the "end" of something such as a relationship or marriage, money problems, a job, hardship and strife, being taken for granted, or even the end of your travels.

The card also reminds us of ritual farewell, the end of an era, acceptance of something being done and finished, adopting a way of being that accepts the inevitable, or out-worn regrets needing to be put aside. This is the card of initiation, shedding old attachments, and learning to be less egotistical. Await the rebirth of a new you. With regards to timing, completion is near. However, there could be a sense of mourning or sadness at the prospect of change.

9. The Flowers/Bouquet

Traditionally the Bouquet symbolises joy being presented into one's life. You will receive a token of appreciation that will make you happy, one that could take you by surprise. In the past, flowers were used as a secret code to relay a person's intentions to another in their life, especially of a romantic nature. The different combinations in a bouquet of flowers spoke in a Lenormand-like way in a special coded message. We must remember that hidden symbols were very much in the psyche of the people of the day. In the so-called language of flowers, we would see the iris, red rose, and ivy together mean a messenger (iris) of passion (rose) and fidelity (ivy).

Figure 26. The Bouquet

"Say it with sentiment or not at all." A sign/expression of appreciation, it could be for romantic considerations or merely for services rendered. Take care to express how much you value a thing or individual in your life; have you a special occasion or celebration coming up? This card is a reminder of being alive and aware of nature's simple beauty, and taking time to "smell the flowers." It could be advising you to take a simplistic, natural approach to gaining that certain somebody's affections; avoid the materialistic way (leave the Caribbean trip till later). A thoughtful act may bring about positive changes. Feminine energy is swirling. If clarity is needed with regards to a venture or project, good dividends will be rewarded after your work is done.

10. The Scythe

Traditionally in the Lenormand, the card of the Scythe cuts and clears; it is an indication that something will be cut out of your life, and will be no more. It may come as a shock. However this clearing is not all negative, as it will allow the growth of something new. It could be a new lease on life. This can be in regards to a relationship; the heartbreak of the end of a relationship opens you up to new opportunities, and you may have the chance to meet somebody new. If this is applied to work, the loss of a job can lead to you reassessing your life and the taking up of a whole new career.

Figure 27. The Scythe

"A blunt blade makes work." This card speaks of a call to action and to be prepared for the work ahead. That very thing you have been delaying will soon manifest and will need dealing with before it gets out of hand. Do not underestimate the work involved and what you will be up against. This card's appearance in a layout draws attention to the cards around it, highlighting timing; it can be an indicator of a need for expediency. Placed next to the Snake, for instance, it could be saying to act as soon as possible to confront an individual who has been quietly devious. If the Scythe is placed to the left-hand side, hold back, take a more logical approach, try to reason. If on the right-hand side, confront in a more emotional way.

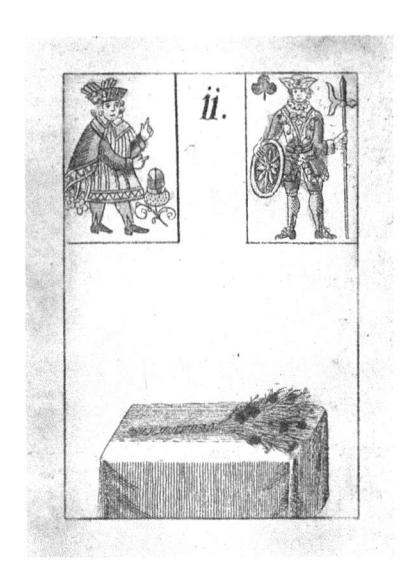

Figure 28. The Rod, Birch, or Whip

11. The Whip

A card of trouble, bad words being spoken, unrest, and argument. In some cases it can signify service.

"No pain, no gain." This is a card that heavily emphasises the importance of motivation and discipline resulting in achieving our goals. There are ways and means of making progress, and they rarely involve an easy route to success. We have to master our own weakness and turn it into strength to serve us in our endeavours. The ancient Egyptians associated the whip with the emblem of power; therefore this card speaks heavily of self-mastery. Additionally are there areas of our life that we need "whipped into shape"; if so, this card is saying "get to it!" If this card is placed next to the Scythe, this is a double whammy.

The Whip can bring strife and disagreements. There may be a battle for somebody in the relationship either at home or at work to maintain the upper hand, the "whip hand." Such a power struggle in a relationship could manifest as a difficult boss, and the card that embodies this is the Bear. Also be very wary if this card appears in close proximity to the Snake—betrayal could be in the cards.

In a very literal sense, a reprimand is on the way. You may have to pay for some past transgression. The whip is a hard task master that commands discipline. The traditional meaning of the card is strife and disharmony, and it indicates that turmoil will be "whipped up." If the discord is at work, it could mean that morale is at a low, and back-biting and disagreements are making the environment a very unhappy one indeed. This card could also indicate that something or somebody is being whipped up into a frenzy. It could speak to a need to control things in your life.

12. The Birds/The Owl

The Birds card signifies conversation, communication, and chatter.

"Age-old wisdom, being awakened when others are asleep." This card conjures up Alfred Hitchcock's *The Birds*, especially the scene where the heroine looks out to see the birds that have lined up on the wires. This was very much a metaphor of communication—are we getting the message? If you think about this a little bit deeper and look at it from the view of the original short story by Daphne du Maurier, this story was about the danger of not being in tune with the natural order of things, being spoilt by technology.

Figure 29. The Birds

This card is saying "listen to your intuition," that which comes naturally and is not forced. The law of correspondence works on all levels. Block out the external noise, and listen to the wise one, the hidden, and the sacred. See beyond, starting from within.

In modern use, this is the card of chatter, gossip, backchat, and real-time communications (unlike the Letter). The card is full of buzz being passed along the grapevine from one person to another.

The Birds means that news spreads fast (particularly with the Rider), via telephone, text message, Facebook, and of course—Twitter.

Where the Birds card appears, everything close to it is already in the air or being broadcast; there is no stopping it.

Figure 30. The Child

13. The Child

The Child card literally represents a child in the sitter's life or, at a symbolic level, a childlike nature. This is innocence and play-power.

"First tentative steps into the world—a living legacy." True honesty, integrity, pure heart, being nonjudgemental and authentic, this is a state of being untainted by cynicism and bitterness. Make a fresh start; it is never too late to learn new things. Be part of new experiences, cast aside the fear that holds you back, go for childlike abandonment. Have trust in the process; those first tentative steps are only just the beginning. The focus for relationships is to be more trusting, authentic, and to come from the heart, not the head.

In a work-related question, this card will show that spontaneity and fresh ideas are needed.

14. The Fox

The card of cunning and trickery, something is always afoot when the Fox is in play. The position of this card in a reading will dictate whether it is you who must be wary, or if others are already out-foxing you. Either way, it is a call to prick up your ears.

The Fox is the entrepreneur of the Lenormand deck; he does not miss a trick, and in fact he is ready to play a trick at any time. The qualities of the fox are quick-wittedness and dexterity in avoiding taking the flack in any situation, especially so at work.

We all know a Mr. (or Ms.) Fox in the workplace; he is full of good ideas, innovation, and has an attitude of self-preservation in life. He is the one waiting to take your promotion when your back is turned, and he will always take the last slice of cake on the plate. All in all, this sort of behaviour has given him a lousy reputation, and he has a good few enemies in life and in the workplace.

The Fox possesses energies you either love or hate, and when he is in a position of influence in your reading, you may be a little wary of what he is up to! However, remember that he's not all bad, and if you put the Fox with Clover for example, it could be foretelling "innovative ideas that come up lucky."

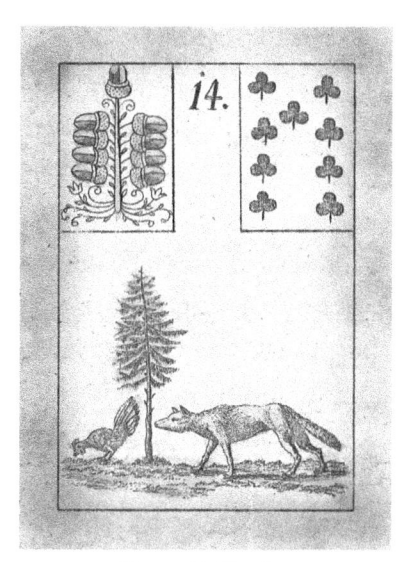

Figure 31. The Fox

15. The Bear

The Bear is a symbol of power and authority. It can stand for a male figure of stature in the sitter's life, such as a boss. It can also, when combined with the Lady, signify the Mother, and the Gentleman, the Father.

In alchemy, the Bear corresponds to *nigredo*, a blackening process. Therefore this would indicate a cruel and crude energy at play in a situation that is plaguing the sitter. This entanglement could result in primitive instincts being awoken, the sitter or somebody around them being quick to anger, or a situation that could easily become troublesome if not handled with care.

Be wary of not expressing your dark shadow, for as Walt Kelly so wisely wrote, "We have met the enemy, and he is us." The most we have to fear is that which lurks within.

The Bear can be symbolic of business and finance—take for example, a "bear market" in share trading, where when the value of stocks is down, which is seen by some in finance as an opportunity to take advantage by buying up shares when they are at a low, later selling when a profit can be made.

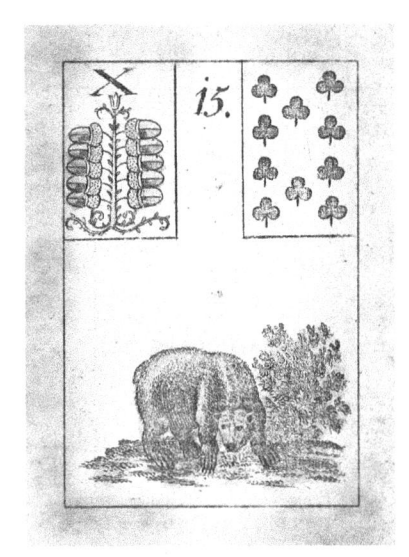

Figure 32. The Bear

16. The Star

The Star is the possession of clarity in all things near and far, and a longing for hope and wishes to come true. It is vital to maintain a positive outlook in work-related ventures. Be aware that just because something looks desirable, appearing to offer abundance, big and brash as it may be, do not take for granted that in reality it is so. In astronomy, it is known that the brightest, largest stars are the ones running out of fuel.

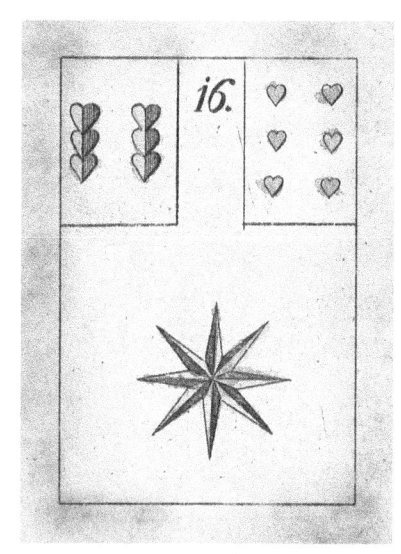

Figure 33. The Star

> *The light that burns twice as bright burns for half as long—and you have burned so very, very brightly, Roy. Look at you: you're the Prodigal Son; you're quite a prize!*
> —Tyrell, from *Blade Runner*
> (dir. Ridley Scott, 1982)

The Star card advises us that we need to assess our lives; are we living at too fast a pace, are we too driven to be brighter and better than others at the expense of our own wellbeing? If we apply the science of a star to ourselves, we are, like the star, at risk of burning out too soon, using up fuel too rapidly in order to maintain our brightest appearance. Remember to plan for the long game!

In general readings, the Star is a card of clarity and vision, blessed with a destination in mind. Follow that which inspires you, do not live life without a sense of purpose, and do not let yourself stray from your destiny.

> Take the joy and bear the sorrow,
> looking past your hopes and fears:
> learn to recognize the measured
> dance that orders all our years.
> —*Archilochos: To His Soul*, translated from the Greek by Jon Corelis

Figure 34. The Stork

17. The Stork

The presence of this card in a reading indicates deliverance from a difficult situation, or the delivery of good productive news. The Stork was believed to have significance to the Romans, who considered it a symbol of filial piety.

Within the Lenormand, the Stork may speak of the delivery of good or bad news, influenced by the cards in its proximity. The news could materialise in many ways, the most obvious one being the news of a birth. There is an emphasis on a strong family or friendship, one that may imply that your family and friends will be there for you; they can be relied upon in a time of need, and this help could come in the form of a gift.

On the other hand, you may find yourself in a situation where the presence of the Stork may mean you receive news of something being taken away from you for someone else's benefit. For example, you could receive news that you will have to find new accommodation because your landlord is moving his family into the apartment. If the Tree, House, and Scythe appear too, the influence is stronger.

Any reading will make more sense if we look at the character of the Stork; it has a reliable reputation and it will return each year to the place where it has always nested. The Stork is known in the Hebrew language as *chasidah*, the "faithful one." She is one who will always come back, and it is interesting that the word "chasidah" also relates to the Hebrew *chesed*, which for those of you who have some knowledge of Kabbalah means "loving kindness." The stork is known to naturally show acts of kindness toward its fellow storks by its propensity to gift food. However, this behavior is of a selective nature—the stork steals food from other species of birds to fulfil this "kind" act!

Yea, the stork in the heaven knoweth her appointed times; and the turtle and the crane and the swallow observe the time of their coming.
—Jeremiah 8:7

Figure 35. The Dog

18. The Dog

The Dog symbolises loyalty, dependency, and the presence in your life of a trusty friend or loved one. This is the person in the sitter's life who gives unconditional love, but may be a little overly needy. In a more negative way of reading, is there a certain somebody you have welcomed into your life who may end up biting the hand that feeds them? There is a need to take charge and let others know you are top dog!

The dog is a faithful companion who coexists naturally with humans yet still maintains a primal nature. Dogs are able to make the best of both worlds—primal and domestic. If you look after a dog well, it will reward you with endless attention and an open, loving heart. However, the dog is a pack animal: it needs to know its place in the pack, otherwise it takes leadership, thinking you are of a lower rank.

When combined with workplace or authority cards, this card can bring to our attention issues of hierarchy and group in-fighting.

19. The Tower

The Tower indicates a need to be aware of what is going on around you, to be ready for any eventuality. It is true that forewarned is forearmed. This card is saying you have the upper ground; you are in a good position to ensure that your security is safe and sound. The Tower is the place to be—you find yourself in an elevated position. This is a card of caution, expressing the importance of maintaining higher ground in a situation.

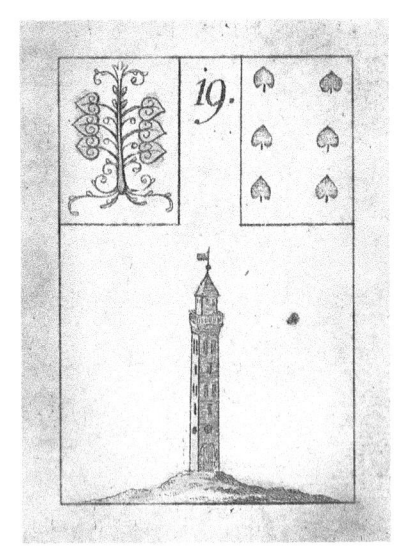

Figure 36. The Tower

This card could speak of an overly defensive stance that could leave you well-protected but out of favour. If this card appears in relation to a health issue, it could be indicative of the immune system's defensive role. It could also indicate the need to withdraw physically as well as emotionally from other people in order to rest and recuperate.

From another perspective it can be about the need to look beyond the present situation we are in to project our situation into the long term. We need to be more analytical and more objective in our planning, maybe even strategic. If the Ring followed the Tower, it would be saying, "Plan and survey before committing yourself to a contract." A signet ring would apply the seal to the deal! In combination with the Letter card, the need to be sure of the situation before going ahead is consolidated.

The Tower can speak of power and bureaucracy and having to face something far greater than ourselves. We may find ourselves up against a well-established system that is unyielding and seemingly uncompromising. It could manifest itself in the form of a tax department. If we are protected by the system, we become part of the machine itself.

20. The Garden

The Garden card is about getting out into the world and being social in some capacity. It is the card of networking, sharing, and coming together with like-minded people. In the matter of romantic relationships, this could indicate a romantic date or a place with other people such as a party or a meal out.

More generally, the card, particularly in the French tradition, tends to signify a "natural life," a life of cultured appreciation. It is often pictured with a fountain, which nourishes one's capacities to enjoy life, and in return is nourished. If this card appeared in a workplace situation, it would indicate that all would run smoothly and harmoniously, even creatively.

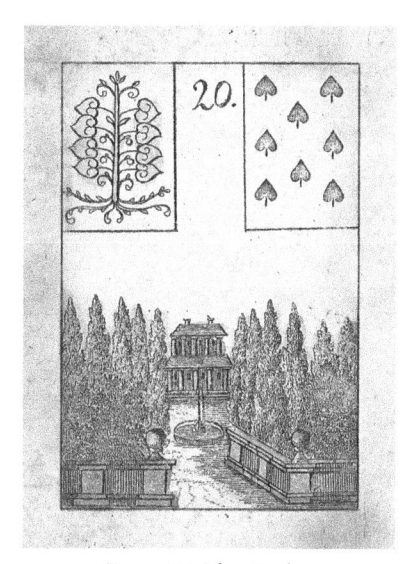

Figure 37. The Garden

It could be indicative of marriage and union, especially when close to the Ring, which is about pledge and commitment. Throw in the Heart and Clover, and it may be a marriage made in heaven, though it will take effort and dedication to maintain, just like the loving care and work put into nurturing flowers and plants in a garden.

The Snake close to the Garden literally speaks of lies and betrayal lurking in a social environment. This is a reflection of the story of Eden, however in mundane terms it is a workplace or the world of social media: Facebook, Twitter. We know that not all news is good news, and a Snake and Garden combination warns of being manipulated by others who only have their own best interests at heart.

Be heartened if the Stork is close by; it could ease the situation. Storks are known predators of the Snake, so their proximity can negate a malicious situation.

21. The Mountain

"Don't make a mountain out of a molehill." The Mountain can represent an obstacle or a diversion. When attempting to reach a goal or commitment we sometimes have to surmount various challenges. A particularly difficult blockage or obstacle can tempt us to retreat, but the context of this card will tell us if retreat is best or if we should find some other way to get over it. Invariably, the best line of action is to grit our teeth, head on up, plant our metaphorical flag, and get to the other side.

The Mountain is also a symbol of durability and the might needed to withstand life's constant wear and tear. The Mountain is seen in some traditions as representing the structure of bones, i.e., the bones of the earth. In relation to health, this could point to rigidity and being inflexible. It could relate to issues with the spine.

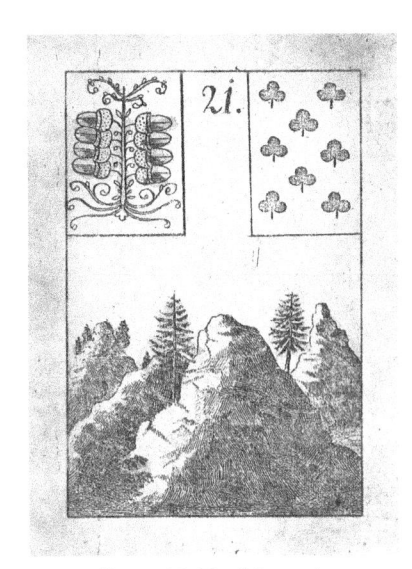

Figure 38. The Mountain

If the Mountain card is placed alongside the Mice, an obstacle that may once have seemed great and insurmountable will be put into perspective, and the problem will be seen for what it is. This is especially so if the problem is related to a verbal obstacle or a stubborn situation, where neither party is prepared to give way. There may have been a falling out or words spoken that were threatening and have caused fear.

Take note of these words taken from Aesop's fable, the earliest version as below:

A mountain had gone into labour and was groaning terribly. Such rumours excited great expectations all over the country. In the end, however, the mountain gave birth to a mouse.[**]

[**] From Aesop's Fables: http://mythfolklore.net/aesopica/perry/520.htm

If you ask the Lenormand about your lack of progress in your career and the Mountain appears close by your significator, it is confirming that you have an obstacle to overcome. However, what you really want to know is how you can overcome this obstacle to progress. If the Mountain is followed by the Mice, it is telling us to carry on gnawing away and producing results. Combined with the Moon it signifies "recognition" and if those are then followed by the Bouquet and the Fish, it would denote that appreciation is due in the form of money.

The Mountain can speak of the need to rise above where you are at the moment. You need to be elevated, and you may find yourself elevated above others, maybe in the promotional sense. New, lofty heights will be reached, but only with struggle.

Figure 39. The Ways

22. The Ways

"Where there is a will, there is a way." The Ways card is symbolic of choices and decisions to be made as we make our way through life. This card can indicate that you have reached this point in your life, and that now is the time to act. It can speak of a dilemma, a problem that is difficult to solve, or times when you simply cannot get to the crux of the matter. This card when in a place of influence in a reading is summoning the enquirer to exert their will to find a way forward.

When we consider a Lenormand card as indicating somebody's character (for example, when a card appears above or below their significator in a Grand Tableau), then we would see this card as showing an erratic character. It literally indicates somebody always on the move, yet never knowing their destination. It can also be (in one German tradition) a sceptic. Certainly it is somebody we cannot pin down to one place. If it were found in combination with the Ship, it might indicate someone with itchy feet, and with the Anchor it would show someone afflicted with unfulfilled wanderlust.

The Ways is reflective of its own nature in a reading; it is influenced by the cards around it, thus it could indicate willpower, bravery, and courage to follow one's way in the world (if combined, say, with the Bear, the Ship, or the Heart). Combined with the Child, the Tree, the House, or the Mountain, however, it might indicate someone who prevaricates, it is neither one thing nor another, and cannot be found to make a fixed decision.

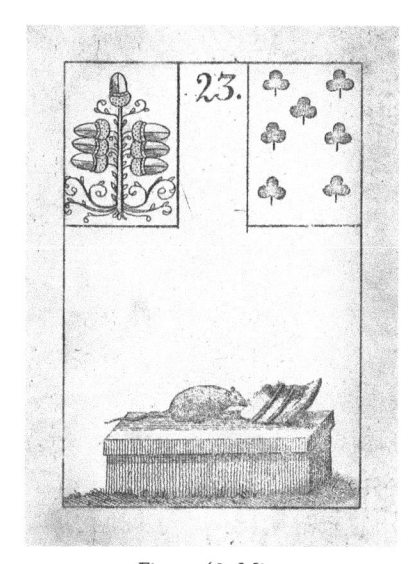

Figure 40. Mice

23. The Mice

This card is negative, and it warns of missing details whilst being distracted by the big picture. Those mice are already eating away at your resources, your confidence, whatever they're nearby. If it's the Ship, for instance, your holiday plans may be unravelled by missing one piece of essential detail (tickets, anyone?).

In a professional or family context, the Mice card shows that people we have recently come to know may be nibbling away at our position. If combined with or in proximity to the Snake or the Fox, then this is certainly a warning card. We would look to the Bear to see how our authority could be maintained in this war of the animals!

The Mice also indicate loss, lack of resources, and poverty. In modern parlance, this might be "limiting beliefs" but we see the literal Lenormand as just that—whatever the cause, psychological or spiritual, the result is the same: you are not going to be able to afford to attend that retreat centre if the Mice are not run out of the House. If the Mice are close to the House, it may even indicate a theft of some kind, in traditional usage.

The Mice card possesses the energy of productivity and doing tasks in bite-sized pieces. The mouse is a tiny little thing but is capable of infesting a whole house in no time at all without you even knowing about it. This card in a position of influence could be drawing attention to something going on in your environment you are not managing. You may be letting little things overwhelm you, so much so that you are going to be left with an out of control situation. Come down from that chair of avoidance and fear so you won't be a mouse in your own house!

24. The Heart

The Heart of course speaks for itself; it is a symbol close to us all. When this card is heavily prominent in a reading, it is all about love, relating, and creating a union of some sort, especially when close to the Ring, the Garden, and the Clover.

We tend to look at the Heart's situation between the Gentleman and Lady cards to indicate the nature of a relationship, if such is the question asked. We would obviously prefer the heart to be the only card between the two people in relationship! Truly, every three out of five questions you will be asked as a sybil will be of this nature.

In a question with regard to a profession, this card would signify to us that someone is looking well upon the sitter, that they are a likely supporter and sponsor on an emotional and connected level, rather than simply a logical or practical one. The combination of the Bear (power), Tower (authority), and Heart (harmony), would show us a very passionate and powerful workplace.

When the Heart is around other positive cards, its influence is magnified; here it truly shines as the centre of attention—our emotional world is fully satisfied. However, if it is drawn close to negative cards, particularly a majority, rather than "tempering" the cards, as we might be tempted to do in proactive tarot reading, it unfortunately and literally indicates that the heart will be open to negativity. Thus the sitter will experience suffering as a result, more so than if the heart were not in that position.

Generally speaking, in all traditions, the Heart is a peaceful symbol of harmony, whether between two companies in a merger, siblings, romantically involved people, or the result of a court case. The Heart stands for equality and satisfaction.

Figure 41. The Heart

25. The Ring

The Ring is symbolic of making a commitment, a pledge, and forging a bond. It can relate to love and marriage, matters of work, contracts, and business generally. As with the Heart card, we would look to the Ring and its position between the Gentleman and Lady cards to denote the nature of a relationship in terms of commitment. If the Ring and the Heart were found only behind the Lady, and the Gentleman was rather close to a Snake, we would have a very recognisable situation. If his card, the Ring, and the Tower were all close together with the Bear or the Fox (if self-employed), he may be wedded to his job too much. Of course, this applies to the Lady card also.

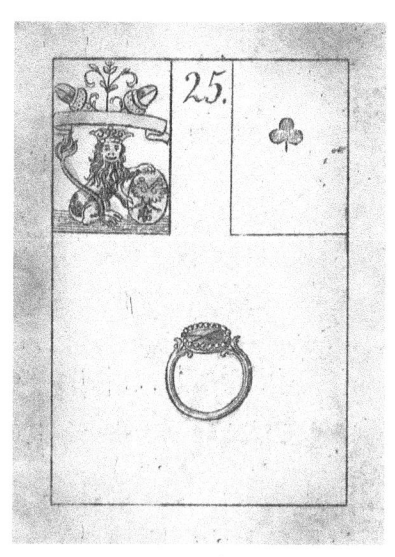

Figure 42. The Ring

However, this card could be looked at as if somebody is stuck in a situation where they feel that somebody else is "running rings" around them. This goes hand in hand with the traditional image of a ring expressing the commitment of marriage or betrothal, but in a negative view it can be seen as being a habit that is difficult to break.

The sitter could find him- or herself in a situation from which they are having difficulty extricating themselves, such as being unable to get out of a contract they have signed. However, if the sitter asks about signing a business contract, this card followed by the Anchor, Clover, and Bear speaks of a commitment to a secure, successful (lucky), and powerful business.

As an example of how the Lenormand cards can be interpreted in a health reading, the German reader Iris Treppner sees this card in such a reading as indicating a family bind, something about an illness being connected to the family or environment.

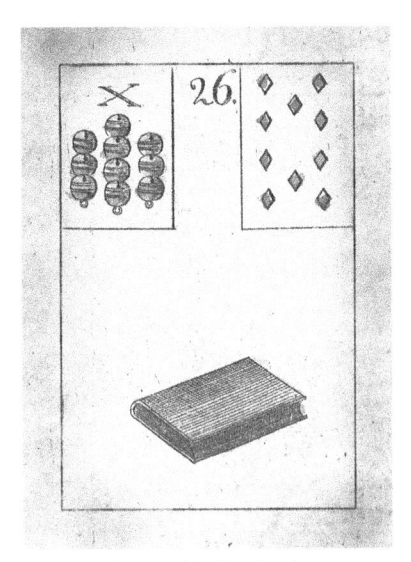

Figure 43. The Book

26. The Book

The Book is a card of secrecy and knowledge. If your deck has the book "open" then perhaps it indicates more about knowledge and revelation. If it is "closed" then it depicts more of the hidden nature of knowledge. Some readers use the direction in which the book is "open" to read what knowledge is being disclosed. As an example, if the book was drawn with the spine to the left of the image, and the card to the right was the Child, then it would indicate a childhood secret or old secret about to come out into the open.

This is a card of learning and using the imagination to go beyond what we know. A book of fiction can transport us to a whole new world where we can experience life beyond our wildest dreams. Nonfiction book can teach skills ranging from the most mundane to the totally way-out—basket-weaving to accessing the secrets of the universe. The Book is power and a ticket to liberty, bringing learning, and learning brings freedom. Therefore, it is a key to unlocking ourselves, particularly when combined, obviously, with the Key.

The influence of the Book in a reading can be a prod to learn something or become better informed. There is something you should know—cards around it would tell you where that knowledge may be obtained: the Tower, for example, would be a school or institution; the Fox, someone with natural ability in the subject of interest.

The Book in close proximity to the Birds and the Rider card says that you should look out for signs (Birds) and the arrival of news (in the form of the Rider) that will inform you of something of which you should be aware.

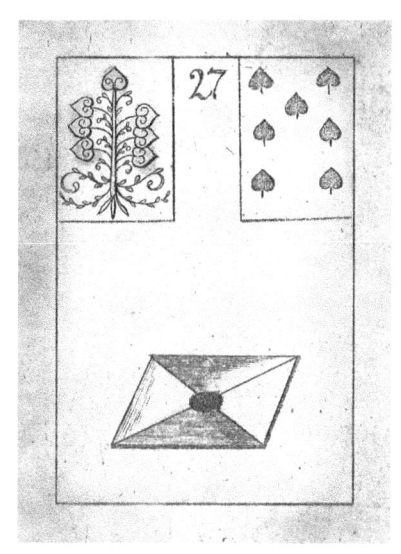

Figure 44. The Letter

27. The Letter

The Letter signifies to us the written word. It is thus a literal card of connecting in a concrete manner, be it email or any other written form. In the French tradition, it is a card signifying invitations, such as to a dance or party. If received for an employment question, it would indicate at least a response, the cards around it indicating the nature of the response—the Sun and Moon being positive in this respect, for example, the Mountain and Ways being a resounding negative.

The Letter is a card that literally puts pen to paper, a form of communication and expression that requires considerable care and sentiment. There is something quaint, old-fashioned, and almost precious about letter writing. It calls up images of bygone times when the world was a much smaller and slower place. A letter would be the only way of keeping friends and loved ones informed of your life.

This card expresses the importance of communication, especially the formal written kind. Close to the Ring, it symbolises a contract, whereas next to the Birds or the Rider, it could signify email.

On the negative side, this card modified by the Fox or the Snake could mean difficulty in the fine print of things, particularly if joined by the Mice.

Figure 45. The Gentleman

28. The Gentleman

The Gentleman in the reading can be the male Significator or the significant other of the female sitter. In a wider sense, it is a sitter's brother, father (combined with the Bear), or close male friend (combined with the Dog).

A few readers use the court cards of the tarot on the Lenormand cards to indicate people and their relationship to each other. We cover this in our courses, as it probably would require a book in itself given the possible combinations and different schools of reading playing cards.

It can also be symbolic of forceful male energy. This could indicate the need to be more assertive in a situation, or be even less so; say for example if a sitter asks advice on how to deal with a situation where they feel they are being taking advantage of in some way, causing anger and temptation to confront the aggressor. If the Gentleman card is behind the Scythe, it may mean that the sitter needs to "cut" the aggressive behavior.

Figure 46. The Lady

29. The Lady

The Lady in the reading can be the female significator or the significant other of the male sitter. In a more general sense, it is the sitter's sister, mother, or close female friend (particularly combined with the Dog). If combined with the Child, it is obviously a younger lady.

As with the Gentleman card, the Lady is given more detail by surrounding cards. A Lady close to the Garden and the Birds is someone who enjoys social gatherings and gossip. A Lady close to the Bear and Tower may have issues with authority, and so on.

At a more abstract level, it can also be symbolic of nurturing feminine energy in a situation, an energy which needs to be applied to resolve a problem.

Figure 47. The Lily

30. The Lily

We find the Lily one of the strangest cards in the Lenormand for its symbolism, as it can range from the sacred to profane. It can represent purity or sex, it can represent a good spirit or passion. In effect, it is a placeholder for the whole range of virtue.

The Lily card in a reading can symbolise fertility, or pure and virtuous intent. If the question posed is regarding someone's integrity, the Lily could imply "virtuous intent" followed by the Heart, which is symbolic of love and union, or "all will be well" if followed by the (lucky) Clover.

31. The Sun

The Sun is a highly positive card in Lenormand readings, and predicts success in our work, particularly after effort (Scythe), struggle (Cross), obstacles (Mountain), or troubles (Mice). The Sun can radically turn a reading into a positive situation when it appears at the end of a line of cards. It shines, saying it will all be worth it.

So, here comes the sun! The Sun is the life-giver and provider of warmth and well-being. In a reading it symbolises growth on all levels and maintaining a positive face to the world; it promotes confidence and willpower. The Sun's influence in a reading is its ability to throw light on a situation. Next to the Moon card, it is indicative of perfect balance. If these cards are on either side of the Heart card in relation to a question about emotional well-being, this is very good indeed.

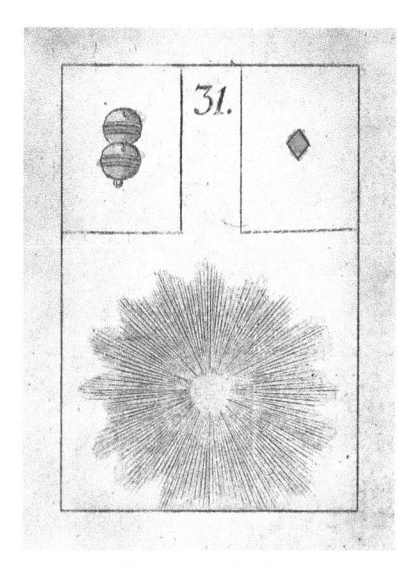

Figure 48. The Sun

The Sun and Moon on either side of the Fish is indicative of a good balance with money, finances, and resources. The Sun above the Garden is good for nurturing growth. The Sun as a timing card is a year.

In a professional context, the Sun indicates advancement and recognition, although again with the Moon, it would provide prediction of a publically recognised advancement. The Sun is a pat on the head, while the Moon is a round of applause.

32. The Moon

The Moon is symbolic of emotions and creativity. It can also represent the idea of letting ourselves be carried away by dreams and fancy. The Moon followed by the Mice can indicate the presence of an emotional obsession that has become repetitive (Mice), rather like the constant chewing of nails—a symptom of some other stress.

We are heavily influenced by the Moon itself, from the ebb and flow of the tides cycles, to the influence it exerts on our physical and emotional states. In regards to an enquiry on a relationship issue, the combination of the Heart, Moon, and Clouds together can indicate that the Heart is heading toward emotional change (Clouds). It certainly sounds like an emotional storm

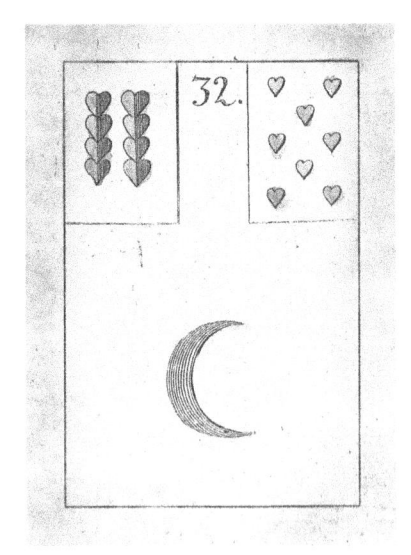

Figure 49. The Moon

is up ahead for our sitter. The Moon can be used as a timing card, indicating a period of twenty-eight days, or around a month.

This is also a card of needing recognition and appreciation. Such a state is highly reactive and always results in constantly looking around to see what others are doing or thinking. Worries of being unable to exert enough influence on others may follow.

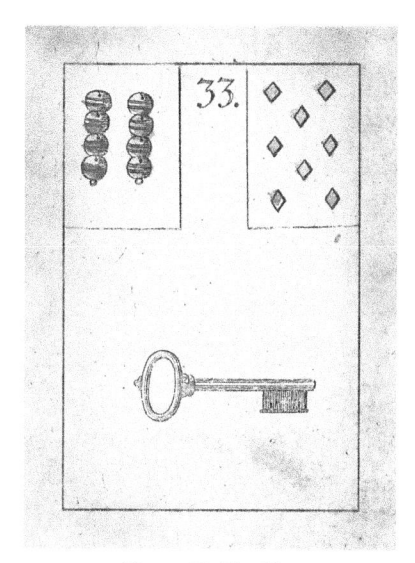

Figure 50. The Key

33. The Key

The Key denotes opportunity, a figurative unlocking of a situation, although some may read it as a locking up also. To receive the Key and the Heart, for example, means a literal unlocking of the heart by someone, whereas the Book and the Heart might signify someone keeping themselves closed off from you. In the latter case, they are a "closed book" to you, emotionally. The Key and the Ways cards together provide opportunity and choice.

The Key is symbolic as a tool for unlocking something that is closed to you. In times of old, a certain status of authority was attached to the key. The lady of the house would be given the keys to all the doors of the house for safekeeping. In a reading regarding moving house and security, the Key card followed by House then Clover indicates the opening (Key) of the new property (House) will be secure and content (Clover).

The Key can also be symbolic of unlocking knowledge. In a reading, it can confirm that something will be unlocked, and you will be able to make sense of something that has until now puzzled you; you'll have a "Eureka!" moment. In a reading with a question similar to "Will I be able to sort out my current problems and have a peace of mind?" one might receive it as a positive response; the Ways "dilemma" unlocked by the Key, followed by the Star, would indicate the bringing of clarity to the situation.

34. The Fish

The Fish card is symbolic of money and good fortune. It is a literal symbol of resources that can be drawn upon and used in plenty to "feed the people," as was told in the biblical parable. Sometimes in a reading this can represent time as a resource, or other capital. For example, as combined with the Moon in a business situation, this card would represent good will or the recognition of ability as a resource.

The Fish announce a change in the tide, bringing a realisation of projects, particularly those with material results. In a reading relating to emotions and relationships, they can indicate the relationship's almost playful nature (or person whose card they affect), seeking joy in life through being with a partner.

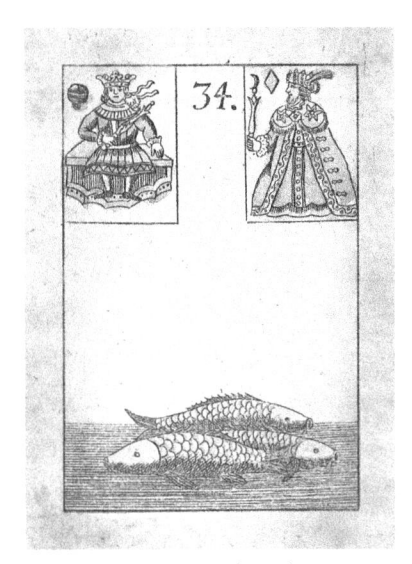

Figure 51. The Fish

In a more psychological interpretation, the Fish swim in the depths of the unconscious, so they represent hidden desires, feelings, and deeper currents. In a Grand Tableau, where the cards above the significator can show what is beyond their control, this card in that position would indicate the person was being driven by needs not fully known to themselves. If it were found below the significator, it would perhaps indicate a person in touch with their deeper emotions and currents.

If the sitter asks about the likely success of a business trip, the Ship card would indicate travel and speculation, perhaps the Whip would signify "work in service," and then the Fish "resources, money, and good fortune." All in all, these cards would be indicative of a successful business trip.

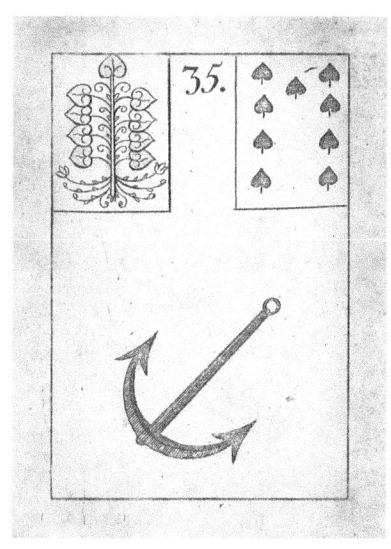

Figure 52. The Anchor

35. The Anchor

The Anchor is the key symbol of the Game of Hope; it is *the* card of hope. In the game, landing on it was the aim, rather than overshooting, which would mean landing upon the Cross.

In the German tradition, this card is the symbol of work in the sense of one's vocational career—the anchor to life, something that provides stability in a storm yet can also keep you in one place. The card is thus, as are all cards in the Lenormand, modified by the card next to it and surrounding it. The Anchor is a fixed point in a reading, whereas the Ways is the freedom of choice. Where these two cards are in relationship to each other and the sitter's significator card can tell us a lot about their ability to make choices in their current situation. The cards around the Anchor and Ways can also tell us what influences their decisions.

In a literal interpretation, this card can be the significator of career and chosen employment, whether it be through working for a company (Tower or Bear) or for oneself (Fox).

The Anchor is a stabilising influence that takes into account the conditions at play. It is urging caution, especially if the Ship and the Clouds' uncertainty and change are close by. It may be a time to reassess the situation that you are concerned about before venturing into uncharted waters! If this combination was followed by the Sun, it could indicate a waiting period of up to a year, but this could also imply that there will be positive growth with the Sun's presence when the time is right.

36. The Cross

In the Christian backdrop of the original Game of Hope, written into the rules of the game is the notion of the Cross as suffering and adversity. It is more the cross of the gravestone than the cross of sacrifice. It is symbolic of finality without redemption, rather than the more positive reconceptualisation as faith. The Cross, then, is read as struggle, perhaps asking us to maintain faith in the advent of difficult times. It is very much about getting down to the crux of the matter, and is also a card of restriction, fastening us to one place, person, or situation. When combined with the Anchor it may denote a long-term burden.

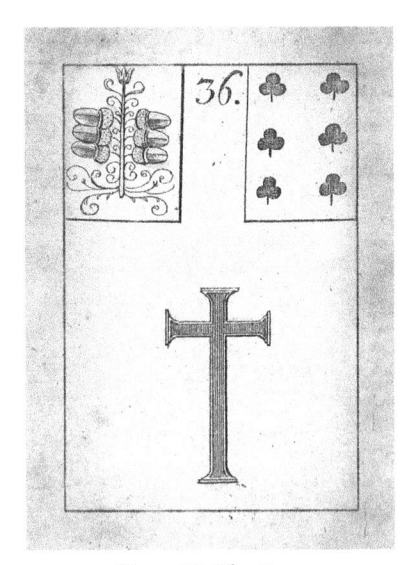

Figure 53. The Cross

It denotes the issue burdening us, weighing us down. It could be something on our mind, something we need put down. It is also a card that—as the Stations of the Cross—indicates a whole string of obstacles, one after another; more so than the Mountain, which is one big obstacle, causing us to seek a diversion. If the Cross is combined with the Mice, it is a series of small setbacks causing cumulative trouble.

The Ways is also of importance to this card's meaning when combined together, especially when taking into account the crosslike appearance of the signpost on some illustrations of the Ways, particularly in The Original Lenormand. The Ways alleviates the Cross somewhat, providing some option of movement. If the Cross indicates staying true to faith through burdens, the Ways will keep you true to your path.

Now that we've looked at each card individually, we will look to further ways of getting you to explore your own meanings for the cards with the use of fortunetelling verses based on traditional forms.

Exercise: Fortunetelling Verses

Many older cartomantic and fortunetelling books use a particular verse form for their oracles. This is not quite the same as used in German verses for the Lenormand cards, nor English equivalents such as those on the US Games Systems deck, whose verses were written by Stuart Kaplan himself.

The other interesting note is that these verses were often in two couplets, the first applying to a man using the book, the second to a woman.

Your exercise is to create verses in this particular format for your Lenormand cards—it's fun and helps you learn the cards. It could even provide an oracular game in and of itself at parties: people choose a card and you read them their verse from your own fortunetelling book.

The format of the verses is very simple, and those who have been on our other courses will know we teach a lot of poetic patterns from haiku to Norse sagas, so this is another to add to your repertoire.

For each card, write a four-line verse composed of two rhyming couplets. The first couplet applies to a gentleman sitter, the second to a lady. The lines of both couplets should be seven syllables. This gives a very simple meter and stress to the verse, suiting it to our salon-style delivery. As an example of the form:

> It's very easy to do
> Writing this for me and you.
> The deck you can make complete
> With these rhymes so short and sweet.

And here's one from a fortunetelling book:

> By this four we clearly see
> Four brats must be laid to thee.

She who gets the same will wed,
Two rich husbands, both well-bred.

Or another on the Ace of Spades, boding ill for both ladies and gentlemen:

Thou who gets this Ace of Spades
Shalt be flouted by the maids,
When it is a damsel's lot,
Love and honour go to pot.

So have a try, remembering in each that the first two-line couplet applies to a male sitter, the second to a female sitter. Here's one for the Bear card:

When the bear is pulled by you,
Health and wealth are in your view,
When faced by a woman's wiles,
It portends a life of smiles.

Exercise: Triplets

As a further exercise for this chapter, we'd like to encourage you to continue to work in montages and scenarios. So here's a practice method that can build up what we call "chains" in the skillset of the Lenormand sibyl.

- Shuffle your deck.
- Take three cards.
- Lay them out face up in a triangle.
- Create a story, scene, or situation involving all three cards.
- Take another three cards.
- Create a separate story for these three cards.

- Now look at both triplets and chain one card from each together by seeing how the two stories might connect through those two particular cards. It can be obvious or surreal—there is no need to make meaning, only connection.

Here is an example, where the storytelling remains as a fable.

Figure 54. Two Triads for Triplets

We drew the Fox, Bear, and Bouquet for the first triad.

"The fox had a lousy reputation; it puzzled him greatly. Wherever he went, his reputation dogged him; there was no getting away from it. He only ever lived up to his own nature, and that is not a bad thing to do. People criticised him for being crafty, manipulative, and cunning; they said he was not ever to be trusted. How was his natural behaviour any more unacceptable than the Bear, who was often seen as cute and cuddly when in reality he was a big, brutal beast? All the Fox wanted was some recognition of his good qualities; it would be good to receive a show of appreciation, like a bouquet of flowers."

For the second triad, we drew the Key, Mountain, and Stars.

"Once upon a time there was a rumour that at the top of the tallest mountain in the world was hidden a key that held the secret to possessing vision that normally only the stars can see."

Now here is how we bridge the two stories together:

"The Fox asked the Bear how he managed to give the impression that he was such an affectionate creature who was portrayed as being lovable. The Bear said, 'Well, it's easy, I journeyed to the top of a mountain and discovered a Key. It unlocked another side of me—the side everyone sees'."

You can keep adding triplets, chaining them through the same or different cards, so long as it is one card only from each triplet to one card from another.

This practice builds up another essential skill in the cartomancer's toolbox.

Exercise: Popular Sayings of the Lenormand

In this exercise, journal what comes to mind from popular culture for each card. We can start with listing contemporary sayings that go with each card. You can also consider song titles, famous pieces of art, even advertising jingles. Anything that associates meaning for you with the card image will deepen your ability to extend that card in context to real life.

1. Rider—Never look a gift horse in the mouth, no news is good news

2. Clover—Rolling in clover

3. Ship—Ship shape

4. House—As safe as houses

5. Tree—You cannot see the woods for the trees

6. Clouds—Every cloud has a silver lining

7. Snake—A snake in the grass

8. Coffin—Another nail in the coffin

9. Bouquet—Coming up smelling of roses

10. Scythe—Make hay while the sun shines

11. Rod, Birch, Whip—A rod for your own back

12. Birds—A bird in the hand is worth two in the bush
13. Child—Child's play
14. Fox—Cunning as a fox, foxy woman
15. Bear—Bear with a sore head
16. Star—Wish upon a star
17. Stork—He who invites storks must have frogs in the house
18. Dog—Dog-tired, a dog's dinner, a dog's life, a dog's breakfast, dog-eat-dog
19. Tower—Towering above others
20. Garden—How does your garden grow?
21. Mountain—Don't make a mountain out of a molehill
22. Ways—Where there is a will, there is a way
23. Mice—As quiet as a mouse
24. Heart—Heartsick, broken heart, full of heart, absence makes the heart grow fonder, losing heart
25. Ring—Running rings around someone
26. Book—In the book, book learning
27. Letter—A red-letter day
28. Gentleman—A gentleman gentle does
29. Lady—Faint heart never won fair lady
30. Lily—Lilies that fester smell far worse than weeds
31. Sun—The sun always shines on TV, sunny-side up
32. Moon—Mooning around, moon-faced

33. Key—The key to everything, it's a key part of the plan

34. Fish—Fishing for compliments, a fishing trip, see what we catch

35. Anchor—Anchors aweigh!

36. Cross—A cross to bear, we all have our crosses, don't cross me

Exercise: Scenes from a Life

In this exercise, in which we start to learn combinations of cards, simply take a scene from real life or a movie and try and describe it in two to four cards only. If we think of a famous scene from the movie *E. T.*, we might consider it quite aptly described by the Child, the Moon, and the Key, as the government agent in the film was identified by the jangling keys on his belt. Any *Lassie* film can be summed up by the Dog card!

What about trying it the other way around? If you had a scene involving the Lady, the Gentleman, and the Ship, which film or event might come to mind?

Figure 55. Three Cards for a Film

Exercise: Performing a Simple Literal Reading

Now that we've covered the basics of the cards, let's see if we can perform a simple practice reading using the idea of similies. This is also a good journal exercise that can lead to real readings. You do not have to have every keyword memorised; you can do this by literal interpretation of the cards when using this method.

Consider a situation about which you require some clarity and direct advice. It can be as simple or complex as you wish. In our example, we will consider having a lot of deadlines to meet—we wonder if we should drop some projects now or continue with all of them and attempt to meet the deadlines.

Consider the situation as **two** separate aspects, "my deadlines" and "my projects." It does not matter which order you place these two aspects in the sentence to follow, so long as you write it out first.

Write "[My projects] are to [my deadlines] ... "

Considering these two aspects, shuffle your deck and select out two cards.

Complete the sentence "My projects are to my deadlines as ... [card 1] is to [card 2]."

We pulled out the Bear and the Snake.

We write "My projects are to my deadline as the Bear is to the Snake."

Now consider the actual reality of the **literal** objects on the Lenormand cards, or use their keywords from whichever system with which you are working.

In a literal sense, a bear rarely encounters a snake. If it did find one threatening, would likely kill it. The weight of the bear would probably make it reasonably immune from a poisonous bite.

As such, we can divine that our projects and their scale (pardon the pun), outweigh the insidious thoughts of deadlines—which may poison the work slowly, even killing it. We therefore write to one publisher and tell him his project requires a change of deadline to be done properly. This was not something we had considered in our original question, but it now seems very obvious—and works!

The Lenormand appears very literal, and it can be used to dictate immediate action in its stark simplicity. We hope you have found this chapter encouraging in the way you choose to learn Lenormand, tarot, or anything else. Do not forget—there is no "is."

Exercise: Five Levels of Reading a Card

Whilst we can keep Lenormand pretty literal, we can also layer readings. We will look at an example of reading the Ship on five different levels: literal, simple, symbolic, extended, and secret.[23] You can repeat this exercise for all cards, as your own extended and secret levels of the card will be unique to you—this is a great journal exercise.

- **Literal:** A person arrives to board a ship. Setting sail from port to travel to an exotic island, all aboard are happy to go on the journey. The destination is the Canary Islands where the yellow-feathered Canary bird lives. The ship takes us quickly without trouble—all is well.

- **Simple:** Will hear good news about future travel. Will go on a trip. Will move. Will be taken by somebody else to a good place. Transport. Journey. Travel.

- **Symbolic:** Somebody will be lucky enough to find their way in life. Transport or journeying, moving, on your way but in between two worlds. There is a haven of happiness waiting; you will find contentment, a place of your very own that you can call home, where you feel you belong. Be aware however that you may find yourself amongst those who may gossip about you, perhaps they may envy your happy life—shown by the bad side of the Birds card.

- **Extended:** It has been said in Greek myth that the Canary Islands were one of the so-called Fortunate Isles or the Isles of the Blessed (Hesperides), a blissful winterless paradise, the santuary of mortals who were deemed to be heroes and had been reincarnated thrice. This card of the Ship then brings us perhaps for the third time to a place of blessing. We may have ignored the signs before or been offered an opportunity previously, and now it calls for us again—will we board the ship this third time and transform our lives?

- **Secret:** Another connection with the ancient world is that the Canary Islands were supposed to have given birth to the Greek myth of the Garden of Hesperides. Legend also has it that one of the twelve labours of Hercules was to go to the end of the world and bring back golden apples guarded by the Hesperides (daughters of evening), offspring of Hesperis and Atlas, the latter a Titan in Greek and Roman mythology who gave his name to the Atlantic Ocean and the Atlas mountain ranges in Morocco. Hercules supposedly had to go beyond the Strait of Gibraltar (named the Pillars of Hercules after his smashing the mountain, forming the pillars) to reach the paradisiacal home of these maidens. Hercules carried out his task and returned from what many later thought could only have been the Canary Islands—about the only place to fit the ancients' description.

It is interesting that the twelve labours correspond to the twelve of the Bird card, which the Ship leads to, and the Ship is 3, corresponding to the threefold reincarnation of the heroes. Those who played this game originally and used it for parlour divination would have been very aware of the classical legends, and it is no surprise to see them connected in this way.

In a deep reading then, this card signifies the potential we all have to engage in a heroic journey, if we can give up the daily burden (as Hercules gave Atlas the world to hold upon his shoulders). Can you discover what responsibilities are attachments and remove yourself from them to discover yourself?

Before we conclude looking at the individual cards, we can also consider them in sets of meaning, which helps us learn the cards in groups and provides more weight for their meaning in a reading.

Negative, Neutral, and Positive Cards

In the Game of Hope and following traditions, certain cards in the Lenormand have a definite positive or negative (favourable or unfavourable) connotation. There is no layering of "this is not a problem, it is an opportunity" language into the literal Lenormand. A snake is an evil and poisonous creature, a mouse will eat you out of house and home. We will list here the various cards in these groups:

- **Neutral Cards:** 1, 17, 19, 22, 25, 27, 28, 29

- **Positive Cards:** 2, 3, 4, 9, 13, 16, 18, 20, 24, 30, 31, 32, 33, 34, 35

- **Negative Cards:** 5, 6, 7, 8, 10, 11, 12, 14, 15 (in some traditions this is a very negative card), 21, 23, 26 (generally), 36

Whilst these associations may be tempered somewhat by the overall context of the cards, as we will see in the following chapter, to stay close to authentic use, they should be treated in the style of definitely good, bad, and indifferent. These groupings may be used to denote if a single or few card layout is generally answering a positive or negative outcome to a straight fortunetelling reading.[24]

We will next start to put these cards together in context, when they really start to speak.

FOUR

Reading the Cards in Context

....

*Mouse—This symbol denotes poverty caused through lack of initiative.
Do not wait for the opportunity to come to you—go out and seek it.
Near the "house" a mouse foretells loss through theft.
—The Complete Book of Fortune, on "Reading the Tea-Leaves," 1936*

....

The Lenormand cards are taken as pieces of an alphabet, and we build them up into words and sentences to generate meaning. It is important to learn the cards as a separate language. In this chapter we will take a look at the basics of the Lenormand language to see how cards are modified by the cards near to them and their location in a layout. This approach to reading in context and combination may have been inspired by tea leaf or coffee grounds reading, and those in turn through far more ancient meanings ascribed to objects for divinatory purposes, including dream interpretation and oracular utterances.

Some of these exercises and methods of reading the cards are not used by every reader, so you should try out as many of them as possible to see what really works for you to unlock the cards' meanings. You may find you have a particular skill or understanding in one of these areas, just as you might in learning a foreign language.

Order of Reading

There are three ways in which you can read Lenormand cards when laying them out in a row of two or more cards. They are:

- Blended/Merged
- Linear/Left to Right
- Affected by Following/Right to Left

If we take a simple two-card example of the Clover and the Fish, we can see how these orders take effect. The most important thing is to choose which method works best for you in different circumstances.

Figure 56. The Clover and the Fish

If we blend these two cards together, we generate a lucky fish, perhaps a talisman of good luck. There is a lucky event of some description with regard to our finances and resources, our general material well-being.

102 • FOUR

If, however, we read these cards in a linear left-to-right sequence like a storyboard, we would say, "First the Clover, then the Fish." That is to suggest that we will have some lucky event that will bring more material benefits thereafter, good resources or work. The lucky event itself—the clover—may have nothing to do directly with what follows; it could even be something like a marriage, which brings financial reward in its own way!

When instead reading from right to left, in effect, we consider that the first card is the object (and this is usually, as it is the nearest card to our significator, or the significator itself, in reading lines in a Grand Tableau) and the following cards each have a roll-back effect on the cards preceding them.

In the simple case of the Clover and the Fish, it is the lucky event that is the object, and the Fish (resources) is applying to it. That might indicate more precisely that the nature of the lucky event will be one of resources—a winning lottery ticket, the finding of a lost wallet that brings reward, and so on.

When this applies to longer sequences, each card modifies the card before it, so the final card in a row is the most influential; it really tells us the most likely outcome and the general deciding factor. A long sequence of generally negative cards that ends in the Star may indicate that our hopes will ultimately be realised through struggle, whilst a sequence of generally positive cards culminating in the Mountain would suggest that we will face obstacles throughout the situation with little absolute result—just another obstacle.

Negative and Positive Cards

Whilst every card in Lenormand is influenced by its position and context, unlike tarot where most cards are given a positive aspect (e.g., the Tower is not just disruption, it is clearing the air to see new horizons), some cards in Lenormand are generally negative, such as the Snake.

You might like to read the instructions for the Game of Hope given in the appendix to this book to see which cards set you back and which cards move you forward in the game. It was definitely the case that some cards were favourable and others unfavourable.

There are other cards that might be considered more neutral, such as the Clouds, which are affected by their facing. These cards also show a lack of clarity or confusion, which is neither good nor bad, although it again depends on the surrounding cards.

Exercise: Near and Far

First, we're going to play a game of "near and far," or "hot and cold." This will make sense as we approach the Grand Tableau method later and instill a good habit in reading Lenormand, where combination and context is so very important to interpretation.

It is a simple game based on Japanese grammar, where the distance of an object changes the very word you use to speak about it. We think this is unique to Japanese, and it is very useful to learning the language of the Lenormand.

Imagine a bear. You are looking at it on a screen or from a considerable distance, separated by something. What comes to mind? The bear's movements, perhaps the way it shambles? Make a note in the table below the words that come to mind, "shambling" or "strolling."

Now imagine the bear in the room with you, or very close up! What comes to mind? Other than "Run!"? Perhaps "strength," "power," or "fear." Write that in the other box below.

Then you can repeat the exercise with the following selection of cards:

OBJECT	FAR	NEAR
BEAR	Slow movement, strolling	Roar, power, fear
TREE		
MOON		
GARDEN		
MOUNTAINS		
HEART		
GENTLEMAN		

If you are journaling your discovery of the Lenormand cards, you can of course do this with all the cards to discover your own interpretation of objects near and far to you. It can also be instructive to go back over your keywords and kaleidoscope words and plug them into the near/far table to consider how, for example, the Mice (choosing a keyword such as "disruption") would work under your nose *and* at a distance. After a while, you can practice near and far with combinations, such as for a question about a sales job. Mice and Bouquet near to you might signify self-doubt if the cards were close at hand (Mice as worrying, Bouquet as self-appreciation in this case), or someone giving you false leads if the two cards were at a distance (an apparent gift like flowers, but something that actually gnaws away at your foundations, the mice).

We will now introduce you to the relative significance of cards depending on their position in what is called the Grand Tableau. We will do this by playing a game we call *Le Tableau Vivant* or "living picture."

The word *tableau* means both "table" and "picture," so it is a wonderful word for our grand spread.

The Grand Tableau

There are many ways to read Lenormand cards, however, unlike tarot they rarely depend on a fixed positional meaning. That is to say, there are not (yet) whole books of spreads where for example the card in position 3 indicates the sitter's hopes or the card in position 9 represents how others see them.

Lenormand cards are read usually in lines (linear Lenormand), curves (horseshoes), circles, or in tableau, usually laid out in a block. We are going to start in the deep end and look at the tableau; it is the best way to teach the cards in relationship to their relative positions.

So, let's scare ourselves *un petit peut* first by seeing what we will end up being able to read when we have finished. Take a deep breath, and…

Now, whilst that may seem a little scary—all thirty-six cards laid out with not a positional meaning to read—that's only because most of us are tarot readers or entirely new to cartomancy.

Before we go ahead and learn some practices so we can develop our skills, and then return to apply them to this method, just a few words about the Tableau.

There are several ways of laying this out. The two most widely used are the 9 x 4 (nine columns in four rows) or the 8 x 4 + 4 (eight columns in four rows with a fourth row of four cards below). We will use the 9 x 4 for this lesson and return to the other method later, as at present we are only interested in relative positions. We hope you did your "near and far" exercise earlier, as it will help you now.

Figure 57. The Grand Tableau

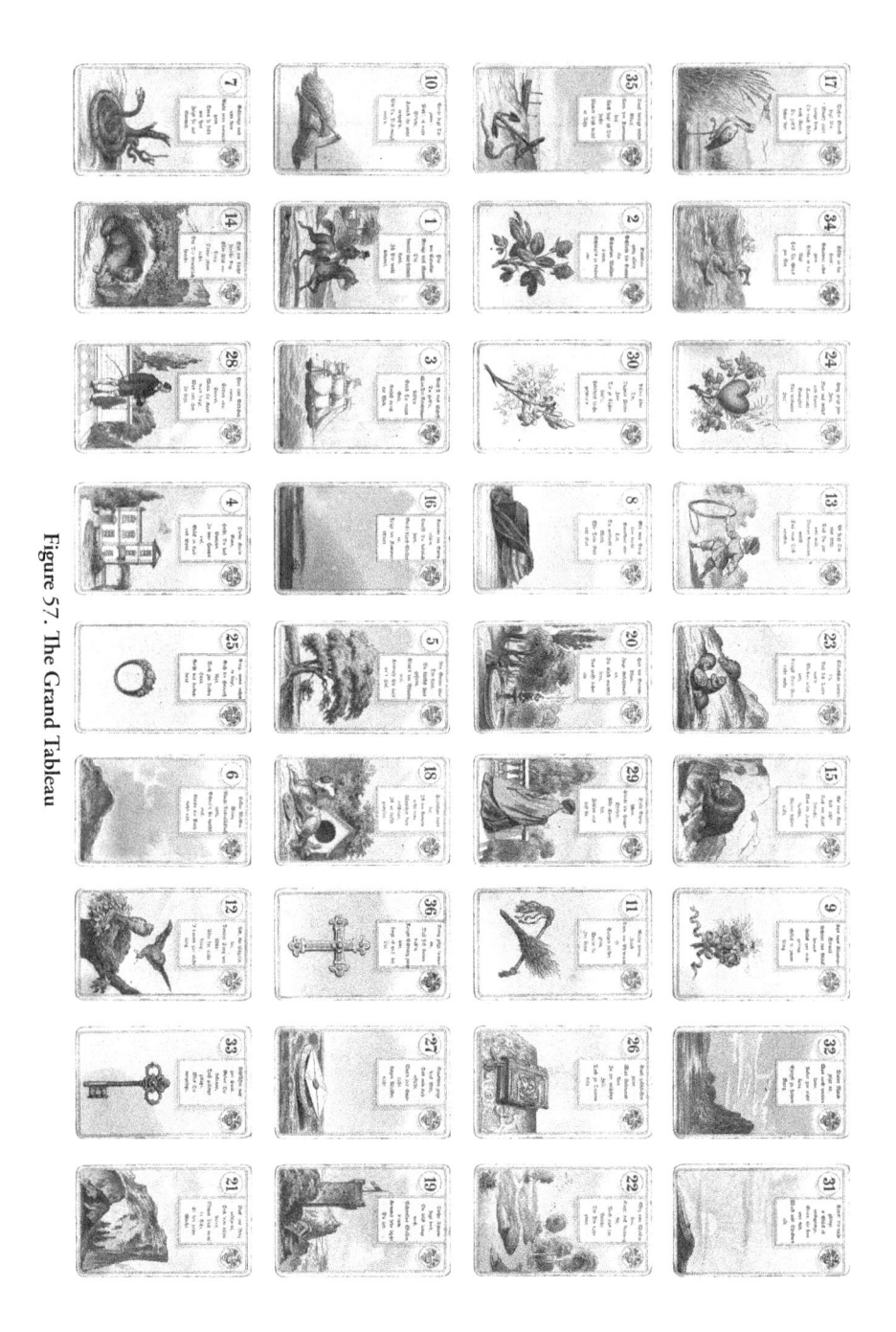

106 • FOUR

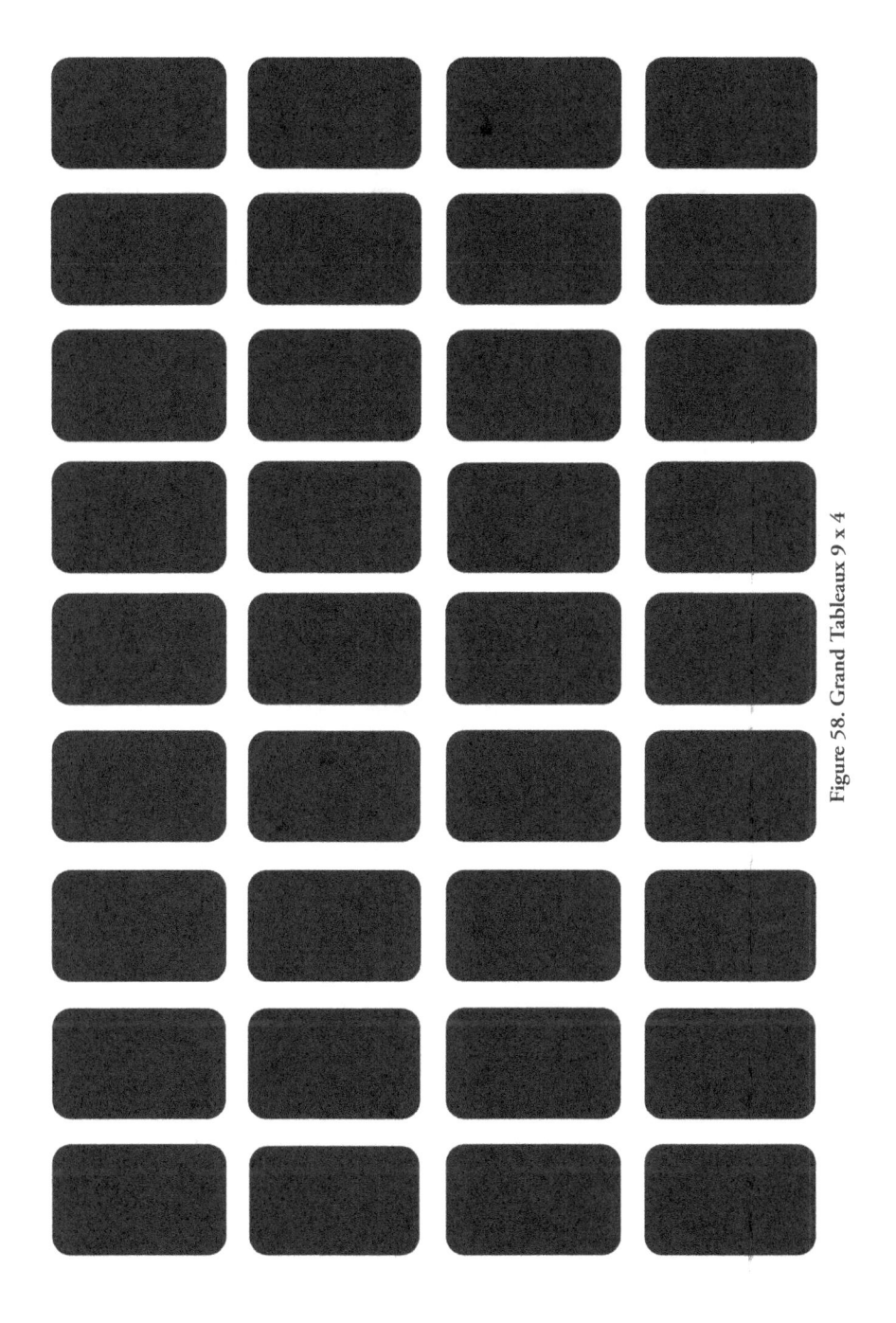

Figure 58. Grand Tableaux 9 x 4

READING THE CARDS IN CONTEXT • 107

Figure 59. Grand Tableaux 8 x 4 + 4

Cherchez la Femme

The clichéd phrase *cherchez la femme* actually first appears in a novel by Alexandre Dumas set in Paris whose crime inspector regularly uses the phrase, as often the key to any investigation is a woman! So it is fitting we start to investigate our tableaux and relationships by playing a little "search the woman." In Lenormand, the sitter is represented by either of two cards, the Gentleman or the Lady, as befits their stated gender. We will see later how we can charge the cards and ask the Lenormand questions for a specific purpose, situation, or issue, using key cards such as the Bear for questions of health, for example. For now, we will start with the Gentleman and the Lady.

In most decks, these cards face particular directions, so we can see how they are "looking forward" or "leaving behind" other cards, for a start. How cool is that?

One way of reading is to presume that what is to the left of the sitter's significator (Gentleman or Lady) is the past, and what is to the right is the future.

Figure 60. Determining Past and Future

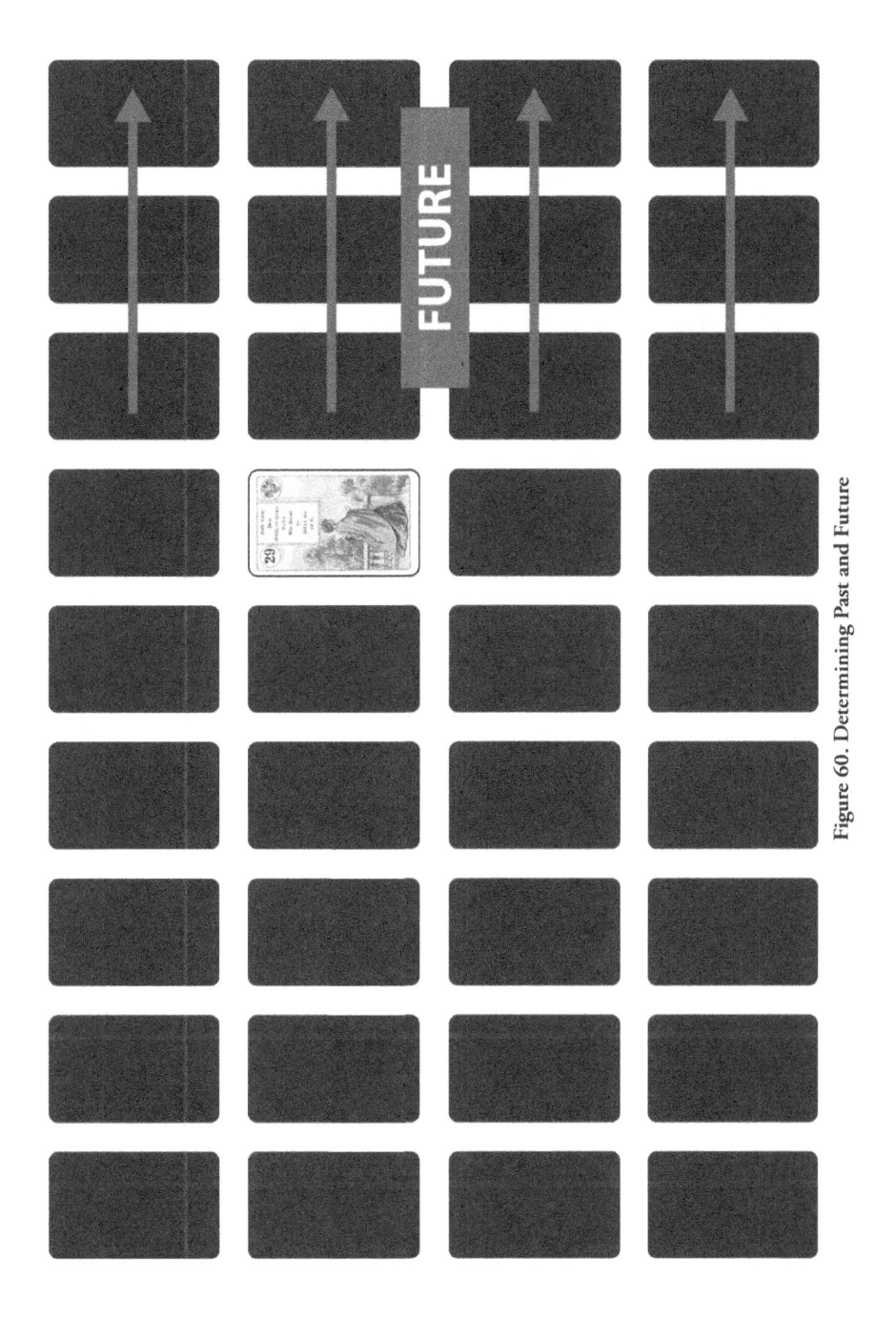

READING THE CARDS IN CONTEXT • 109

Time Issues in L-Space

As an important side note, we should here explain that L-space is very different, yet somewhat similar, to T-space. This is what makes it tricky. We must remember that a lot of what we know as tarot methods derive in part from the Golden Dawn era, where counting cards, dignities, and all manner of esoterica was introduced. The Golden Dawn itself was basing their correspondences on their reading of earlier cartomantic methods, with an added Industrial-Kabbalah flair. So when we look at Lenormand (and not that much is known as to how the cards were actually read) and the cartomantic methods of the time, we see a lot of echoes, people using the same ideas, that later come back up on the other side of the Golden Dawn synthesis into popular T-space. It can be mind-bending.

The question is simply "where is past and future in a reading?" particularly when we use the Grand Tableau. As ever, there is no "right" answer, just a preferred methodology. We'll give some background that may help you make a decision—which you are free to later change after practice!

Early card-reading books have sections called, for example "Look to your right, and to the left of the consultant" (this from an 1872 book), which is quite fascinating because they are not related to time, but to **influence**. Certain cards one side of the consultants card mean one thing, and to the other, something else. The books are usually written in such a way as to reveal certain patterns, e.g., "should there be two aces, it indicates you have enemies" but not provide a totally comprehensive scheme or teaching.

They certainly tend to a "right to left" linear reading style that combines cards with no fixed idea of past and future, just a "fortunetelling" presentation: "I perceive that you have a suitor who is dark-complexioned, and this will result in an argument between two women, and your sister will come to no good."

A more recent compilation in 1903 reveals a simple past-present-future spread by dividing a playing card deck into three piles, reading the pile to the left being the past, the middle present, and the right being the future.

In the Golden Dawn, in the Celtic Cross positions for past and future—in the original method, using Golden Dawn court cards as signficators, which faced one way or another—the querent card faced the future and had its back to the past, meaning that things depended on the direction of facing of the court card. This got horribly confused when Waite published the method as "another method of divination" in his own book accompanying the deck he created with Pamela Colman-Smith, where the court cards do not necessarily face one direction or another. It has led to a century of silliness about which side is past and future in the Celtic Cross.

In the real world, as we might deduce from neuro-linguistic programming (NLP), people are found to have different notions of time-space. One of our *Tarosophy* methods asks people to think about their past and future by asking questions such as "did you find it easy to get here this morning" or "where are you going to be for the holidays" and watching eye movements to naturally discern how the querent represents time. We then lay out a freeform spread based on his or her own unconscious representation.

It is sometimes a straight line (where people get the idea of a timeline), and often left-right/back-forwards. All sorts of shapes are possible, however, say for example with bad memories being held in a quarantine zone far away from the timeline.

Anyhow, the gist of it is that there's no single right way. If we stick with tradition, we tend to use the direction the sitter's card is facing to denote the future and what is "behind" them to denote the past. We do not think that a Grand Tableau has little about the "future" just because the sitter's card is right on the left, facing the edge. All it means is that everything about their potential and future is to be discerned from what is behind them. Such is often the case in life.

Think of it like a tiller on a ship. We may navigate to what we see ahead, but our direction is made by where the tiller behind us is positioned. The trick is to have both navigator and steersman working together—and the Grand Tableau (hereafter GT) can let us see this, no matter where the sitter's card is positioned.

We need to move from T-space to L-space in this context, where the whole GT tells us about both past and future, even if it presents only what is before or behind the sitter. In doing so, when we return to T-space, we may even bring a new perspective to our tarot readings.

Now let's add the Gentleman card, and assume that we are looking at a situation about a relationship—which we know will be three in five questions asked of us in the salon.

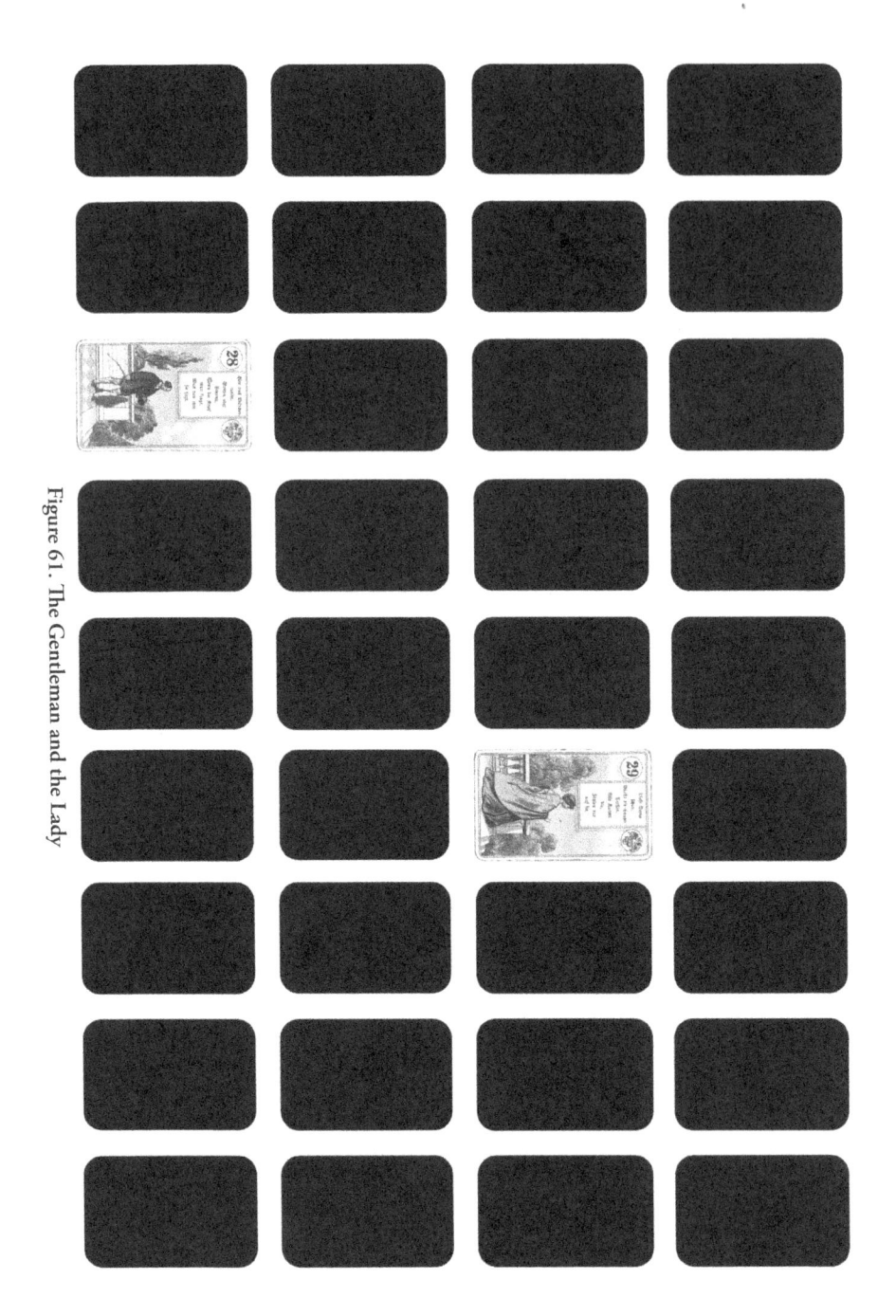

Figure 61. The Gentleman and the Lady

112 • FOUR

Here we see that the man is having to look up to the woman, who in turn looks away from him. The man sees the woman in his future, however the woman cannot see the man in hers. This can be read as literally as it appears, if you wish.

We can already see, we hope, that we need more cards to clarify this situation, and that is a big difference between Lenormand and tarot readings—the more cards, the easier it actually gets to read once a few basic skills are under our belt and we have practiced our methods.

Let's now have a bit of a refresher of a few cards so we can use them to create our own life maps.

The Gentleman

When the sitter is male, this card relates to them; when the sitter is female, this card relates to their significant other, such as a romantic interest, or a male figure in their work/social/home life generally.

The card also indicates in a general sense a certain formality, an adherence to social expectations and at worst, a somewhat aggressive dominance in the situation. The card at best shows cultivation and careful attention.

The Lady

When the sitter is female, this card relates to them; when the sitter is male, this card relates to their significant other, such as a romantic interest, or a female figure in their work/social/home life generally.

Again, the card shows a certain formality, yet perhaps not so much as the Gentleman card. It relates to the Ace of Spades in cartomancy, and in the earliest known publication listing meanings for cards, we have this:

> You that draw the Ace of Spades,
> Shall be flouted by the maids;
> When it is a damsel's lot,
> Wit and humor go to pot.
> —*Dr. Flamstead's and Mr. Partridge's New Fortune-Book*, 1710

An 1872 book on fortunetelling in our library gives the Ace of Spades as also signifying love and relationships, matters of the heart (where one might expect these to apply to the Ace of Hearts), and when reversed, the Ace of Spades signifies pregnancy, maternity, and conception.

Having looked at the main characters of the Lady and Gentleman, we'll look at the Heart, Cross, and Ship cards to build a basic relationship reading between this pair.

The Heart

The keyword for this card is courage. In a relationship query it signifies being true to your own heart and having the courage to express your feelings to a significant other. People often speak of not having "the heart" to tell somebody something, in case it results in hurt feelings; the sitter in question may have to bite the proverbial bullet and speak the unspeakable.

This card also signifies "goodness" and virtue, being authentic and true to oneself.

The Cross

The keyword for this card is faith; this card signifies a state of keeping faith, whether it is in relation to a romantic endeavour or the sitter being able to keep true to his or her own true intent. However, as not all acts of faith turn out to have a favourable outcome, this card can also signify a burden that may have to be carried before there is any resolution.

It can be the sign that a belief, for example, is limiting or outworn, depending on the cards about it and its relationship to all other cards, as we will come to see.

The Ship

The keyword for this card is adventure. In a reading, it can signify a longing to break free from the life presently lived, and to find success and opportunity on new horizons. This card is effectively a calling card for transition.

Its position in a reading shows where movement is possible, despite any obstacles indicated by the cards around it. It is the go-to card for showing where choice may still be found and one's own course plotted in a given situation.

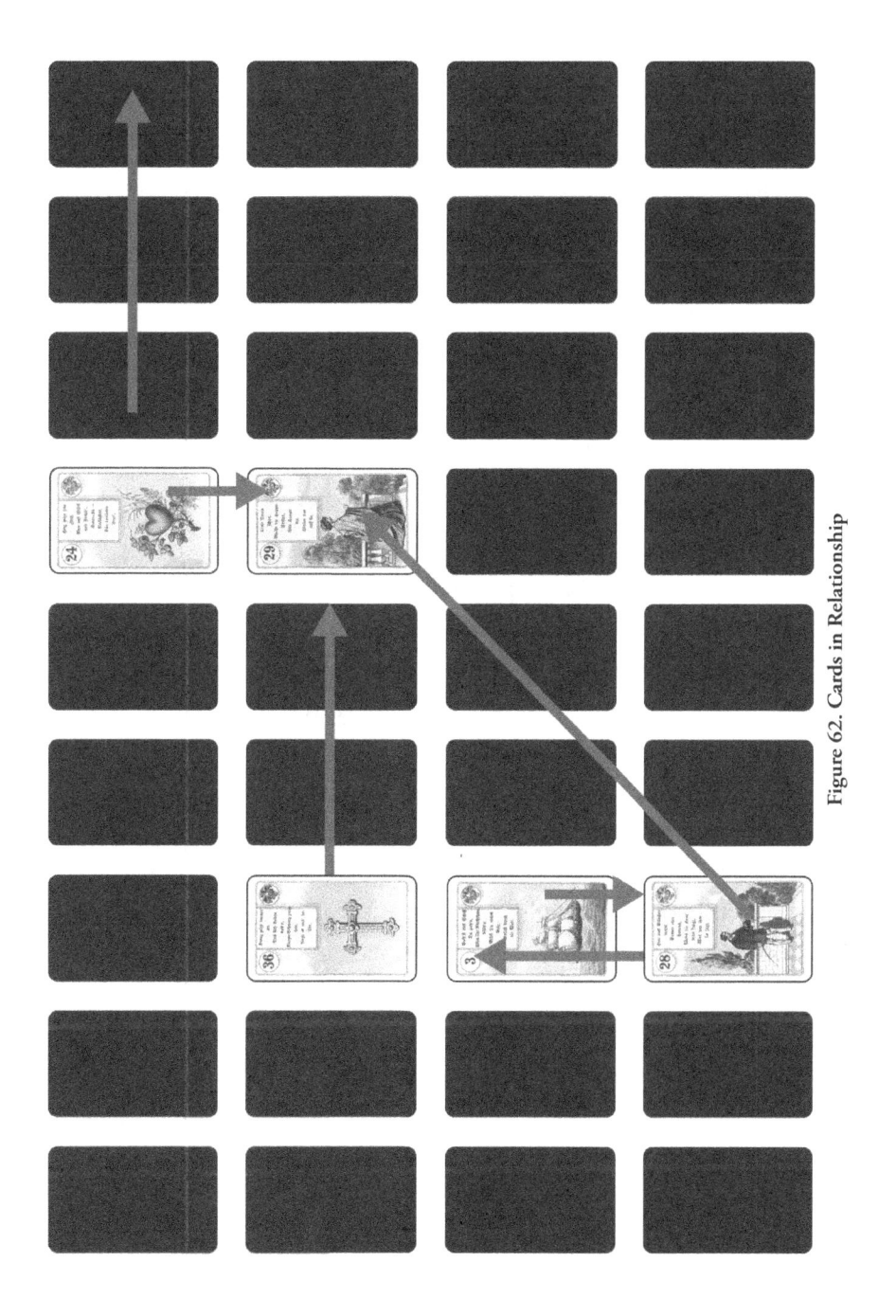

Figure 62. Cards in Relationship

READING THE CARDS IN CONTEXT • 115

Now let's take a look at these cards in relationship to one another. It is very important to look at the relationships and positions of the cards relative to each other, and in each case, in both directions. What appears above can influence what appears below.

In a later chapter, we will cover "knighting" movements and other more complex arrangements and patterns; here we can simply look at our first obvious layer of straight lines and a little bit of diagonal. As they say, that's "something racy for the gulls" (a little bit of extra for those who look for it)!

The woman looks away into the future, but the man is not there. The heart of the matter belongs to her—it is closer to her. If you did the "near and far" exercise, you might interpret that her heart is too close to her, that she wears it on her sleeve. It is also *above* her, perhaps indicating that she is ruled by it, and easily—there is no deep consideration, just emotional response.

We can see too in her past (to her left) is the Cross, indicating something interesting—perhaps there was a loss of faith in her past and she's moving away from it. We know this only because of the overall picture; there is nothing in that particular card that explicitly indicates faith or the loss thereof—it just makes sense in the overall context.

We think that is a good example of how our ability as "sense makers" and storytellers works to interpret Lenormand against the more structured and sometimes singular patterns of tarot.

What about our man, the sitter in this particular example? He has to look up to the woman—perhaps indicating a certain idolisation from afar. It is possible he has not even spoken to her yet. This is probably the question—"What will happen if I speak to Danielle?" Often in Lenormand it is better to have an exact question because it provides context for the interpretation.

He is also *below* the Ship, showing that it is at the same time providing him clear access and freedom, yet it is overweighing him because it is right on top of him—he is spending too much time thinking about something that he is totally free to do. Again, we look up further and see that same Cross card—he has a big issue with his faith in himself and his own freedom (Ship).

And here's the nice thing—the man and the woman share that Cross in common, though in different ways. If we were to offer advice from this reading, it would be to approach Danielle with the spirit of a shared doubt—one she has recently experienced, and one with which he himself struggles.

There is a saying in alchemy: "through the cross to the rose." Here we may see that saying play out in a real-world relationship. Are you interested in seeing all the other cards now so we might read even more? Well, not yet … let's practice!

We will give you three vignettes, like short stories. We'd like you to lay out the five cards we have used above (Gentleman, Lady, Ship, Cross, Heart) to illustrate the vignette. In this way, we break the usual way of teaching cards, by applying real-life to the tableaux first. We talk to the Lenormand, it will talk to us.

Don't forget, these must be laid out within a 9 x 4 grid. Place each card where you think it would best suit the vignette.

You can also optionally add any one card from the Lenormand deck to help you illustrate each vignette.

Exercise: Mary et John

Mary is married to John and they are talking about their future. They want to share it together, yet they struggle because John has a gambling issue. Their house is now at risk and he has started drinking. Mary is at her wit's end and cannot see any future.

Exercise: James et Cristobel

Let me tell you about the budding relationship that is unable to progress forward for James and Cristobel. James is in a quandary; he is in a relationship with a special woman. However all is not ideal, as they live thousands of miles apart, he in London, and she in Sydney, Australia. He has just received a letter from Cristobel, who is sick of being in a long-distance relationship. She has written asking him to move to Sydney to live with her. (She likes old fashioned letter-writing for affairs of the heart!) He is loathe to do this, however, because he has built a successful business in London, and all his family and friends live there. James does not know if he can take the risk and move to Sydney to be with Cristobel. Despite how much faith he has in the relationship so far, he does not feel brave enough to do this—after all, there's no guarantee that things will work out. He knows he needs to resolve the situation soon, but James cannot bring himself to talk to Cristobel about his feelings in case he upsets her, creating a distance between them in more than geography alone, as Cristobel is feeling increasingly rejected.

Don't forget too that the relationship and distances between cards can describe the strength or weakness of feelings, whilst their position above and below each other shows dominating or conscious influences over lower (in control or unconscious) influences. The tableau should always come together as a whole, like a jigsaw puzzle.

Exercise: Alan

In this vignette, we have only Alan as our sitter; no woman is involved, so the Lady card here stands for intuition and emotional response.

Alan is a businessman and has a long history of success. However, he has recently been made redundant from his company and is at a bit of a loss. He wants to travel but feels he needs his security and should find another job as soon as possible. He has no time for his own emotional life and just wants a logical way to make the right decision.

How would you describe this situation in terms of a tableau?

In this section, we have seen how the cards speak *langue Lenormand* by being in context with each other, and how combinations of cards can be given particular meaning depending on their position and relationship. We will start to weave this together in the next section, looking more at the whole Grand Tableau.

Saboteurs and Silhouettes

In these optional exercises, we'll give you a bridge to the next lesson and also something you can apply to other styles of Lenormand reading outside this introductory book.

When we look at combinations of cards for linear readings and horseshoe readings where we can pair cards together (much as the Golden Dawn did in their Opening of the Key spread) we can come up with meanings for pairs of cards. However, these "flip" depending on which card we present first.

We have given below some of our own personal meanings, both directions—saboteur and silhouette—and you can complete the missing pairs and create your own if you wish. A "saboteur" is a card which works to influence the first card without being recognised itself. It may also provide a "silhouette" in that it provides an outline or framework in which the first card comes to life.

- The Rider/Messenger + Clover = Wisdom begins by knowing oneself.
  [The Clover to us is about "identity" as much as "luck"]
- Clover Leaf + Rider/Messenger = Sense of self awaiting validation from another.

Here the silhouette reading is changed because we have the Rider following the first card, meaning there is still some delay in the manifestation of the first card, here the "sense of self" or identity.

- Ship + House = Speculating wisely for the future
  House + Ship = Living for today in case there is no tomorrow
- Tree + Clouds = Midlife crisis looming
  Clouds + Tree = Transitory resources
- Snake + Coffin = Spiritual emergency
  Coffin + Snake =
- Bouquet + Scythe = Appreciation brings change
  Scythe + Bouquet =
- Whip + Birds = Working toward revelation
  Birds + Whip =
- Child + Fox = White lies and cunning behaviour
  Fox + Child =
- Bear + Stars = Aggressive behaviour creating bad energy
  Stars + Bear =
- Stork + Dog = Expect questions over loyalty to be brought up
  Dog + Stork =

- Tower + Garden = Imagination creates good company
  Garden + Tower =

- Mountain + Ways =
  Ways + Mountain =

Don't forget that you can go back to the list of single keywords and the keyword kaleidoscope to help you create your own combinations for these cards. Then, see what happens as you consider them each in opposite order of presentation. Lenormand is all about patterns and the big picture.

Reading Cards in Any Context

Generally speaking, questions will always focus on one particular area, be it someone's relationship, career, finances, health, travel, lifestyle, and occasionally education and legal issues. In this section we will show how two selected cards can be taken in each of these areas, by themselves or in combination with a number of other cards in sequence.

The Rider in the Context of Work

The Rider card is symbolic of the delivery of communication in many forms, either through the physical delivery of news via the postman or verbal communications in day to day conversation. It can signify the delivery of gossip, where we are reminded of the old saying "don't shoot the messenger."

This card is the effective relaying of communication across various networks. It can also be the phone call you receive, the email, or the text message. News good or bad is delivered a lot swifter these days than via the old-style horseback messenger.

The appearance of this card in the context of work puts a great emphasis on effective communications, making sure the person who needs to get the message gets it loud and clear. The person who needs to get the message could be the one in the office who never listens to what you say. So the Rider can stress the importance of delivering your ideas with clarity.

The meaning of the card of course changes by the influence it takes on from those cards around it. The Rider with the Whip may say "news is troubling," which could be news about unpaid overtime or a form of servitude; you may feel you are being taken advantage of at work. The Whip can be about trouble and strife in your life.

Switched Sequence

- Whip + Rider may say "trouble delivering news." It also may imply trouble getting something across, itself causing strife in a work environment.

Rider in the Context of Finances

- Rider + Whip + Fish = News is troubling regarding money

Switched Sequence

- Fish + Whip + Rider = Money trouble news

Rider in the Context of Health

- Rider + Whip + Coffin = News of troubling illness

Switched sequence

- Coffin + Whip + Rider = Illness that is troubling news on the way

Rider in the Context of Relationships

- Rider + Tree = News of family

Switched Sequence

- Tree + Rider = Family news to come
- Rider + Heart + Gentleman or Lady + Clover = News of love from Gentleman or Lady will bring luck (well-being)

Switched sequence
- Clover + Lady or Gentleman + Heart + Rider = Luck (well-being) at finding Lady or Gentleman for love and possible marriage as dating agency delivers match.
- Rider + Whip + Heart + Mice = Gossip delivered (news) brings strife, gnawing away at you.

Switched Sequence
- Mice + Heart + Whip + Rider = Gnawing feeling that strife will result from gossip in future (news)

Rider in the context of travel and lifestyle
- Rider + Ship = Postman delivers travel tickets

Switched Sequence
- Ship + Rider = Holiday travel tickets on their way

The Fox in the context of work
As mentioned earlier, the Fox is the (somewhat opportunistic) entrepreneur of the Lenormand deck. Remember, however, that this card is not all bad—if you put the Fox with Clover, for example, it could say you will have innovative ideas that make you lucky. As with most divination, there is no "good" or "bad," it's all in how we read it.

- Fox + Garden = Crafty behaviour expected at a conference

Switched sequence
- Garden + Fox = An innovative conference

Three Cards with the Fox
- Fox + Garden + Tower = Crafty behaviour during a conference—watch out for yourself

Switched sequence
- Tower + Garden + Fox = Be on watch at the conference for crafty behaviour/sly tricks

Below we have added Clover to the sequence, which modifies the meaning, putting a more positive slant on the interpretation. Every Lenormand cloud has a silver lining, which is why it is so important to read cards in combination. Otherwise it's akin to tearing the last page out of a novel and never having the full story.

Four Cards with the Fox
- Fox + Garden + Tower + Clover = Watching out at the conference for crafty behaviour/sly tricks could prove advantageous.

Having introduced ourselves to these sequences and combinations, as well as the general layout of the Grand Tableau, we will now move on to the GT itself. You may feel you *need* a G & T to tackle it, however, we are now reasonably prepared!

FIVE

The Grand Tableau

A reading that you see in front of you may appear wildly improbable, and totally at variance with what you know of your consultant. Pay no heed to this. Your business is to read exactly what you see. Simply that and nothing more… The cards know a great deal more than you do. There is always something fresh to be learnt from each "fortune" you read.
—Cicely Kent, *Telling Fortunes by Cards*

We will now introduce the Grand Tableau, which you may be surprised to find that you now know how to read using the skills we have covered in our previous chapters. Though it will take practice, you have the essentials already in your head, so let's apply them.

Simpler Layouts
Leading to the Grand Tableau

We have seen that the Grand Tableau can be laid out in at least two or three different manners, so we will continue to keep things simple with the 9 x 4 layout. However, before we start, we will look at some simpler layouts, starting with the 3 x 1 three-card layout.

We also need to introduce the idea of "charged cards" now—that is, cards that act as compass points, about which we navigate and find our bearings. These are somewhat similar to the significator in a tarot spread, but they're different enough to require explanation.

A charged card is taken out of the deck by choice to relate to the question being asked. In general cases, this is the Gentleman card for a male sitter and the Lady card for a female sitter. In other specific instances, the card is chosen according to one's correspondences and keywords. Here are some cards for you to consider.

Charged Cards (Key Cards)	
Relationship	The Heart
Health	The Bear
Spiritual Life	The Coffin (sometimes used for immediate health issues)
Career	The Fox
Home/Domestic	The House
Education	The Book
Contracts	The Ring
Relocation/Travel	The Ship

The appropriate card is first taken out of the deck and "charged" (in rune work we would call this "loading") by concentrating on the card. There are various other actions one can take to charge the card, but they aren't covered here and a moment of concentration will suffice.

The card is then replaced in the deck so we know what we are looking for when it is laid out with other cards in any form of layout. It provides a beacon for us to use in highlighting the tableau. Consider it a lighthouse, shining brightly on the cards around it (but perhaps missing those right next to it) and less brightly on the cards far away from it.

If we are performing a quick three-card spread, we simply shuffle and go through the deck face-up until we find the charged card. We select the card above it and below it, and lay these out together for our reading.

In any case of shuffling, you may wish the sitter to shuffle, or you may shuffle and allow the sitter to then split the deck into three piles (with their left hand) and then restack them into one deck.

Three-Card Reading (Career)

Let us imagine our sitter has asked about his or her career. We are to perform a three-card spread. We charge the Fox card, and then shuffle (or allow the sitter to shuffle) and perform a three-deck split. When the cards are placed back in a single pile, we turn them face-up and work through them carefully to locate the charged Fox card.

The card immediately above it, we place down on the table, then the Fox itself, then the card immediately below it. Of course, you can select two cards above and below for a five-card layout; three cards above and below for a seven-card layout; and so on.

Figure 63. Three-Card Career Reading

In this example, the Letter is to the left and the Child to the right of the Fox. Using our essence keywords, we see this as "an innocent sentiment." As a sentiment is a combination of beliefs and emotions, we read this as being completely guileless with regard to career (the young child.) Unless this sitter is looking for employment in childcare or other related fields (for example, entertainment) this does not bode well for job-hunting.

THE GRAND TABLEAU • 127

The Letter itself may be read literally that the person will receive an offer but going into it wide-eyed is ill-advised, as otherwise they will be eaten. (The fox has caught the bird in the central image.) This is very much a warning.

Nine-Card Reading (Romance)

In this next reading, we look at a charged card for relationships, the **Heart**. Whilst generally we would look mainly at the placement and relationships between the Gentleman and the Lady cards for matters of romance, we can also look at the Heart card to see the sitter's emotional state within the situation.

In this nine-card reading we have placed the heart at the centre of the cards for the purpose of teaching—this will make sense later in this lesson. For now, just work with us *un moment* and examine this layout.

Take a look at these cards in relationship to each other. One thing that immediately strikes us is that bearing down on the emotional state of the Heart (reading right to left) are the top three cards, together showing "a proposal of faithful reliability." The sitter's highest expectation of relationship is to be given a long-lasting statement of trust. When we look at the three cards below, we might see that they have reached a standstill in their self-appreciation (Anchor + Bouquet + Coffin), the Coffin doubly signifying a recent change of state (perhaps a divorce or other breakup) and also their self-initiation and image. With the Bouquet "appreciation" is turned into a self-image and self-worth state, rather than someone else's appreciation.

We hope you can see how we must read the cards **together** first, in batches, sets, montages, vignettes, scenarios, scenes, and tableaux. It makes it much easier.

Now, what about the **Ways** and the **Stork** either side of the heart? Is there something promising in the sitter's emotional life?

Figure 64. Heart (Emotional) Nine-Card Layout

THE GRAND TABLEAU • 129

Nine-Card Reading (Travel)

Let's do another nine-card reading, this time for a question about travel. A sitter has come to ask us about their prospects for travel: should they look to travel or settle down?

Travel relates to the Ship, so after charging that card, we could first place it on the table and shuffle. Then we'll cut and draw eight cards to surround it. We could alternatively shuffle, find the Ship, place it on the table, and surround it with the next eight cards in the deck. There's another method you'll learn at the end of this lesson, but for now, let's look at this next layout together.

Let us also add that our sitter in this case is a young man, so we can immediately see that the Gentleman card with the Clouds ahead of him shows change and transition. Whilst he will likely seek stability (the Tree) on the other side of that rapid change, he will be forced to travel anyway, as the Ship is above him.

How about we use our keyword kaleidoscope to see what the Snake might mean here? We take a look at Snake + Ship + Clouds as they corner the Gentleman. That's:

- Stealth + Adventure + Transition

- Stealth + Adventure = Spying

- Adventure + Transition = Exploration

- Stealth + Transition = Disguise

We can collapse our kaleidoscope into one word: Spying + Exploration + Disguise = Safari. It certainly looks like the cards are suggesting a high-octane adventure-type trip where the sitter will have to dress up for the climate or culture.

Now do the same for the Scythe, Sun, and Messenger in the top-right corner. They are further away from the Gentleman but influence somewhat his activities with regard to travel, being on the shadow side to him (the Ship).

Figure 65. Ship (Travel) Nine-Card Layout

THE GRAND TABLEAU • 131

Nine-Card Reading (Education)

Let's take what we have learnt and practiced in these nine-card methods and now apply it to a sitter who has come to us to ask a question about education. The sitter wishes to leave her current job, but is unsure how to go about retraining or learning, whether she should invest, do it full-time or part-time, or stick with her current career. Whilst this is related to career, it is more about education and upgrading skills so we'll charge the Book card.

In this case, let us first imagine a cross of vertical and horizontal lines; take a reading as to what is directly influencing the sitter's perspective on her education. Next, we'll look at the diagonal cards to discover any possible routes.

We cover this more later in our chapter on diagonals, but for now, let us use it as a way of applying our skill in two separate examples.

So here we can read the Stork and the Tower either side of the Book indicating a "delivery of vision"—almost like receiving a clear plan of the future. This shows that the sitter already has all the information required to make the decision, like a syllabus of life.

The Letter and the Lily top and bottom together show a "pure invitation," an offer that will be absolutely what the sitter requires.

We have not done anything here other than put together our essence keywords from the earlier chapter, but now we can work on our interpretation, perhaps by placing these phrases together to read "you will receive an offer that will meet your vision, and you are advised here to commit yourself to it absolutely cleanly, separating it out from all other concerns. It must remain yours and be done for your own self-worth, not for others."

Let's now clarify this insight with the diagonals.

The Fox and Coffin seem to be the most "negative" images here, however, they are not so when taken en masse; the cunning of the Fox with the Book shows rapid learning to good effect and the Coffin shows a transition or new state of affairs that will arise from the new education. Again, it is suggested the sitter quit her current job and make space for the course alone.

Similarly, the Ring and the Lady here show that the proposal will be pleasing and emotionally satisfying.

Figure 66. Book (Education) Nine-Card Layout

THE GRAND TABLEAU • 133

Figure 67. Book Layout Cross Cards

Figure 68. Book Layout Diagonal Cards

THE GRAND TABLEAU • 135

Try using the keyword kaleidoscope on the four corners together, or other combinations of the nine cards in this layout. You can see how powerful these simple 9 x 9 layouts can become with just a few simple skills and practice. We will also see how the concepts of near and far come into play at the end of this lesson.

So far, we've covered career in a three-card layout, then romped through romance, travel, and education in nine-card layouts. Now let's take a final look at further layouts of 3 x 3 for two other perennial topics, health and spirituality.

In these two cases, we will give you a couple of pointers, ask you to look at the readings, and apply your skills and practice to interpret the layouts.

Nine-Card Reading (Health)
Exercise: Bear Reading

- What will be good for the sitter's health, according to this layout?

- What tends to draw the sitter to practices that are bad for their health?

- What is the importance of the Mice + Birds + Scythe?

- Look at the images of the Bear + Broom.
  What does this say about willpower?

Exercise: Coffin Reading

- What might flowers of all kinds signify to the spiritual life?

- What is the difference between a house and a garden?
  What could that mean?

- Compare the two columns, left and right. What might these suggest?

Figure 69. Bear (Health) Nine-Card Layout

Figure 70. Coffin (Spiritual Life) Nine-Card Layout

The Grand Tableau

We have seen how we can derive so much meaning from 3 x 3 card layouts, and you may be wondering when you will build up to the incredible 4 x 9 thirty-six-card Grand Tableau. Well, *mesdames et messieurs*, we have a surprise for you—you have already learned the Grand Tableau! *C'est vrai!*

It is indeed true. Take another look at all those 3 x 3 layouts you have been reading, and then take a look at the following single Grand Tableau.

That's right! Every single reading you have done in this chapter—whether it be three cards for the career of the sitter, nine cards for health or spiritual purpose, relocation concerns or their romantic life—*they are all from the same single Grand Tableau.* This is the incredible scope of learning Lenormand; one singular layout can be used to read the entire range of concerns and issues any sitter may present.

You don't have to keep laying out different cards or spreads as you might in a tarot reading; the method is actually a lot simpler than shuffling and searching for charged cards, counting piles, or anything—just lay out all the cards and read the tableau. In between each significator card being read for health, wealth, or love, we reset our meanings for the other cards. In other words, the Fox can now mean something entirely different in the next part of the reading. The way meanings may change is one of the most fundamental differences in practice to tarot. It also makes for a reading that can last two hours at least, so it is best to take time into consideration if you are interested in adding the GT to a professional practice.

Figure 71. The Grand Tableau Master

Exercise: Near and Far

If you have completed the previous two exercises, you may consider how the various 3 x 3 layouts relate to each other—where they overlap (and how you read the same cards differently in each case!)—and where they are far apart. Which charged cards are near and far to each other, and how might that add another layer to your reading? Which cards that caused concern in one part of the tableau also cause concern in another?

It may take a while to realise just how powerful a method this is, and how you can now profoundly apply the essential skills you have already learnt to interpreting a full tableau. In our next chapter, we will deepen our reading with an introduction of the houses of Lenormand, although it is suggested you practice for a while without using the houses.

We also recommend you continue to practice with full tableaux, even if you only read part of them. Do not get into a habit of laying out only a few cards; this sort of laziness leads your brain down a more limited avenue.

SIX

The Houses

....

We give this method of fortune-telling for what it is worth. It may be either a pastime seasoned with a flavour of mystery, a study in the weird ways of coincidence, or a test of skill quickened by intuition. We would have all our readers amused and interested, but none saddened or enslaved by it.
—Professor P. R. S. Foli, *Fortune-Telling by Cards*, 1903

....

In this chapter we will introduce the houses, using our existing knowledge of the cards to add another layer or lens to our GT reading. Again, we must completely disconnect our T-space head to enter into L-space, which is here very different. We'd also like to touch on a slight difference as well in our own style rather than the usual book-given methods (usually in German or French) or online explanations.

You'll soon appreciate how the use of houses widely opens up your readings and provides even more depth and possibility to interpretation.

The Houses

In the 1903 book we quoted at the start of this book, Foli is introducing the cartomantic student into a "Master Method" that appears toward the end of his book on card-reading. It simply provides a thirty-six-card layout where each position has a particular meaning.

This is the only method in the book that uses positional readings; all those prior are layouts and lines where one looks at pairings of cards, their reading in a line, the types of cards and their frequency, et cetera.

THE MASTER METHOD.

Table of the Positions and their Several Meanings.

No. 1. Project in hand.	No. 2. Satisfaction.	No. 3. Success.	No. 4. Hope.	No. 5. Chance. Luck.	No. 6. Wishes. Desire.
No. 7. Injustice.	No. 8. Ingratitude.	No. 9. Association.	No. 10. Loss.	No. 11. Trouble.	No. 12. State or Condition.
No. 13. Joy.	No. 14. Love.	No. 15. Prosperity.	No. 16. Marriage.	No. 17. Sorrow. Affliction.	No. 18. Pleasure. Enjoyment.
No. 19. Inheritance. Property.	No. 20. Fraud. Deceit.	No. 21. Rivals.	No. 22. A Present. Gift.	No. 23. Lover.	No. 24. Advancement. A Rise in the world.
No. 25. Kindness. A Good Turn.	No. 26. Undertaking. Enterprise.	No. 27. Changes.	No. 28. The End (of Life).	No. 29. Rewards.	No. 30. Misfortune. Disgrace.
No. 31. Happiness.	No. 32. Money. Fortune.	No. 33. Indifference.	No. 34. Favour.	No. 35. Ambition.	No. 36. Ill-health. Sickness.

77

Figure 72. The Foli Master Method

We can thus infer that earlier cartomantic methods were more often nonpositional than not. It is only in our T-space that many readers have become used to "the card here relates to your future" or "the card at the top of this layout is your outcome."

We know that the Golden Dawn Opening of the Key method that derived from these earlier methods was nonpositional, and it was only a member of the Golden Dawn who wanted a shortcut (or a method that could be used with nonmembers without revealing the secret correspondences) that devised the Celtic Cross with its ten fixed positional meanings.

The Surprise Card

In earlier methods, a "surprise" card was drawn and left face-down until the rest of the reading was performed, after which it was then turned over to reveal an outcome, final verdict, or "surprise" (perhaps a key to interpretation) to the sitter—and the sibyl.

This may be a method you use with smaller readings of the Lenormand. It provides a novel twist, yet is rooted in early cartomancy for salon-style readings. Tarot readers might find this practice difficult whilst moving about in L-space, and we are going to give it another jolt again in this lesson.

We are also going to provide another cartomantic revelation:

You correspond the *arising meaning* of the card with its house—*not* the individual card.

Many sources give a simple method of using houses, but this can lead us to a narrow avenue if we learn it, so we want to ensure you learn the wide way! Let's look at what the houses actually are first—you'll see an echo of Foli here.

The Thirty-six Houses

The houses of the Grand Tableau are very simple. They are the "meanings" of the thirty-six positions given by laying out all thirty-six cards in order. That is to say, the first house is that of the first card, number 1, the Messenger/Rider. The second house is that of the second card, number 2, the Clover. The final house is of course number 36, the Cross.

You can see the houses laid out numerically in the following diagram, left to right.

Figure 73. The Houses

146 • SIX

Now, each of these houses has a particular meaning that obviously relates to the card corresponding to the position. Before we go into those meanings, however, a note: whatever card falls into a particular house in a GT is **not** like a card falling into a position in a tarot spread. We do *not* simply "pair and compare" the card and the position, a T-space behavior that will limit what you can do in L-space.

As an illustration, if we laid out the GT from the previous section (Figure 71–The Grand Tableau Master) and now read it with regard to the houses, we do not simply take the first card, the Mountain, which is in the House of the Rider, and pair the Mountain (meaning in itself "stability" for example) with the Rider, meaning "communication," etc. We know many sources may teach this because it appears to be a simple way of presenting the houses—but it is not (*à mon avis*) the most powerful way to use houses in L-space.

You can start in this way, if you must, and you can also do it intuitively. Here the Rider is seen riding over the Mountain—what might that mean?

If you recall our previous exercises, you will remember that the Coffin showed a positive transition as a result of learning and education—a new state of mind was to be reached. Now we can see in the houses that in the previous layout, the Coffin is in the House of the Mountain. If you read our own take on this house in the list below, you'll see how even a simple card comparison can be layered by the house; the Coffin, showing how our sitter will be changed by new education, in this house informs us that the change will be long-lasting and not without opposition. The person will have to find sanctuary and dig deep into personal resources to "survive" courses or learning for a longer time than anticipated. This is useful information to impart to the sitter, a warning to take steps to prepare and pack for an "unexpected adventure."

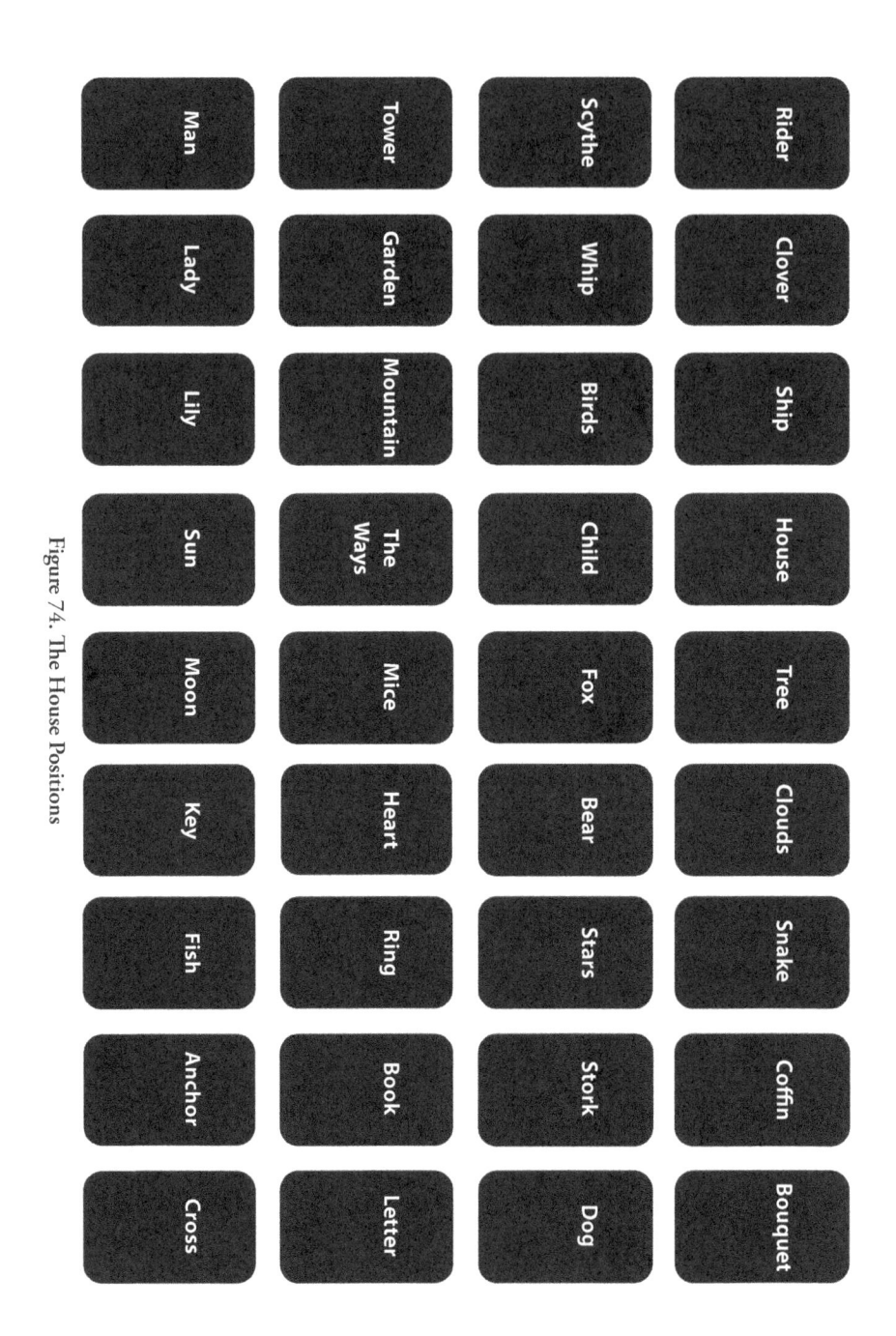

Rider	Scythe	Tower	Man
Clover	Whip	Garden	Lady
Ship	Birds	Mountain	Lily
House	Child	The Ways	Sun
Tree	Fox	Mice	Moon
Clouds	Bear	Heart	Key
Snake	Stars	Ring	Fish
Coffin	Stork	Book	Anchor
Bouquet	Dog	Letter	Cross

Figure 74. The House Positions

Cards in Their Own House

What do we make of the Key being in its own house (compare the Key card in the layout of figure 71 with the house positions in figure 74)? Again, head back to the previous lesson and see how we might add the **Key** to that reading (which we didn't read in the lesson as it was not close to a constellation we were examining, such as the Bear for health, etc.). This is the only card in its own House—usually there will be one such card.

A card in its own house can be a double whammy or a feedback loop; depending on the context, it can provide a point of significance or a black hole of wasted energy. For now, just take it as a card as calling attention to itself, like looking at itself in a mirror and saying, "Hey, check me out!"

So, whilst we can read in a simple manner with the houses, what we must rather do is see the Mountain in the context of the other cards first and its overall significance in the Tableau. This includes those cards surrounding it through the keyword kaleidoscope approach, diagonals, shadow cards, and near-and-far (some of which we haven't done yet), and only then place its *arising significance* into the context of the House.

Having said that, it will be easier to explain after we have looked at the meanings of the Houses, and their "focus" individually.

The Meaning of the 36 Houses

1. The Rider/Messenger: Communications/Liaison
   This house relates to the sitter's engagement with the world.
   It can indicate the message being transmitted to the world
   by the sitter's behaviour.

2. The Clover: Identity
   This house relates to self-discovery and belonging, who you are,
   who you will become, and where you are going.

3. The Ship: Adventure
   This house is about your purpose and the processes you will go
   though to fulfil your true destiny.

4. The House: Security

    This house is about what makes you feel safe. It is related to what keeps you grounded and secure, what you work toward to maintain a happy life. It can also be the centre of your spiritual being; it is you and it contains your own inner light, your soul and your strength; it is your earthly anchor.

5. The Tree: Longevity

    This is the house of the ancestor, the source of our life blood; it is testament to our survival. It is related to family and the support that comes with being part of a lineage.

6. The Clouds: Transition

    This is the house of change and movement. It is all about the times in between, where we rest and take stock of who we are, what we want, and where we are going on our journey.

7. The Snake: Stealth

    This is the house of temptation and timing: knowing when to act on your impulses and when not to. "Slowly, slowly catchee monkey." One who waits will gain the prize.

8. The Coffin: Initiation

    This is the house of facing your inner demons and looking within yourself to hunt them down. This is the house the shadow world, where you take the step beyond fear itself and turn and face it. This is the house of harnessing great power if the sitter approaches the situation or experience with awareness.

9. The Bouquet: Appreciation

    The house of awareness that we are not alone, that if we appreciate and recognise the needs of others—and they do likewise—the world would be a more generous place. This house could be said to be the house of philanthropy.

10. The Scythe: Clearing

    This is the house of regeneration. If we do not clear out the old, there will never be a place for the new. This has always been and always will be the way. This is the law of creation, life, and nature.

11. The Rod/Whip: Service

    This is the house of discipline, work, maintenance, and striving toward the good of the whole.

12. The Birds/Owl: Divination

    This is the house of looking out for signs and being aware of the meanings behind your dreams. The ancient Romans would watch the movement of birds to interpret the signs behind their behaviour, known as "taking the auspices." It is therefore the house of the spiritual messengers. This house warns to consider well before making decisions; check that "auspices" are good and true.

13. The Child/Little Girl: Ingenue/innocence

    This is the house of purity and action without guile, the realm of doing something for the pure joy of it without care of result. This is a world devoid of superficiality.

14. The Fox: Cunning

    This is the house of the scavenger and opportunist. It is here that situations will arise where you may need to be wary of the behaviour of the flatterer or the charmer. Do not let down your guard easily.

15. The Bear: Headstrong

    This is the house of stubbornness and situations where you will find no joy in trying to change someone's mind. You could find yourself up against an immovable force you had not planned to meet.

16. The Stars: Creation

    This is the house of beginnings and endings. With the death of a star comes great brilliance.

17. The Stork: Deliverance
    This is the house of benefiting from something you worked toward earlier; it is a house of timing and productivity coming together to create joy and continuation.

18. The Dog: Codependency
    This is the house of need and being needed in return. There is a strong emphasis on loyalty and responsibility.

19. The Tower: Vision
    This is the house of getting the bigger picture, being aware of what is going on in your life and in the neighbourhood. It is the world of seeing beyond the obvious.

20. The Garden: Communing
    This is the house of getting out and about and mixing in the world; this is the world of social engagement and entertainment.

21. The Mountain: Durability
    This house relates to and describes the enduring nature of survival and growth. Mountains were carved out by glaciers and stand as testament to great strength. Essentially, this house shows the sitter's backbone. It is a place of sanctuary and protection from hostility. It also shows the potential for drawing upon hidden resources that are naturally available when we are forced to extract them.

22. The Ways: Choice/Decision
    This is the house of making decisions and acting upon them, and considering the long-term implications of these choices. It can also indicate a "road less traveled" that may turn out to be the best one. There is no right or wrong way, but you must choose. Take your pick, because you cannot go both ways at once.

23. The Mice: Productivity
   This is the house of being busy and getting work done. It is the house of the silent worker, the one slaving for the good of the whole who is often not recognised. The work is often done by the little people who get little reward in return.

24. The Heart: Courage
   Like the Cowardly Lion in *The Wizard of Oz*, this house is the centre of your courage and being true to your own self. It is the house of exposing your centre and being strong in the broken places. Here lies within all the wonderful things connected with having heart, courage, kindness, consideration. If the matter is addressing the underlying energy of a question or issue, it means that heart is at the crux of it. Getting to the underlying house of an issue will open the door to a solution.

25. The Ring: Continuity
   The Ring gives this house the sense of sealing a deal. It is the house of the pledge and shines out into the cards above and around it a sense of commitment, a cause, bond, and oath. It can be a promise to oneself that has to be made in the context of the cards that fall in and around this house.

26. The Book: Knowledge
   The House of the Book shows where knowledge may be gained—within or without. It gives the cards above it and around it the light of clarity and preservation. It can mean that any information required is easily found and shared.

27. The Letter: Sentiment
   The House of the Letter is where considered communications must be made. The card in this house must be more considered than not, and those around it should be seen in the light of consideration and sympathy.

28. The Gentleman: Analytical

    The House of the Gentleman is the masculine house with all the stereotypes and archetypes of masculinity.

29. The Lady: Intuitive

    The House of the Lady is the feminine house with all the stereotypes and archetypes of femininity.

30. The Lily: Purity

    What falls in and around this house should be considered in the light of memory and the past. There is a certain honour required in this House.

31. The Sun: Will

    The Sun shines brightly and illuminates the card in its house, giving it focus, intent, and more power than it might otherwise warrant in a reading.

32. The Moon: Mediumistic

    The Moon reflects into its own house and gives the card above a deeper meaning that should be delved into below the surface.

33. The Key: Access

    The House of the Key can easily unlock the rest of the reading, so give due consideration to this card. It can also lock something, so the cards around this house may be barriers.

34. The Fish: Resources

    The House of the Fish is where resources can be drawn upon.

35. The Anchor: Standstill

    The House of the Anchor is where the reading may be held firm or fastened, depending on the questions and the interpretation's context.

36. The Cross: Faith
The House of the Cross shows the resolution and acceptance of the reading, the context, and the cards. It is the grace surrounding resolution.

Now that we've seen how the houses might be considered another layer to our overall reading, let us look at an example of how the House of the Owl might be seen in two very different readings. This will give us a good way of seeing how flexible this approach is, as well as its intuitive and powerful qualities—particularly if you do not fix yourself to comparing a card to the card of the house.

There are many other methods of using houses; for example, to bridge from a card being read to its house, then to read the card in that house, and bridge to the house of *that* card until you return to a card that has already been read.

Figure 75. Work/Career in the House of the Owl

A Career Question in the House of the Owl

In this example, we have simply imagined looking at a spread (or part of a GT) where the central card is in the House of the Owl. There is no particular significance of this other than to demonstrate houses. Any card can fall in any house in any reading of a GT, whatever the question.

In this scenario, the sitter's question is regarding work life; she wants to know if all her hard work will pay off in the long term.

Looking at the nine cards arranged in a 3 x 3 grid, we can interpret an answer using the keyword kaleidoscope and our own intuition. Again we must consider each card and image as part of the whole—unlike tarot, these cards cannot be read singularly.

So let us consider that the Child here represents her determination to succeed at her venture, but we must look at the cards around her and the influence they exert on the issue at hand. We see how her enthusiasm is driving the Fish (resources) onward, which can be seen as positive, but there could be too much willpower being exerted or the danger of being perceived as pushy. Directly beneath her is the House; security is assured, the stability of a house's foundation beneath her as long as she stays focused on the goal.

The Key behind her indicates that play-power (not power-play!) is a means to unlocking fulfilment in the long-term. The key that unlocks the house points to the grown-up Lady who looks toward the security of the House. She is the same child, now matured. She stands in the grounds of the House, a part of the cycle.

The play-power can be seen to have been paid off, then. The Anchor card emphasises rest and recuperation on the journey, maintaining the purity/authenticity of the Lily, childlike innocence, keeping simple faith (the Cross) of convictions but taking some care to feather the nest (the Birds). The overall influence of the House of the Child on the cards around it is one of forging on with childlike authenticity.

Thus the advice is for the sitter to be resourceful and feather her nest but rest in between. Doing so will bring success, well-being, and satisfaction—making an opening for long-term security.

Adding the House of the Owl

Let us now imagine that the central card here is in the House of the Owl. As you have just learned, a house adds a tincture to the overall taste of the interpretation.

The Owl could be said to have an influence of hidden wisdom, indicating a need to look for signs and portents. This does not mean anything in isolation for we are not reading it as a card, merely a nuance to the interpretation. Sometimes this will give an added layer to the reading, sometimes a new twist or solution, and sometimes new depth. There is no single rule.

In this example, we sense that the Child in the House of the Owl would indicate that the very situation is its own solution. The energy of keeping the loop going—the momentum—is a sign and portent of the problem itself. The Owl is not a creature that lives in a house, so it indicates that the security of the situation must be observed from a greater distance—the sitter cannot see it.

In fact, thinking about it in this light, we are reminded that the stick keeping the hoop of continued momentum upright and moving is the very same rod that can become a spine for your own back.

Perhaps the Owl also looks upon the Child playing (and scaring the Fish away) and opines, "She will never catch anything that way." We would tell our sitter that she needs to learn to perch and swoop when the time is ready, to not be overly enthusiastic. In order to "feather the nest" (as we saw in the combination of Lily, Cross, and Birds) the House of the Owl tells us that there may be another solution. In fact, **it is that Owls do not build their own nests**—they inhabit old dwellings; in this, the deeper answer to whether the sitter's hard work will pay off is "lessen the work, and build on the work of others."

If we were giving advice from this reading, we would ask the sitter to look at taking over a failing or abandoned piece of work, make it her own, and use that project to demonstrate her capability. This would get her out of her loop.

Here are some of our reading notes for this session, showing how it was built up:

- Fish + Birds + Anchor = Resources + feathering nest + recuperation = Well-being/satisfaction

- Cross + Key + Lady = Faith + Access + Feminine = Openness

- House + Lily = Security
- Birds, influenced by the House of the Child: Too eager and impatient for signs
- Anchor: Being too reckless and not heeding the conditions, not putting down anchor
- Cross: Too reliant on blind faith
- Key: Too much responsibility
- Lady: Too sensitive or responsive to emotional stimulus
- House: Too driven by desire for security
- Lily: Hot-housing, forcing artificially, not being natural
- Fish: Over-fishing, not replenishing resources.

In this next example, we will ask you to consider how the same House of the Owl might influence the following 3 x 3 constellation of cards in a Love/Relationship reading. Here our sitter has asked us about matters of trust in relationship and how it affects her new relationship. Don't forget, this is not a method or reading; it is a scenario for practising the houses in a particular manner—to get you using them as a layer for the overall meaning of the cards in combination.

Figure 76. Love/Relationship in the House of the Owl

Exercise: Love in the House of the Owl

The sitter is represented in the tableau by the Lady card; she looks ahead to the Stork expectantly. The Stork looks ahead to the Birds card as it to point to her listening to her inner wisdom, to read the signs. This is confirmed by the presence of the Tower card; it advises her to look around and await developments.

The Ring, Sun, and Bear—proclamation, will, and strength—speak of being true to one's own core values. The Bear looks down on the Coffin, a sign that the sitter needs to have strength to rely on the natural order; she needs to put aside old doubts and stop questioning other peoples' intentions to be able to welcome new relationships. The Garden is below the Sun, which illuminates it. The Garden is open and friendly, a place of liaison and meeting people.

Now look at the Garden card in the House of the Owl, having already read the Garden in this context—this context provides a different type of garden, function, and reading than other readings you will do—this is the power of the L-space. And when you have this unique garden appear in this one reading, then you can see it in the house in which it falls, bringing with it all the other cards.

And of course, the same goes for every card in every house; they all interweave in a massive matrix of potential perspective and meaning—our methods only provide the most illuminating lines of sight.

Exercise: The Ship in the House of the Book

For your second exercise, go back to the Grand Tableau in chapter 5 and consider the reading relating to travel we gave to the young man. We used the charged card of the Ship, which we can now see fell into the House of the Book. Without doing a simple comparison of Ship + Book, look over the whole tableau or just the 3 x 3 square of cards around the Ship, and come up with ways the House of the Book may provide deeper insight into his travel.

Beacons: Cards in Their Own Houses

The thirty-six houses in the Lenormand could be compared to the use of an underlying theme in story writing; more so than its meaning or context, the theme is the backdrop of what is going on under the surface of the divination. If we take the Rider card as an example, the underlying theme of the Rider card as we see it is "getting the message." When a card falls upon its own house in a reading, it is the divine's way of flagging something you really ought to come to grips with in life. It is saying that you need to really pay attention to something. It acts as an alert or warning. Conversely, it can be a confirmation that you really are doing just fine, exactly where you should be.

1. The Rider in the House of the Rider

   Are you getting the message?

   Urgent or important news arriving. Communications/liaison. This "like attracts like" influence has a magnetic force to it; it is trying to get an important communication across. Ask yourself what are you may be ignoring, what you are allowing to pass you by, a person who is trying to tell you something whom you're ignoring. The combination heralds news that will be life-changing.

2. The Clover in the House of the Clover

   Rolling in clover

   This is a very fortunate combination; it confirms that whatever you do will turn out beneficial. The Clover placed in its own house confirms that you are in the right place at the right time; the positive energy that you put out into the world comes right back to you magnified. This perfect combination of "luck" and "origin" that is being where you are supposed to be comes naturally. In relation to friendship and love, this is about being around people you love, and they love you; this is one big love-fest.

   Identity/origin, confidence and self-belief will grow and grow; believing in anything being possible will bring abundance and good fortune. You are satisfied with your situation; this may even be seen by others as being self-satisfied.

3. The Ship in the House of the Ship

   Just do it–set sail, do not waste time!

   This is not just a Ship, this is a fleet, and it is ready to set sail. It is not how but when, and this is very soon. The Ship's presence in its own house, overseas distance is magnified. This indicates not just holiday travel, but adventure at its greatest, the desire to move on, move away, and be a pioneer. With regards to timing (as with all of the cards in their own houses), time is of the essence. There is urgency, after all, it is slap-bang on itself, not to be ignored or cast aside. The matter requires giving serious consideration; action is needed. Conditions are perfect for getting out into the big wide world.

4. The House in the House of the House
To be as safe as the houses
The House in the House is solid! This is double-strength security; what a wonderful position in which to find oneself. It isn't just four walls but eight to keep you safe! If you or the sitter has a concern about security, this combination occurring will put the mind at rest. If there is a question as regards a house purchase, this is very favourable for success ahead. The downside to this combo can be feeling trapped by your good life; sometimes being safe can get to be a little boring. There may be a person in your life or that of the sitter who is over-controlling. It may be saying in a quirky way you need to get out of the house more; the life you have is becoming somewhat stagnating. It could also be a warning to make one's house more secure. A warning to ensure it is doubly safe.

On the other hand, this also speaks very much of being too dependent on security, not wanting to get out. There could be fear of the outside world.

5. The Tree in the House of the Tree
Let there be spaces in your togetherness, and let the winds of the heavens dance between you. Love one another but make not a bond of love… And stand together, yet not too near together: For the pillars of the temple stand apart, and the oak tree and the cypress grow not in each other's shadow.
—Khalil Gibran, *The Prophet*
The Tree in its own house can speak of over-reliance on your family; there could be a case of not wanting to make a life outside of the family.

It may speak of adult children who just won't grow up, who expect to be supported by their parents and are dependent way beyond the norm. In all its positivity, the mighty Tree can offer shelter and support outwards whilst drawing on resources deep down from its roots as does the ancient Methuselah Tree. Think of the tree and how adequate space is crucial for its survival, as other trees cannot be planted too close to avoid competition. Trees also need light, and if they are deprived, they grow upwards too quickly instead of outwards and overall growth is stunted.

The positive aspect of the Tree in the House of the Tree is that it has an overall energy of protection and longevity. Any question that draws out this combination speaks of a force to reckon with. If the question is about relationships, the future stems from strong roots.

6. The Clouds in the House of the Clouds
There are no rules of architecture for a castle in the clouds.
—Gilbert K. Chesterton

The Clouds in the House of the Clouds can portend entering a period of seemingly disruptive change after a long period of the same old thing. This long-term buildup will result in a release of held-in emotions. There may be tears and a lot of disruption when you finally let go, but something has got to give, and this card coming together in its own house is the indication of the big shift required in your life. This combination is your calling card for unavoidable change. Do the things that need doing; don't let those clouds get in your way; make them work for you. Change is a liberator, not a force to be feared; embrace it.

7. The Snake in the House of the Snake
The world of men is dreaming, it has gone mad in its sleep,
and a snake is strangling it, but it can't wake up.
—D. H. Lawrence

The Snake in its own house speaks of the energy of the creature consuming its own tail, the *ouroboros*. It may be that you are in a situation where you keep repeating the same thing over and over again; no matter what you do, you cannot get out of this loop. The cycle could be one of obsession or impulsion, a desire you cannot resist. This combination can spell out an obsessive situation or relationship, especially if placed between the Gentleman and Lady cards. Its presence in a reading on finances can indicate that an individual is able to be self-sufficient. In a work situation, it means that one is able to work alone and be self-motivated.

This combination could be trying to magnify and draw attention to the aspects of ourselves that embody the energy at play we would rather not acknowledge; sneaky behaviour can be easily recognised in ourselves. We may dislike the person who gossips, but we still find ourselves acting out this very behaviour. The Snake in its own house means the behavior is magnified whether we like it or not. On the positive side, attention is drawn to it, allowing us to change behavior.

The Snake card and its reputation of lies and deceit brings to mind the words of Walter Scott: "Oh what a tangled web we weave when we first practice to deceive," and its appearance in the Snake's own house speaks of a web of deceit in which you or the sitter may be entangled. It could warn of a person in your life who is best avoided or a dead-end situation that is not going anywhere. There is some disentangling to be done or some reconciliation.

Perhaps there is a need to express some kundalini energy. The Snake in the Snake House could be kundalini energy within one's own body.

The *ouroboros* is a dramatic symbol for the integration and assimilation of the opposite, i.e., of the shadow. This "feedback" process is at the same time a symbol of immortality, since it is said of the *ouroboros* that he slays and brings himself to life, fertilizes himself and gives birth to himself. He symbolizes the One who proceeds from the clash of opposites, and he therefore constitutes the secret of the *prima materia,* which unquestionably stems from man's unconscious.

8. The Coffin in the House of the Coffin
   Wake-up call
   Like the Death card of the tarot, the Coffin card has a little of an unfounded bad reputation. The Coffin is not all doom and gloom and the end of life as we know it, no more than the Death card of the tarot means literal death! At number 8, the Coffin of the Lenormand is very much about energy flowing effortlessly.

   When the card of the Coffin appears in its own house, this is the "über-energy" of regeneration and recycling your resources. Momentum is at work if the matter regards a question about love, work, or health. The indication is that you or the sitter is in a good place right now—the ball has started rolling, and the progress must be watched. The Coffin in its own house could be trying to draw attention to a health condition. A change of lifestyle could be required: a whole new way of living life, the start of a new beginning. Maybe it is about burying something that should have been buried a long time ago, something you are hanging onto. The Coffin in the House of the Coffin is drawing attention to it.

9. The Bouquet in the House of the Bouquet
   Coming up roses
   This is the scenario of receiving an award at a ceremony. The Bouquet turning up like this in its own house is about receiving appreciation from your own peers. The work you have put in to make your career and creative endeavors thrive is going to pay off big time.

10. The Scythe in the House of the Scythe
    Never cut what you can untie.
    —Joseph Joubert

    The Scythe in the House of the Scythe appearing in the layout is shouting out to you to get working on clearing out your environment and your life in general, and that something in your life is tripping you up.

The matter may be about cutting down on cutting down; it could indicate that perhaps somebody is trying too hard to lose weight, cutting down too many calories, and that "cutting down" has been taken to the extreme. This combination could advise moderation in all things (including moderation) and to not be too extreme in attitude, belief, or behaviour. More simply, maybe someone is working too hard!

11. The Whip in the House of the Whip
    A rod for your own back
    The Whip in the House of the Whip could indicate you have found yourself in a situation where you are making a whip for your own back. You have put yourself out too much to make life easy for other people, at the expense of your own well-being. You may be in a work situation you have fought very hard to achieve, maybe even in charge in some capacity, however you have to answer to somebody with a bigger whip to wield. The presence of this combination should drawe your attention—maybe the situation is possibly abusive.

12. The Birds in the House of the Birds
    A wise old owl sat on an oak. The more he saw, the less he spoke. The less he spoke, the more he heard. Why aren't we like that wise old bird?
    —Edward Hersey Richards

    The Birds in the House of the Birds is very much a sign to be applied the way that birds in ancient Rome were used for oracular purposes. It can indicate the need to be more of a channel for the divine or perhaps return to the roots of oracular tradition. You need to take on a bird's-eye view of the world, see things from a greater perspective. The Birds in the House of the Birds can be a confirmation that you are at one with your spiritual values, and are where you are supposed be right now.

13. The Child in the House of the Child
    Child's play
    The Child in the House of the Child could be a bit problematic: there

is an overabundance here of childlike behavior. Perhaps somebody is not owning their responsibilities, shirking their duties. A house needs to be run by an adult, not the child. Boundaries need to be set in life to avoid complete chaos in the person's life. There is very much an issue of immaturity here. This combination could also stress the need for discipline and structure in someone's life.

14. The Fox in the House of the Fox
Doubly duplicitous
The Fox in the House of the Fox has the making of being in a den of deceit and mischief. This combination could be confirmation that you are correct in your fear that somebody you had doubts about cannot be trusted. It could be a person who has hurt you before, but to whom you have given the benefit of the doubt, telling yourself the person has changed. You can take the fox out of the fox house, but not the fox house out of the fox! This is the warning.

15. The Bear in the House of the Bear
A bear with a sore head
The Bear in the House of the Bear could mean that you find yourself in an intimidating situation where you have to be strong and assertive. This could speak of an environment such as a workplace where you have to push to get what you want. Such pushing could mean you must compete (for promotion or otherwise) against other much stronger bears. You need to channel your inner bear and keep your inner mouse well out of the house. Trust your primal instincts you need them right now.

The Bear in its own house could be trying to draw attention to financial matters—a "bear market" is where securities fall and people sell their shares. The resulting paranoia and pessimism has an echoing effect, causing other investors to panic and sell theirs. The only ones who benefit in this kind of situation are those who hang on and wait for long-term benefits. The Bear in the House of the Bear could be saying to avoid being negative because it will consume you. Live like the Bear, be strong, and you will see results.

16. The Stars in the House of the Stars
    A celestial haven
    Wow, this is one starry place to be! What a perfect place for this card of stars to fall. It is a beneficent sign, and something good will come of this configuration. This state of wholeness, *Gestalt,* is a place of hope, vision, and brilliance in abundance. It gets brighter and brighter. On the other hand, take care that you do not burn yourself out—remember that the brighter a star, the less time it will have to shine. It is important to pace yourself and create balance in your life. Take stock in the knowledge that wherever you are in celestial space is exactly where you are supposed to be. It is written in the stars!

17. The Stork in the House of the Stork
    Good things come to those who wait
    The Stork in the House of the Stork possesses an underlying context of all ways returning back to whence one came or an instinct to return to the nest. The traditional way of looking at the card is the delivery of good news; however, there will be disruption that accompanies it, bringing about changes that will require adaptation with time. The combination is of giving and receiving.

    To be on the fortunate side of receiving this special combination in a reading, you may rest assured that you will not be short of gifts in their many shapes and forms. The double whammy of Stork energy will draw vibrant young energy to the house. You or the sitter may feel rejuvenated. Expect this to go on for a good eighteen months (double the gestation period). This combination could also mean that something you have always wanted in life is going to be delivered to you; expectations will be fulfilled.

18. The Dog in the House of the Dog
In the dog house
The Dog in the House of the Dog speaks of steadfast loyalty and intense need. This is a very reassuring state of being. The downside is that the loyalty and love you are immersed in may become stagnant and restrictive—a lot of dependency is active here. Somebody may be expecting constant attention.

19. The Tower in the House of the Tower
Being on watch
The Tower in the House of the Tower brings with it the context of being cautious, but overly so, a danger of being hyperalert, almost verging on paranoid. That said, it would be sensible to acknowledge the sensitivity here, as it is advising to take extra precautions. Be alive and aware of what is going on around you. Do not stick your head in the sand to avoid things you would rather not deal with right now.

Remember, as Roosevelt said, "speak softly but carry a big stick; you will go far."

20. The Garden in the House of the Garden
There's no "I" in "team"
The Garden in the House of the Garden is a very positive combination regarding the success of a meeting or conference. Here we have like-minded people getting together to mingle and share their passion. If the sitter has asked about the success of a conference, party, or wedding, this combination bodes well for the event, and it speaks of abundance. However, the event is very much team-oriented—everybody needs to do their bit to make it a success. The downside to that success could be that in too great a number, an event may feel impersonal.

21. The Mountain in the House of the Mountain
Great things are done when men and mountains meet.
—William Blake

The implication here of the Mountain in the House of the Mountain is one of taking the high ground. The Mountain can reflect the quest to achieve something, to take something to a whole new level. It can for some involve the search for spiritual clarity to gain a greater understanding of the human condition, to escape the mundane.

There may be a situation where something is in the way; some large force cannot be overcome or budged, so we need to work out a way to go around the problem. The energy at play with the Mountain in the House of the Mountain is steadfast and inflexible.

22. The Ways in the House of the Ways
Happiness, that grand mistress of the ceremonies in the dance of life, impels us through all its mazes and meanderings, but leads none of us the by the same route.
—Charles Caleb Colton

The Ways in the House of the Ways puts the emphasis on making a decision—and it must be made pretty quickly, it cannot be delayed! The problem here is an excess of choice, making it difficult to choose which way to go. The indecision can be paralysing in itself. The Goddess Hecate is sacred to the crossroads and she was depicted by some as having three heads: dog, serpent, horse.

If your subject of enquiry has this Ways combination and is surrounded by the Dog, the Snake, and the Rider, the overall indication is very powerful. See also the Cross card, which is heavily connected to the House of the Ways. The Dog card is very significant considering the Hecate influence.

23. The Mice in the House of the Mice
Just do what comes naturally
Here we have the Lenormand Mice in the House of the Mice. Mice by their very nature are prolific little creatures, and if the card of the Mice falls in its own house, you should expect to have a very productive

life; creativity and abundance will be unstoppable. This is a wonderful opportunity that should be taken to the full.

The energy of the Mice in the House of the Mice is very tenacious and its configuration brings with it the spirit of just going for it and keeping on and on, even though what you are doing may not be welcome by some people in your environment, either at home or at work. You must do what your instinct tells you.

24. The Heart in the House of the Heart
Where your treasure is, there will your heart be also.
—Matthew 6:21

The Heart in the House of the Heart is the place of intense love. Its appearance could mean your heart is in the right place. In regards to a possible relationship, this is the bullseye! Cupid's arrow has been well and truly delivered. If you or the sitter has asked about a relationship being serious, this is the confirmation that the relationship will go from strength to strength—expect passion and excitement. With regards to health, this person has a very strong life force. This is a positive, open, and giving environment that attracts people of the same mind.

25. The Ring in the House of the Ring
One ring to rule them all, one ring to find them,
One ring to bring them all and in the darkness bind them.
—J. R. R. Tolkien

The Ring in the House of the Ring, the Ring falling upon the Ring, seals the importance of bond and commitment to a person, cause, or career. It could be in the recitation of a pledge or the renewal of marriage vows. From a relationship/marriage perspective, it may be drawing attention to where you are now, or indicate that there are parts of your relationship that need renewing or reconsidering. Are you happy in the House of the Ring? Do you need to ring in the changes? If this is in regard to a contractual agreement, it is a reassurance that all is how it should be.

26. The Book in the House of the Book
Books are the carriers of civilization. Without books, history is silent, literature dumb, science crippled, thought and speculation at a standstill.
—Barbara Tuchman

When the Book card falls in its own House, adult education springs to mind—learning that comes with maturity, life's lessons, delivered with weight and sincerity. The searching you have embarked upon in the past, your own reading of books, and your self-development have all brought you to a place of revelation; suddenly there is meaning in uncertainties that have been puzzling you for a long time. If this combination falls into place when you or your sitter asks the cards about where your life's course is heading, it is saying you are where you are supposed to be. You are learning the lesson that needs to be taught, even if it feels like a curse.

27. The Letter in the House of the Letter
A letter to yourself
The Letter in the House of the Letter combination could mean you need to come to grips with communication. Are you being bogged down with too much? Do you feel overwhelmed? If you have been waiting on an official letter with important news, it will arrive shortly.

28. The Gentleman in the House of the Gentleman
Gentleman's club
This is the gentleman's club of old, very much the "men are from Mars" way of thinking. If this card comes up in a question regarding job opportunities and you are a woman, you may find you are up against barriers, a feeling of not belonging to the club. If you are a man, you may find doors opening for you; as the card is your significator, this is very much about you. Look within yourself—do you have gender-based exclusionary ways of relating to the world?

29. The Lady in the House of the Lady
Women owning their power!
Woman is the moon. It wanes and waxes. Everything grows because of the moon. Everything ripens because of sun. And everything is conceived because of the combination of the harmony and those two polarities of male and female sun and moon.
—Yogi Bhajan

The Lady in the House of the Lady, when the significator, is a clear indication that matters are relating to you. There is also a connotation of the "red tent" ladies-only domain, the place in ancient days where women would take time out during their menstrual cycle and childbirth. In certain cultures, this was considered a sacred time of contemplation and for conversation between women; sisterhood secrets are imparted, wise women have their voice. When the Lady card falls in her own house, it can symbolise sisterhood.

If there is a question regarding relationships and the possibility of one, the Lady in her own house could be stressing the importance of taking time to be with your female friends or a need to spend time on your own. You deserve time to recharge and adjust to changes. A "girls' night in" could be in order. If this combination is in response to a health question, it could point to a gynaecological condition or reproductive health in general. Give reverence to the moon— it is empowerment and being in tune with life's cycles. Also consider whether you you have a "women are from Venus," gender-based exclusionary way of relating to the world.

30. The Lily in the House of the Lily
The lily is all in white, like a saint, and is no mate for me.
—Thomas Hood

The Lily in the House of the Lily is very much about coming from a place of pure intent, a place all your own. Consider that what one person may believe is pure may differ from another person's definition. This theme plays out in the spiritual aspect of the idea of purity, "chastity," calling to mind the Virgin Mary, making the other symbolic interpretation of it being about sexual purity as well. The Lily in its own house is also a symbol of resurrection; is something close to you in need of revival?

31. The Sun in the House of the Sun
He who kisses the joy as it flies /Lives in Eternity's sunrise.
—William Blake

The Sun in the House of the Sun brings brilliance into play; growth and abundance is twofold. You are charged with the power it brings, which can ease the way for any projects or things you want to grow and nurture in your life. This is a fortunate combination if the question posed regards money; it offers security. If the matter is about love, the relationship will grow from strong to stronger. If the matter is related to career, the allusion is to a promotion, as it confirms that you are truly at one with what you are doing. It will bring new clarity in your life; all will make more sense. You are a powerhouse residing in a powerhouse! Be confident and be in your own power; do not doubt what you are capable of achieving.

32. The Moon in the House of the Moon
Once in a blue moon

This is an emotional place to reside. This combination brings with it heightened powers of intuition, and all your hunches at the moment just seem to come true. Revel in creativity and take time to explore this side of yourself. The energy here is most playful by nature. It is very much about doing what comes naturally to you, so with this falling into place, especially if the question posed is love-related, it is saying do what you feel you should. Follow your heart, be true to yourself.

If you have strong feelings for somebody, express them—don't keep them hidden. If the question posed is about pregnancy or fertility, it bodes well. It can also relate to a creative process that could be delivered successfully. This combination could be trying to draw your attention at the time of the reading to the signs that the moon can show in its phases; a waning moon means you need to relinquish something from your life, a new moon is about rejuvenation and starting again, a waxing moon points to healthy growth, and a full moon tells that all has come to fruition.

33. The Key in the House of the Key
From now on, do whatever you want, but do it with awareness.
Easy and natural are the keys. Don't repress anything; be your own self.
—Bhagwan Shree Rajneeesh

This combination is a breakthrough of understanding; the Key is in its rightful place, and all is well. It is a place where you or the sitter has reached a stage in life when you are gaining insights fast and furiously. Those things in life that have been eluding you so far will fall into place, like a key unlocking a door. If you or the sitter has asked about career changes, it is saying go ahead and do it. If the question is about relationships, this combination is saying that you should ensure that you are compatible, a matter further indicated by the cards between the Gentleman and the Lady.

34. The Fish in the House of the Fish
The aquarium or the big, open sea
The Fish in the House of the Fish indicates the place you now find yourself in is quite emotional, and your intuition is heightened. This is a good place to be; good fortune is indicated. If you or your sitter is asking about earning more money, this is a "yes" card—you will attract more money, and situations will occur that will make you materially better off; a inheritance or other windfall may be in store for you. This is a good combination to speculate on; spontaneity is encouraged. You will be amongst good friends who will come to your aid in any way.

35. The Anchor in the House of the Anchor
    Neither should a ship rely on one single anchor,
    Nor should life rest on a single hope.
    —Epictetus

    This is a doubly secure situation to be in right now. If you or your sitter is asking about future security, work, home life, and love, you can be sure that all is pretty good and steady. As long as you keep a cautious eye on the conditions around you and respond accordingly, you will be able to keep this up. Take special notice of the Clouds and its proximity to the Anchor, as this can be a sign to take extra care. The same is also true for the Moon card and the Ship card. The Fish in close proximity also indicates material security.

36. The Cross in the House of the Cross
    The word *crux* is Latin for cross. When this card falls into its own house, it is saying that the crux of the matter can be about how to maintain faith in the difficult times ahead. The cross is known to symbolically represent a bridge, and therefore there is a need to get to the centre of this problem to bridge the difficulty. With this card landing on its own house, the combination is saying you are on the right track; X marks the spot.

    The ancient Egyptian style of cross used in hieroglyphics stands for health and happiness; the religious and cultural meanings behind this symbol are quite varied. This card close to the Ways card ("*cross*-roads") is very significant, pointing to a union or even a reunion in the offing. If the question is about relationships, it could indicate a marriage, especially because the Cross is connected with religious blessings. If the matter is work-related, this symbol points to the signing of a contract—signing your cross so to speak. The Rider, Letter, and Stork close by would indicate the delivery and decision made regarding an important issue.

In this chapter we have seen how the houses provide an expansive template underneath or above the Grand Tableau and how it can act as a multidimensional lens on the whole reading. Every card should be considered a reflecting surface of all the cards around it, and the houses should be considered light sources illuminating not only the card above them, but every card in different ways. This kind of depth and detail is why you may need to book more than an hour to read a GT.

Exercise: Simple House Reading

One quick method to read with the houses that is very suitable for party readings and quick draws where you do not have a table is this simple house reading. Ask the sitter to shuffle the deck whilst considering the issue or situation. They can then return it to you holding it face-down. Turn over the top card, and put it back on the deck facing up. Say, "You have received [name of card] in the house of…" and then turn the deck upside-down so you can see the bottom card. This is the house indicator of the reading, so you will say "… in the house of [name of bottom card]." If we received the Anchor as our top card and the Garden as our bottom card, we would say, "You have received the Anchor in the House of the Garden."

You can then interpret the top card in the context of the bottom card. The limitation here is that you'll never receive a card in its own house, of course, but it remains an easy and quick reading method.

Going Around the Houses

Some readers add a layer of meaning by considering the house in which a significant card falls and then finding and reading the corresponding card in the GT. You can continue to track this journey around the houses by using the house in which a card falls to find its corresponding card until you at last return to your own home—the original significant card.

As an example, we might be doing a general reading for a woman. As we go along, we see that her card, the Lady, has fallen in the House of the Dog. Her loyalty and long-standing patience are indicated, which might be entirely relevant to her situation—even if she has not yet mentioned it. Often with this layer we can tell more about a sitter than they may wish us to speak about, and we sometimes wonder if people realise this when they post their Grand Tableau on the Internet!

We would then look for the Dog card to seek further information about the context in which this loyalty is being expressed. To no surprise, we might find the Dog card in the House of the Snake, showing that the woman is misguided in her loyalty, perhaps to her sister or another significant woman in her life (the Snake card is seen as another woman in some traditions). We could then pursue this revelatory thread by looking for the Snake which we might find in the House of the Bouquet. This would indicate further that the other woman is offering something at least to our sitter, even if the loyalty in response is misguided. Perhaps it is babysitting? We can then find the Bouquet, which might be in the House of the Lady, bringing us full-circle to the house of the original card.

We can trace these revelatory threads around the houses starting with any significant card, such as if we wanted to look more at career steps, we would look at the house in which the Fox card was placed, locate and read the corresponding card, take that to its house, read the card, and so on.

Exercise: Open Your House

Perform a GT for a particular and specific question with a specific charged card. Interpret the GT with that in mind, and then look up the house in which the charged card has fallen, and use that to deepen your reading.

We will now turn to more intermediate techniques that provide additional ways to consider the reading and provide new angles on the situation.

SEVEN

Knighting, Counting, and Diagonals

....

Free will is the key-note of all Dame Nature's efforts, and every one of us is master of his own destiny, within the limitations of his own personality. Bear that in mind when you read the cards. Never state that a thing will happen, but that it appears probable in the present course of affairs.
—Charles Platt, *Card Fortune Telling*, 1921

....

Accessing Your Inner Sibyl

Before we discuss these advanced techniques, we first remind ourselves to access our own inner sibyl. Having set the scene for a reading from the "cards of antiquity," we should be mindful to move ourselves into a particular mindset suited for Lenormand reading—again, one different from tarot.

To access your inner sibyl, you need to release yourself from your own inner critic. You must respect that quiet, sacred side of yourself that has always known what lies beyond the here and now. The inner sybil is the part of yourself that wants to perform without care of what people may think.

It is the side of ourselves allowed to roam with no repression. It does not mean you have to dress in Romantic-style Romani clothes, wearing gold rings in your ears (however this is optional!). It was Heraclitus, the Greek philospher, who spoke of the sibyl's abandonment of speech that was above ridicule. The divine alone would project forth her oracular message:

"The Sibyl, with frenzied mouth uttering things not to be laughed at, unadorned and unperfumed, yet reaches to a thousand years with her voice by aid of the god."

To access your inner sibyl, you must not *try* to do so; it must be something that comes to you. When ready, it will come forth when the words are expected.

Knighting

The idea of knighting appears to have derived from Iris Treppner's work, and the concept of shadowing is something we personally use in contemporary readings of our Lenormand. It is similar in a sense to the idea of reflections, which again comes from earlier methods.

There are many schools of thought you can explore with the Lenormand system, as it is relatively untrammelled in English, perhaps accounting for its new popularity. However, all of them are as constructed or derivative as any other offering, since we do not know exactly how Mlle. Lenormand read her cards, nor do we have consistent "fixed" meanings across different schools, times, and nationalities. Indeed, there is even a Brazilian variant, described in *The Game of Destiny* (2007) by Mario dos Ventos, which equates the cards with Afro-Brazilian traditions.

By the publication of *Etteilla, ou L'art de lire dans les cartes* in 1791, a compendium of cartomancy in which Etteilla wrote the foreword, it is evident not only were the meanings of cards also mentioned by de Comte de Mellett now being stabilised in practice (such as Hearts announcing happiness and clubs, money), but that the practice was changing too. "As early as 1753, our scholar and single Renovator of Cartonomancy has begun by discarding the art of reading cards one by one, substituting the art of card reading from the whole pack laid out on the table." The "scholar" is Etteilla himself, of course, and the word "cartonomancy" was later to shortened to "cartomancy" and entered popular usage at that time.

It is commented in the same 1791 work that Etteilla himself had restored the "meaning" of the Nine of Spades to "victory" rather than it being erroneously assigned to the Nine of Diamonds. Is there a "true" attribution or system of correspondence? Well, this is the province of esotericists rather than historians and mere card-readers such as ourselves.

The Gaming Aspects of Lenormand

It is believed that the Lenormand system of cards derived from an earlier card game, within which certain cards are favourable, unfavourable, or indifferent. The game is played much like any other "race" game, with an element of betting and two dice to determine the course of play.

The players land on various cards and the instruction book provides their progress, forfeit, or silence, so they stay in place until their next move.

The Tower, for example, gives a "pleasant vista," yet costs a little money (or tokens) for the pleasure. In this we might derive the cartomantic meaning of the L-Space Tower as offering insight, perspective, and a wider view of life—somewhat different to the "House of God Struck by Lightning" tarot version of the same name.

Perhaps it is due to this birthing from gaming systems that the reading of the Grand Tableau involves positional interpretations based on chess such as diagonals (the move of the bishop), laterals (the move of the rook/castle), and knighting (the move of the knight). We will add to our repertoire these two additional moves, as we have already covered reading in lines and groups.

Diagonals

Diagonal lines, to us, show powerful influences or convergences of energy into the situation. They allow us to read the ley lines of life in the tableau and they may indicate whether the position is—to borrow the astrological terms—fixed or mutable. They are like the guy-ropes holding up a tent (or snapping in the storm) and can be optionally read to provide additional information in the GT.

You can read diagonals from any card, of course. To begin, however, simply take the key card you are reading or working with, or the Gentleman/Lady card, and read what forces apply.

In the following example, we apply the diagonals to a lovelorn man who wishes to discover what the situation might be with a woman he has recently met. We look to his card, the Gentleman, and see that there are two diagonals above him, bearing down on him.

The first is from the Lady card itself, through the Rider, signifying liaison (in our essence words), so that seems fairly positive. She is certainly having an influence upon him energetically.

Let us now look at the other diagonal leading up to his right.

- 16: Stars—Creation
- 20: Garden—Communing
- 15: Bear—Headstrong

This line—which might also be taken to be his future as he looks to it—shows that there is a force driving him to connect with this woman. The line speaks of a very physical connecting force—it will even prove to be very creative for him.

If we were then to wonder about that Bear, let us remind ourselves of the houses from the last lesson (I always check the houses if I am not sure or in need of inspiration). We see that the Bear is in the House of Clouds, or transition—an opportunity to take stock of one's identity. Something in this relationship is causing a powerful awakening to change in this man, and whilst we could narrate this further by looking at the cards about the Bear, showing the physicality of the relationship, we have read enough for now in our diagonal.

Figure 77. Diagonals on a GT

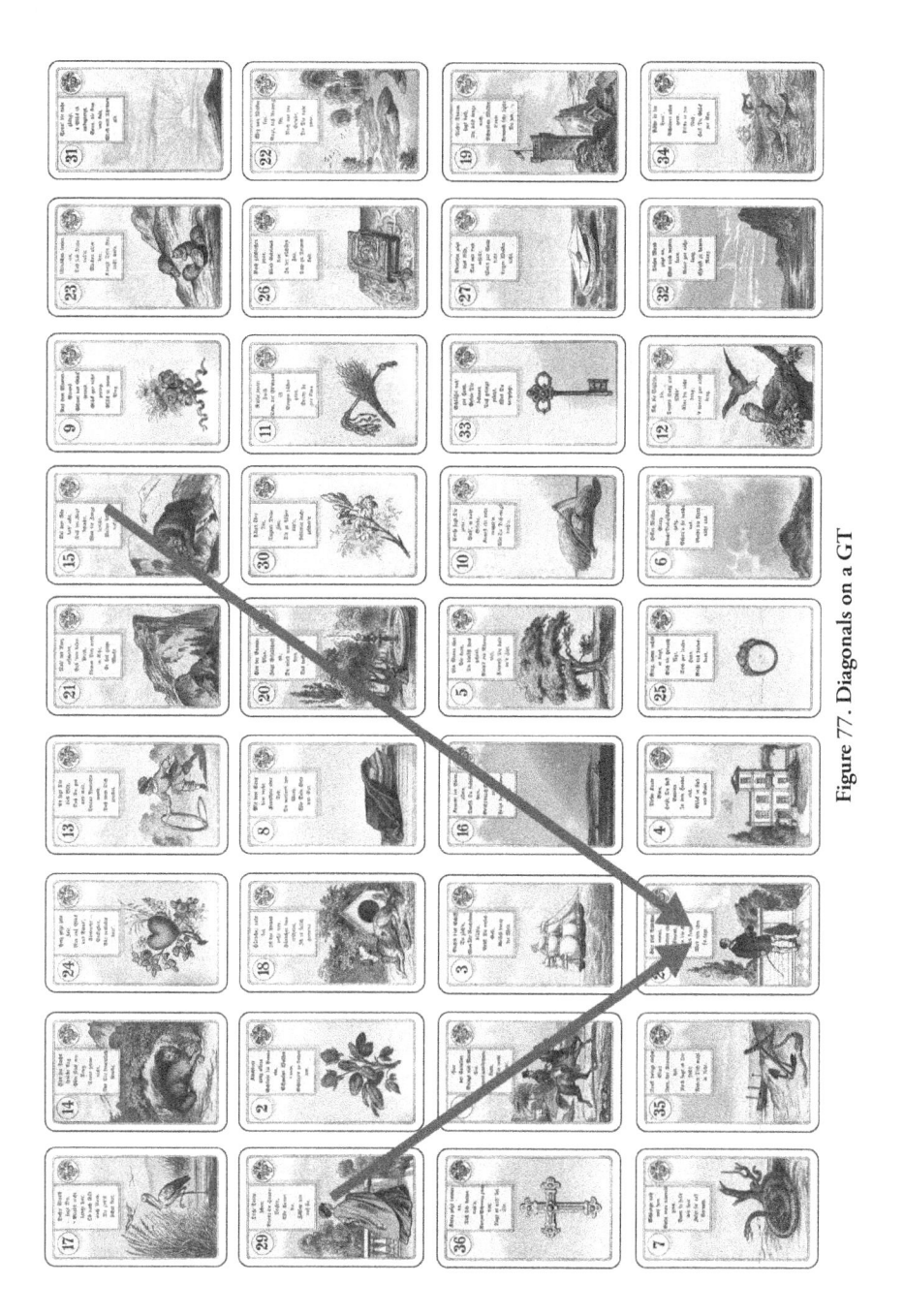

KNIGHTING, COUNTING, AND DIAGONALS • 185

Knighting

To us, knighting is about overcoming obstructions in your life. This aspect of reading replicates the movement of the knight in chess—two moves one way, and one move another in a L-shape. Perhaps the "L" is for "Lenormand"!

We sometimes look at the cards accessible to the Key (charged) card by knighting in order to discern if there is any "out of the box" option available to the sitter that can transcend the constraints of the situation as presented in the GT. If nothing else, it's nice to have options!

Here the male sitter wants to know how he can be with the woman of his dreams. Using the system that we believe Treppner developed, we can discover the obstacles in our sitter's path and how he can act to overcome them.

Let's start from the Gentleman card. If we move directly upwards two cards (the Snake and the Bear) and one across to the right, we land on the Scythe. These three cards combined together, Snake + Bear + Scythe, advise swift action. The sitter cannot wait—he needs to clear out old commitments and make preparations for the future. The message needs to be put out that he's prepared to enter into an emotional relationship. The cuddly side of him (the Bear) is ready, and he is strong and big enough to handle commitment.

Figure 78. Knighting in a GT

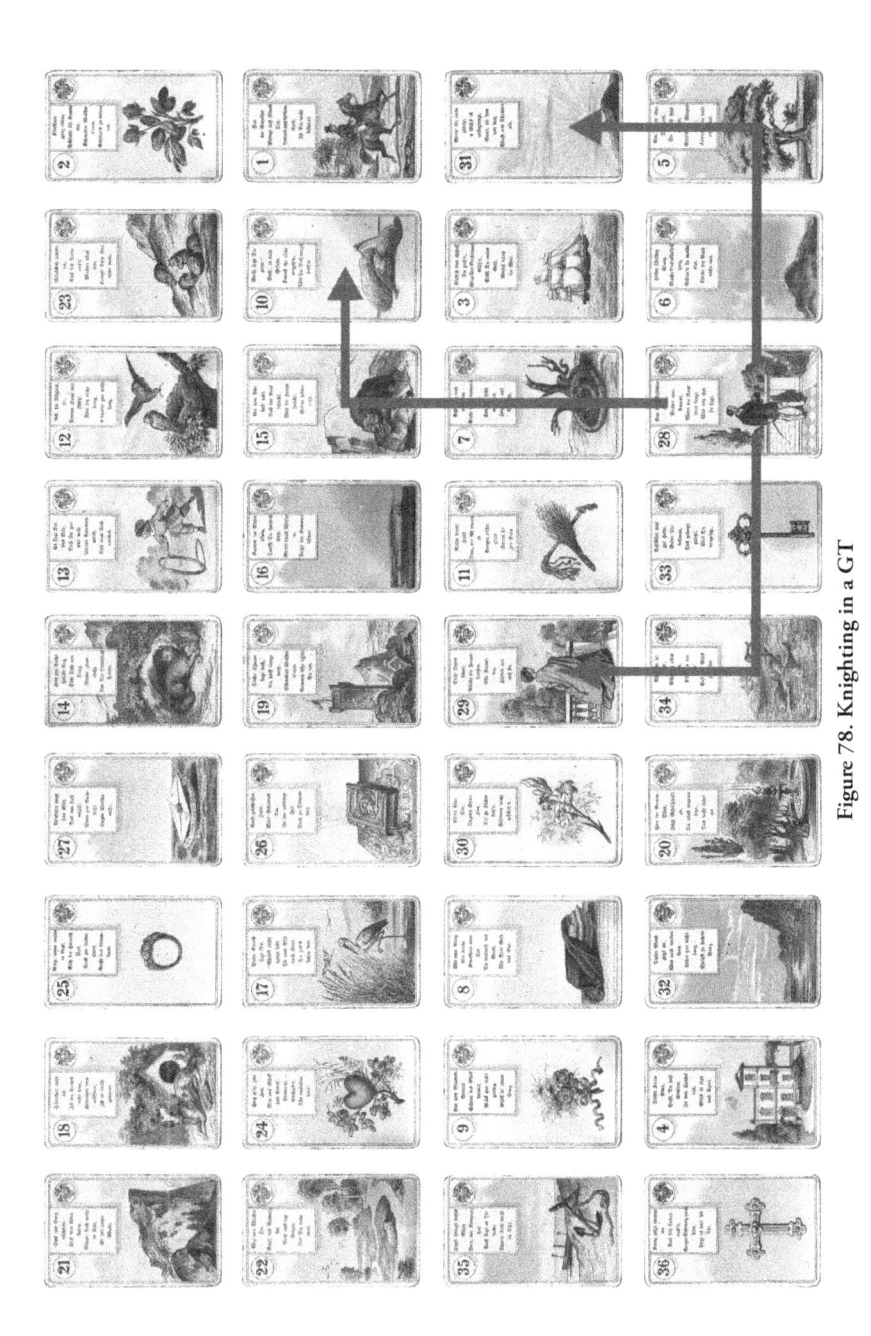

Moving from the Gentleman to the left to the Key, the Fish, and then one movement upwards, we find that our Gentleman is united with the Lady. This of course is an obvious affirmation of union with the Lady. However, the two cards in between—the Key and the Fish—speak of the obstacles that will have to be overcome before a relationship becomes a reality. The Key speaks of first movement, and that he needs to unlock or free up the next card, the Fish, or his resources. He needs to be organising his finances to ensure a secure future with the Lady.

If we *knight* from the right of the Gentleman, the movement is over the Mountain, the Tree, and one movement upwards, to the Sun. The mountain is about strength and endurance; as in the other knighted reading, the message here is that the sitter needs to be committed to what he wants. The Tree is about family and lineage, the Sun is about his will—is what he wants really what he wants? He needs to be sure of his aim, and then he can have the future he needs and desires.

Knighting provides us a means of looking at a situation's wiggle room, the smaller things that can make or break the whole deal. For reference, here are all the potential knighting patterns given from one central position, as seen on a chess board.

Figure 79. Knighting in Chess

Counting

The method of counting cards in part derives from shuffling a deck and laying out only every particular card during a count of the deck. We might shuffle a deck and then lay out every third card, or split the deck into three and select the top card from every pile, and so on.

Once all the cards are laid out, we can simulate this method—usually seen as "cutting to the chase" of the matter or revealing something hidden—by counting from one card to another in a particular manner.

There are many versions of card-counting; here we will highlight one of the most straightforward, which is to count from a significant card through the Grand Tableau by a count of seven. Other variations use counts of three, five, nine, or an alternating count based on Pythagorean-type number sequences (1, 3, 4, 8 …), amongst many other methods. You can also count based on the playing-card insert with the Lenormand card too.

The usual fashion of counting is to count "1" on the starting card itself. Count from there, and do the same from the resulting card. You continue the count until you return to a card you have already chosen. The resulting chain of cards is then read as a linear reading.

Let's take a look at a GT in which a question has arisen about a future trip. Due to the subject matter, we would make the significant card the Ship.

Counting number one on the Ship, reading left to right, and then back to the next row (returning round to the top-left start of the GT matrix if necessary) we land on the Tower as card seven. We then count one again on the Tower, and our seventh card from there is the Fish. We count seven again and return to the Ship.

In this case we would read the Ship + Tower + Fish as a journey that would be rewarding so long as we worked in concert with or within our own authority. The Tower can also signify observation, so we might be counselled by the reading to look out for an opportunity to do some "fishing," perhaps making contacts beyond the original purpose of the voyage.

Figure 80. Grand Tableau for Counting

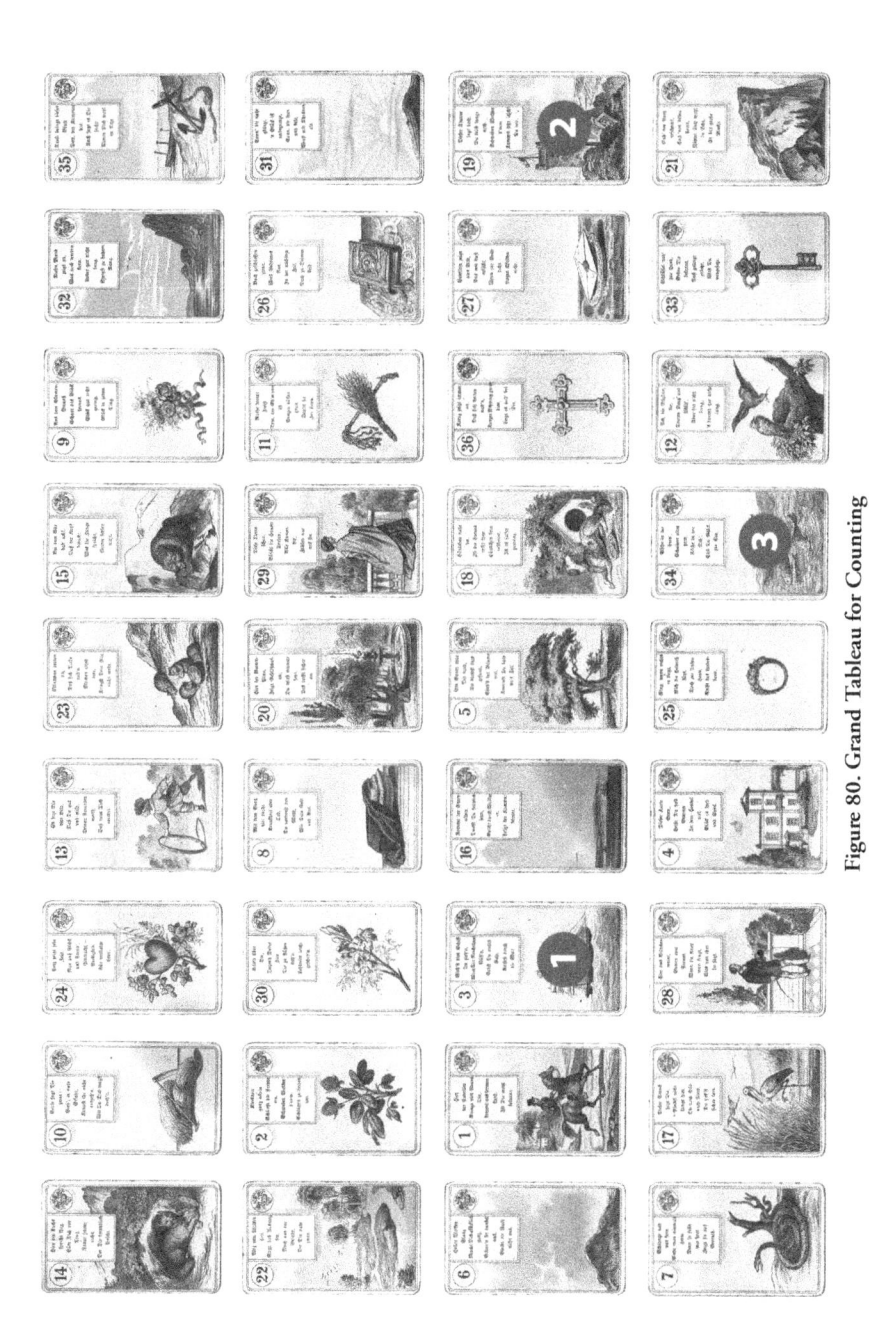

EIGHT

Zones and Shadows

....

Cartomancy is a science which can only be attained through reflection and practice, inasmuch as the permutations of the cards represent thousands of possible occurrences, and it is through comparison of their respective positions, changing at each deal, that we arrive at their full meaning. Spreading before your eyes a panorama of events passed and present, it becomes easy to institute wise reflections on the past and speculate upon events announced to happen. This is one of the aims of the science, which forewarns you of threatened danger, so that you can avert it in anticipation of its occurrence. The panorama of past events shows to us in what we have failed, and hence we must shun past errors. **In a word, cartomancy teaches the individual the art of self-government.**
–Fortune-Telling by Cards, 1872

....

In this lesson we will consider the whole Grand Tableau and a few smaller areas for your practice. We will look at our own personal and contemporary methods of considering the whole GT with zones, making use of correspondences from other systems. Whilst we only cover the basics here, there are many more templates that can be usefully applied to the GT to provide a reading's clarification, correlation, and confirmation.

The Zones

We can consider the GT a scenario that reflects upon all aspects of our sitter's field, form, and fate (see the book of that same name, *Field, Form and Fate* by Michael Conforti). When seen as a field, we can divide it into different zones. Whilst some zones are dependent on how the cards fall, others can be seen in the fixed matrix of the GT. When we layer the two, we get a very comprehensive and flexible way of reading Lenormand.

In these illustrations, we will use the 8 x 4 + 4 layout so we can learn to use this variation by considering the bottom four cards as a new set called "label cards."

In this illustration, we see the cards around the edge of the GT are considered the frame. These are often useful to be read together midway through the reading in order to give some overall context and summary. We can break this frame down into distinct components.

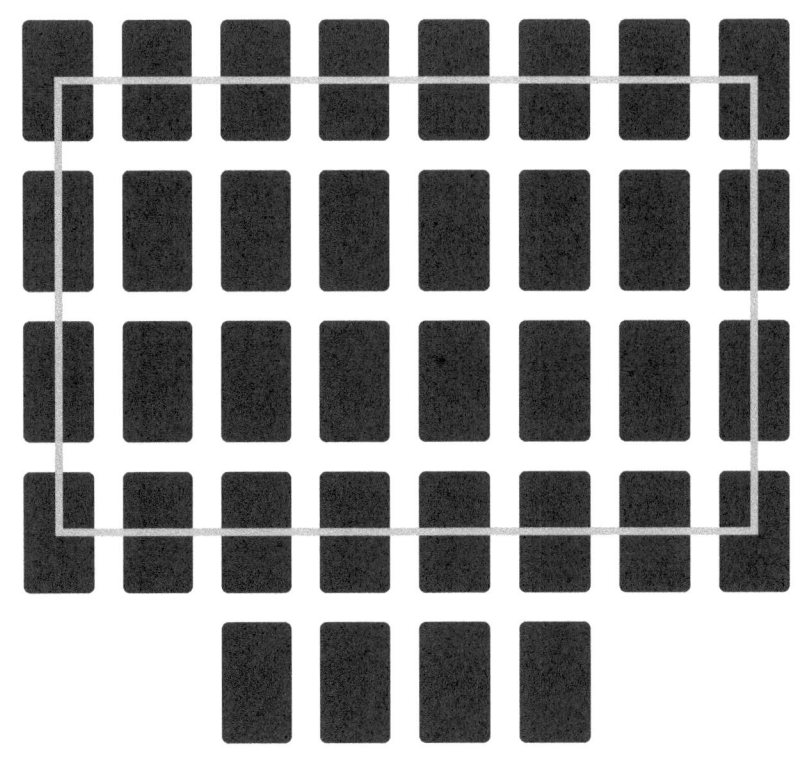

Figure 81. The Frame

Past and Future Frame

Read the column to the left as a past frame and the column to the right as a future frame, irrespective of the deck or other elements of the reading.

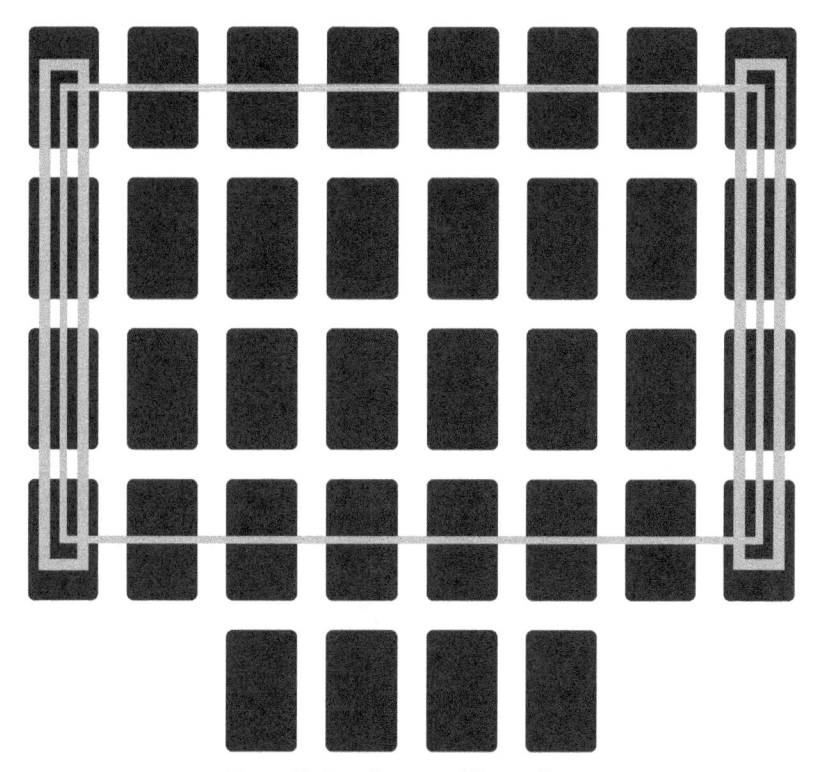

Figure 82. Past Frame and Future Frame

The four cards in the left column give us an indication of the past of the current situation, or effectively what sitters always return to when considering their life, old visions, patterns, habits, strongest memories, etc. This column shows us what has made them who they are in the present as well as what may need uncovering or even redeeming to make substantial changes in the present scenario.

The four cards in the right column give us an indication of the future—where sitters can see from where they are right now. This may be limiting or stretching them, depending on the other cards and contexts we have already read in the GT.

Note that these two columns are sort of different from the past/future columns dictated by the position and perspective of the charged card, e.g., the Gentleman. Where the card falls in a male sitter's reading may indicate that most of the GT to the right is the future. If his card has fallen in the left column and he faces right, it means that he's stuck in the patterns of his past.

As the epigraph of this chapter illustrates, the aim of our reading should be to promote self-governance; the use of these frames in combination with our previous lessons gives a powerful mechanism for layering a GT reading.

Zones of the Spiritual and Mundane Life

You can consider the top and bottom rows as the spiritual frame (highest aspirations) and material frame (manifestation, practicalities), which is useful in some questions, particularly when pairing.

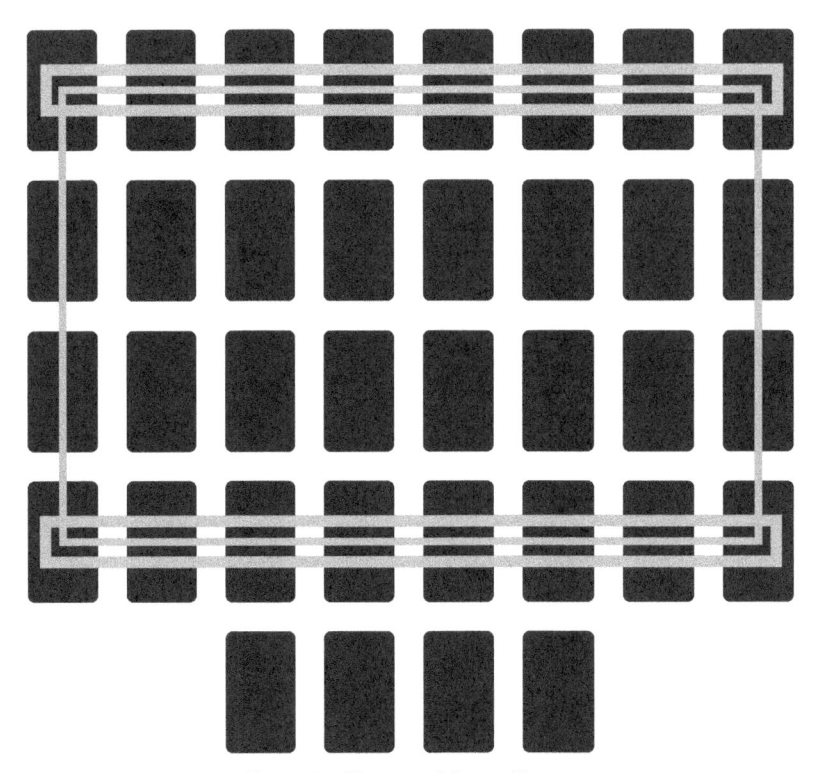

Figure 83. Upper and Lower Frame

As with the past/future columns, you can pair/compare cards to drill down into the detail of the overall reading without losing the gestalt of the whole.

Here is an example of a reading we did where we have taken out just the top row and bottom row of our GT and read them as two rows, then paired.

Figure 84. Example of Above and Below Frame

- The Above Cards: 1, 31, 34, 36, 23, 30, 2, 20

The above cards speak of a spiritual life motivated by the giving of communications; this is evident with card number 1, the Rider. This is powered by the energy of the Sun, so the willpower to carry on is there, and the resources will be provided with the presence of the Fish card so long as the intent is true.

The Cross represents a certain burden that accompanies the journey, yet reassures. The work is done quietly and steadily, prolific and slow in nature, in the spirit of the Mice card. The Lily warns against neglecting one's inner life, and it cautions against thinking the goal has been reached—things have only just begun. It would be better to maintain a life of simple discipline than to aim too high and be left wanting.

This lifetime is about showing the best of what one is, rather than being superficial. As Shakespeare wrote, "lilies that fester smell far worse than weeds." The focus is on not putting off one's duties. The Clover is about "knowing thyself"—personal identity, with the Lily also indicating an inner purity that must be preserved even if taken into the garden of external life.

The Garden is the "social self," which must be presented in integrity with the "inner self" of the Lily. The Garden must not be a place where one is seduced into behaving in an inauthentic manner.

- The Below Cards: 5, 32, 22, 9, 15, 27, 16, 4

In day-to-day life, these cards show, particularly with the Tree and the House bordering either end of this row, the importance of keeping one's resources close to hand. If used wisely, the Tree can provide a self-sustaining resource and shelter—but it can also be wasted and turned into planks which then rot. The Moon casts a light on the sitter's practical life, showing a need to connect to intuition along the Ways card—that inner voice should be listened to, and the sitter should find the Bear's strength in the ability to communicate (the Letter). The Star shows that the sitter's day-to-day life must be steady and not at risk of burnout; the sitter should favor long-term planning and avoid crash-and-burn syndrome.

When we look at the pairs of Above and Below, we can delve into the sitter's most profound spiritual life issues, how it relates to their practical life, and vice versa. I provide a brief note here of what might be explored; you can see that this is a session in itself.

- 1 + 5: Messenger and Tree—the importance of channelling ancestral knowledge and learning from one's own deep history.

- 31 + 32: Sun and Moon—the balance of will and emotive decision-making.

- 34 + 22: Fish and Ways—the sitter's spiritual resources can be nourished by observing signs and acting upon them. Even if the sitter asked, "How should I act?" we can answer this by looking in the original GT at the cards above the Ways card, we could look at the house in which it had fallen, etc. This is the power of L-space: it provides what our first quote of this chapter called a "panorama".

- 36 + 4: Cross and Bouquet—applying appreciation to one's spiritual life with outside observation and practice, showing reverence.

- 23 + 15: Mice and Bear—from humility can be drawn strength.

- 30 + 6: Lily and Letter—putting things off will cause festering within.
- 2 + 7: Clover and Star—returning to one's own original dreams and visions will bring good fortune.
- 20 + 4: Garden and House—finding the balance of inner and outer life.

We hope yet again you will see that even whilst these pairs provide us acres of information to relate to the sitter, we would be best served by seeing them in the full GT and expanding outwards from each pair. In providing these zones, the aim is to give you lots of diving boards into the full ocean.

The Four Pin Cards

We can then look at what we call the **pin cards.** These are the four cards that would pin the GT up if it were hung on a wall, and show a sibyl how the sitter is holding him- or herself in a life situation. These four cards are the sitter's unique signature or strategy for dealing with the stresses (and tranquilities) of his or her life.

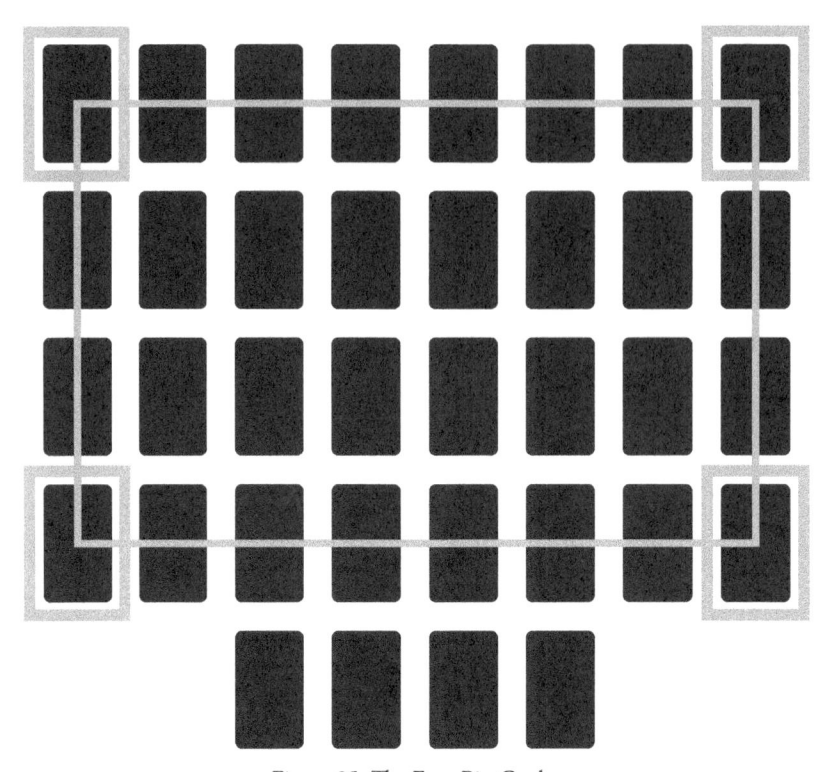

Figure 85. The Four Pin Cards

The Label Cards

Finally, we can also look at those lower four cards in the 4 x 8 + 4 version of the GT, which we call the **label** cards. If we imagine the GT as a picture, a *tableau vivant*, then the four cards at the bottom are the label. They give the essential details or characteristics of the image. In cartomantic tradition, these are the "verdict."

The label cards tell us, in no particular order:

- The **history** of the scenario (Is it in its early stages? Middle? Late or declining?)

- The overall **style** of the scenario, that is to say, is it a formal or informal situation? Is it a matter of the heart or the mind?

200 • EIGHT

- The **subject** matter—what is really being communicated?
- The **uniqueness** at play for this particular sitter. What sets this scene apart from other depictions of the same?

As an example, if we had the following four cards in the label area:

Figure 86. Label Cards

This would tell us the following about the sitter's life:

- History: Heritage, long-standing
- Style: Traditional, following a pattern
- Subject: Creating a space by making decisions—finding your place
- Uniqueness: Being thrust into what the sitter is supposed to be doing and following through.

We would suspect that the sitter had been employed or in a relationship for a long time, and had now been thrust into a totally new situation. Whilst for many it is a common subject to "find one's place,", this sitter has a unique position (the *in medias res* aspect), and any immediate decisions will set the course for some time to come.

You can assign four fixed positional meanings to these four label cards, but we find that closes off the elegance, grace, and profound power of L-space to easily express complex situations.

The Hidden Cross

A more advanced template you can consider is the "hidden cross," which comprises of the following cards.

The four cards in the centre of the GT give the hidden cross its pivot point and can be taken as the "hub" or "crux" of the matter, particularly in the sitter's daily or mundane world. Since these four cards are the "hub" of the matter, sometimes I take a peek at these first before I start navigating the whole GT in order to get my bearings, then I go look at the charged card and read on.

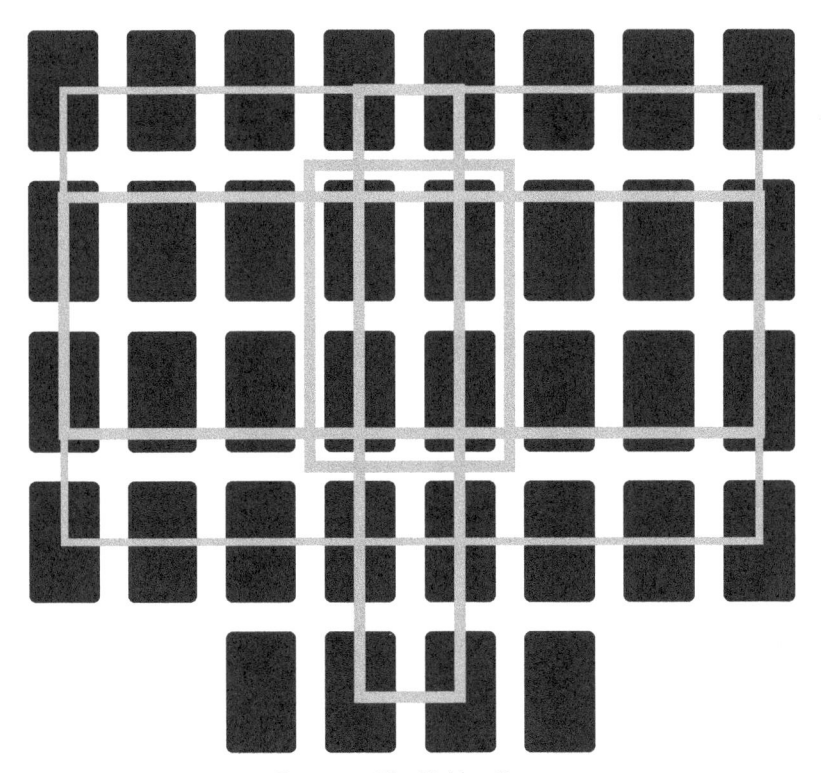

Figure 87. The Hidden Cross

Reading Whole or Linear

In all these templates, the cards are read as we have learnt—**together.** They have no unique positional meaning; they are always arising as a whole scenario. If you lay them out as a block or a row, you can decide if you wish to read them left to right, or right to left, in a linear fashion.

If you do, you need to decide in advance which card impacts on the other. Does the first card apply to the second you read, or vice versa?

As an example, in a linear reading, you might have the first two cards of the Key and the Coffin.

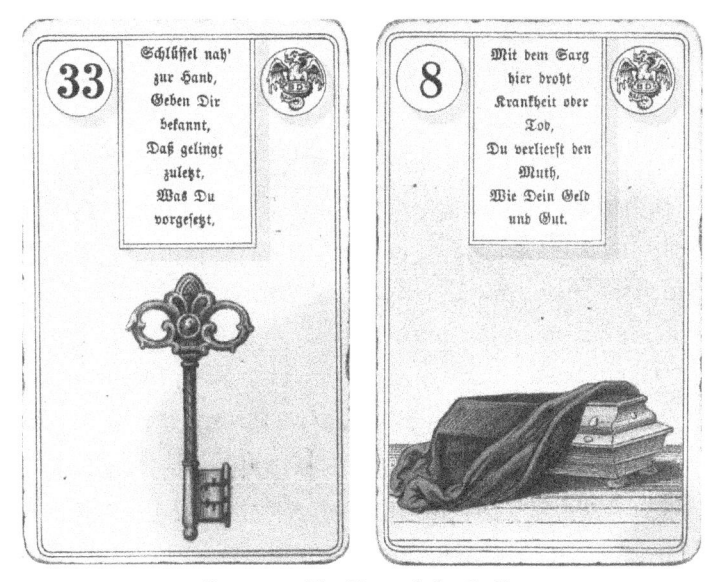

Figure 88. The Key and the Coffin

We might consider it like this: is the Key in the Coffin, or on the outside? It might really make a difference! This is where most of the books remain somewhat unclear—when they provide pairings (many do), they maintain the same interpretation no matter the relative position of the two cards. This is fine in a holistic-type reading where all the cards are seen **together** and as a whole, but it is problematic—well, confusing (mainly to T-space readers)—when reading in a linear fashion. Unsurprisingly, everyone asks, particularly those travelling from T-Space to L-Space.

If we read the Key then the Coffin, according to Treppner, we get a simple interpretation: "It will get better soon." However, if we read the Coffin *then* the Key, we get much the same, but with a proviso, "It will get better soon, [however] there will be a minor misfortune affecting your security, but nothing dramatic." That is to say, the Key (locked) will be breached by the Coffin's impact.

Generally, a good rule is to say the second card applies to or modifies the reading of the first. In this case, "security" *first* from the key, *then* the "change" implied by the Coffin. If we were to read them the other way around, it would be the change of the Coffin being locked down by the Key—quite the opposite interpretation.

As usual, find what works best for you, and once you have decided on a method, stick to it, review it often, and gradually develop your own methodology. We are all unique oracles.

Shadowing

Shadowing is a slightly quirky element I (Tali) have added to my own readings over time, as I believe that when a card is very close to another, it is sometimes not so obviously reading as "strong influence" but rather "too close to see."

As a result, I often read the cards immediately surrounding a card as "shadowing" it. This might be compared very loosely to tarot reversals; it adds a certain angle to readings that often provokes sudden intuitive insight. You might like to try this and see if it works for you also.

Any card immediately next to another can be seen as shadowing it. The potential readings are endless because you may be looking at several cards shadowing your key card, the Gentleman or Lady, or a few cards shadowing a card which you have knighted and is in a particular house of interest—this is where we cannot really give rules.

The best analogy to this is not chess but the game of Go. With just a few very simple rules and a couple of differently sized boards, the mind cannot really fathom fixed rules like chess. Go offers a graceful and elegant flow of patterns and is played through like the best Lenormand reading.

You might like to read *Go! More Than a Game* by Peter Shotwell for more on the game's mechanics and aesthetics. The science of "pattern recognition"—particularly as it applies to chess and tarot—is something Marcus Katz has written about in *Tarosophy*.

1. The Rider/Messenger: Communications/Liaison
   Shadow Words: Noise, chatter, gossip

   An example could be the Bear and Anchor shadowed by the Rider. This might indicate internal chatter, doubts and uncertainty, paranoia, and bouts of depression that may affect health and mental/emotional well-being. Another example could be the Mice and Child shadowed by the Rider: the state of being unaware of an impending problem due to misinformation.

2. The Clover: Identity/Luck
   Shadow Words: Bereft/Misfortune

   The Clover I feel can be about identity, in that the clover (shamrock) is considered as the national flower of Ireland, and the symbol is very rooted in national identity there.

   The Stars and Tree cards shadowed by the Clover could indicate weariness, fatigue, and feeling that your life is dull and no longer what you want. A lack of belonging, alienation, a lack of feeling appreciated, losing track of our faith, spiritual identity. This could be a time of midlife crisis and a feeling of regret for what you have not created.

   It is interesting to note that if the Clover card is combined with the Mountain card, it can signify the discovery and journeying toward spiritual "identity," the reason for this being that "when clover is located upon a mountain it comes to signify knowledge of the divine 'essence" gained by hard endeavour" (Cirlot).

3. The Ship: Adventure
   Shadow Word: Speculation

   A reckless energy could be at work. The Snake and Book cards shadowed by the Ship would be a blatant misuse of information for ulterior motives; however the Ship shadowing this would show that the deception is easily discovered. It might show that someone is risking discovery because they have become carried away with their own cleverness.

4. The House: Security
   Shadow Word: Possessiveness

   The House casts a shadow that, whilst providing cover and sanctuary, also leaves one outside. This cutting-off from resources can lead to possessiveness and neediness through fear of losing security. The shadow of the House then can bring caution, introversion ,and passiveness, the proverbial "sticking one's head in the sand."

   The Key and Stork cards shadowed by the House card indicate misuse of power due to putting too much emphasis on gaining wealth. There could be a misuse of credit cards, spending beyond your means, in order to keep up with those you deem to be successful. Not be able to pay back, not be able to deliver what you have promised!

5. The Tree: Longevity
   Shadow Word: Stubbornness. An act of overreaching and straying from the source.

   The Tree shadowing the Scythe and Heart can mean being too intent on being overly disciplined, overly motivated, and not enjoying life's pleasures as a result. All that's left is exhaustion. Life is also about pacing the journey and enjoying the moment. It is not merely how quickly you reach the destination; take time to enjoy the scenery. Is this a lesson the sitter needs to learn?

6. The Clouds: Transition
   Shadow Words: Unpredictability, variability

   The warning of those we may describe as fair-weather friends. Be wary of putting too much faith in those you do not truly know; they may shift their allegiance. Does this ring true? Stormy relationships portended.

   If we apply this to the Ship and Fox cards, abandonment is very much suggested here—rats abandon the sinking ship, travel is not advised without planning well beforehand. Beware of shifty behaviour; somebody could let you down. Does something seem too good to be true? Invariably, gut feelings are the correct ones, so you must trust these instincts and act accordingly to make changes.

7. The Snake: Stealth
Shadow Word: Sabotage
There are things at work we are hardly aware of; we carry on day to day, perhaps oblivious to the external forces that can wreak havoc. You cannot prepare for every eventuality and just have to accept the inevitable. Or do you?

The Snake shadowing the Mountain and Anchor implies that a longstanding stubborn situation is not going to go away on its own, insidious problems that have built up over time and have not been addressed are going to come to the fore…or the warning could be that this could happen in the future if you do not act now!

8. The Coffin: Initiation
Shadow Word: Tribulation
To step into the unknown brings with it burden and responsibility.

The Coffin shadowing the Dog and Child cards shows a test of loyalty, feelings of being judged by others, losing vigour and enthusiasm, being kept to heel, and not being allowed to be footloose and fancy-free due to responsibilities. Perhaps there is a feeling that all the fun has evaporated out of life.

This shadow is about the burden of codependency and the accompanying pain attributed to the impending fear of losing a significant other or desired state. To love and to be loved back is a blessing and a curse. A loss of innocence is possible as well.

Heaven lies about us in our infancy!
Shades of the prison-house begin to close
Upon the growing boy.
—William Wordsworth

9. The Bouquet: Appreciation
   Shadow Word: Sycophancy

   Casting a shadow over the Lady and Gentleman cards is indicative of a superficial relationship grounded too much in flattery and not in speaking the truth. What is said is done to gain another's favour and affection. A person's motives may be suspect—be wary! Also question the motives if there a whiff of guilt in this emotional equation.

   This card shows sycophantic drudgery at work through the use of superficial words and false affections. One can end up forging their own chain of repression. Ulterior motives may be behind a gift.

10. The Scythe: Clearing
    Shadow Words: Loss or mourning

    This card casting a shadow over the Garden and Lily cards implies that through rash action and curiosity, innocence will be lost that cannot be regained. The indication is painful longing for how things used to be, a state of nostalgia.

    I remember, I remember
    Where I was used to swing,
    And thought the air must rush as fresh
    To swallows on the wing;
    My spirit flew in feathers then
    That is so heavy now.
    —Thomas Hood

11. The Rod/Whip: Service
    Shadow Word: Drudgery

    This card casting a shadow over the Clouds and Ring talks of commitment to something or a duty that ends up changing rapidly from what you originally expected. You may have entered into a relationship or work situation thinking you were in charge of yourself and then find that another person is calling all the shots—and you are doing all the running. The outlook could be dismal if you do not take stock of your life and act on what you really want.

12. The Birds: Divination
    Shadow Word: Receptivity

    There is a saying: "Too much knowledge can be a dangerous thing." The Birds casting a shadow over the the Moon and the Cross can suggest an attitude of intense knowing that lends a false sense of security in dealing with other peoples' sensitivities or emotions. Just because you know something does not mean you should express it without regard for how it may affect another person. The indication here can also be the pain and burden that comes with being sensitive and feeling too much.

13. The Child/Little Girl: Ingénue, innocence
    Shadow Word: Gullibility

    The warning here is of being so naive that the sitter's better nature is being abused.

    The Child casting a shadow over the Ways and the Snake could suggest that an ill-considered decision could end up developing into a compromising situation between the sitter and an untrustworthy person. Now is not the time to be so trusting when the sitter does not know the situation or the people very well.

14. The Fox: Cunning
    Shadow Word: Malevolence

    There is a fine line between ambitious calculation and wishing ill intent on others. It is wise to bear in mind the act of going out and getting what you want merely for selfish ends does not come without repercussion. The Fox card casting a shadow over the Bear and Letter cards speaks of karma and "what goes around comes around." It is never healthy to talk ill of others; news and gossip may grow out of control and come boomeranging home! There is never an action executed without a return.

15. The Bear: Headstrong
    Shadow Word: Unyielding

Ever thought about picking a fight with a bear? Probably not! Think about the Bear casting a shadow over the Tower and the Mice; it is about finally seeing what has been in plain sight all along, right in front of your nose. Perhaps you have been behaving like a timid little mouse—now is the time to release your inner Bear energy. Go on, release your beast, it won't hurt a bit!

16. The Star: Creation
    Shadow Word: Proliferation

There is a school of thought that says we are the creator of our own reality; what we believe, we become. We therefore have to be mindful of what we wish, as one negative thought can create another, and so on. A restless state of mind grows out of control and we are no longer master of our reality, spun out of control into a black hole.

So if the Star card casts a shadow over the Sun and Moon cards, there could be a bit of rollercoaster ride ahead; maybe your imagination gets the better of you and you become overconfident, plunging yourself into a situation well out of your comfort zone. Bear in mind that this stellar triangulation is pretty powerful; put to good use, the outcome could be used to your benefit, so take heed and be mindful of how you wish upon a star.

17. The Stork: Deliverance
    Shadow Word: Reliance

This speaks of the danger of becoming too reliant on others for long-term stability—there is a risk attached to the belief that you will be assured security no matter what. You may have surrounded yourself with people you can rely on, a band of supporters who bolster your sense of self-worth. You may expect them to always be there for you when times get tough. In truth, they may not be there for you when you really need them. This in itself can be devestating to your stability.

The Stork casting a shadow over the Clover and the Ways can indicate insecurity about your identity. You may be aware of where you came from, but what comes next? Questions like "Who am I?", "Where am I going?", "What is my life purpose?", "What's the point of it all?", will be very prominent in the sitter's life. The theme here is a fear of moving forward, potentially losing what one has already.

18. The Dog: Codependency
    Shadow Word: Selfishness

Be honest about your true motivation for doing things for others. Are you being pleasant and friendly merely to achieve a certain outcome? Do you want someone else to do a favour for you and are therefore being extra nice? Is someone your friend on your terms, only on your good side when they tell you things you *want* to hear rather than what you *should* hear?

The Dog card shadowing the Key and the Garden indicates a situation where somebody is being kept in the dark. Something is locked away and hidden to avoid a bad reaction, and it is preventing an opportunity to learn and grow via the the outside world and the experiences it holds. The sitter needs to go out, attend events, meet and mix.

19. The Tower: Vision
    Shadow Word: Surveillance

The ability to have vision can bring with it the burden of seeing too much and knowing too much. The shadow this card casts is one of surveillance—we live in times where everything we do is monitored, recorded, and reported. At times it feels as though there's no place to hide from the prying eyes of the Orwellian Big Brother. We are vulnerable to identity theft, cyber-bullying, cyber-stalking, illegal tapping of communications, and endless other invasions of privacy and boundaries.

The Tower card shadowing the Ring and the Fish speaks of jealous, possessive relationships; somebody could be being stalked. The Tower shadow could also indicate that the sitter is consulting the cards too much; they may expect the cards to impart information about someone else to whom they should not be privy. This shadow could be drawing attention to the dangers of obsessive curiosity, in that there are so things that you or another would be better off not knowing. Curiosity killed the cat(fish)!

20. The Garden: Communing
Shadow Word: Social media addiction

There is a so-called condition dubbed social network addiction, coming off the proposed idea that social media is more addictive than cigarettes or alcohol. Facebook, twitter, et al., have become more and more prevalent, must-have, must-do, essential parts of our lives. They expand and enlarge our toolkit of interaction, but also shrink other types of interaction, namely face-to-face, real-life interaction. Maybe we feel we must invest more and more time "feeding the beast" to receive validation of own social worth.

The Garden card shadowing the Birds and Rider cards speaks of Internet bullying, gossip, and an overdependence on social networking for one's sense of self-worth. You need to get back to the basics of socializing: make a phone call, write a letter, go visit somebody in person. Attend an event and make friends in person.

Social networks have changed the ways we interact with each other enormously. One thing that has changed dramatically is the concept of meeting people. This principle was brought to my personal attention a couple of weeks ago when I met a musician for the first time whom I had casually encountered a couple of times online. Oddly enough, neither of us acted as if this were a first meeting.

Users derive a variety of uses and gratifications from social networking sites, including traditional content gratification alongside building social capital, communication, surveillance, and social network enhancement. The different uses and gratifications relate differentially to patterns of usage, with social connection gratifications tending to lead to increased frequency of use, and content gratifications to increased time spent on sites.

21. The Mountain: Durability
    Shadow Word: Toughness

    We all will have at sometime in our lives been accused of being too tough, not having shown enough compassion or understanding when it may have been more appropriate to do so. We may have learnt over the years that those who are too soft get walked all over. The Mountain depicted in the Mountain card has been around a very long time, and it has survived and proved to be durable. The hardships we go through make us tough.

    The Mountain card casting a shadow over the Fox card and the Lily can speak of being too calculating and overly forceful, not being flexible and giving way for a change. Remember that spoken of lilies by Shakespeare, in his Sonnet XCIV:

    They that have power to hurt, and will do none,
    That do not do the thing they most do show,
    Who, moving others, are themselves as stone,
    Unmoved, cold, and to temptation slow;
    They rightly do inherit heaven's graces.

    And that:

    For sweetest things turn sourest by their deeds;
    Lilies that fester, smell far worse than weeds.

22. The Ways: Choice/decision
    Shadow Word: Responsibility

    The saying "the buck stops here" comes to mind here, meaning that the individual who takes or makes the decision ends up taking full responsibility if all goes wrong at the outcome. We all have to make choices and decisions, and we are aware that along with the process of decision making comes a burden of responsibility. We have to go ahead and bite the bullet.

The Ways card casting a shadow over the Lady card and the Cross card could speak of putting too much emphasis on nurturing and fussing over somebody in our lives, not allowing them space to make their own mistakes.

23. The Mice: Productivity
    Shadow Word: Dilution

It can be very easy to stretch oneself a little too far, to push the limit of our limitations in order to keep up with the unnecessary want that has become the norm of our times. We need to slow down to avoid losing sight of what matters most and concentrate on quality rather than quantity. Less is certainly more, especially if the resource is special. For instance, compare the quality and unique creation of limited-edition handmade craftwork compared to the uniform, mass-produced products that come off the production line.

The Mice card casting a shadow over the Letter and Moon brings to mind the ever-expanding world of social media. We are in danger of losing the personal touch of a phone call or personal letter to friends of old—we no longer have the time. We exist in a cyberworld that has reshaped our reality and sacrificed true one-on-one intimacy.

24. The Heart: Courage
    Shadow Words: Foolhardiness/daredevil

There is a propensity to being courageous, and then there is being foolhardy. Certainly the former can easily become the latter at times. You would have to have courage to walk across Niagara Falls by tightrope, however many would consider the attempt foolhardy.

The Heart card casting a shadow over the Clouds and Anchor would warn against ignoring warnings to take care and advises taking action when the safest course and line of least resistance would be to stay at home and do nothing at all. Is it that you think you know it all? Is your behaviour a bit rash?

25. The Ring: Continuity
Shadow Word: Predictability

When a situation carries on and on without any change, no end in sight, this can result in life becoming very boring. We have such an addiction to or reliance on routine and habit that we have almost forgotten what it was like to be spontaneous. Life becomes very predictable, and we are a prisoner of our own devices. Round and round we go in our vigorous little circle, never moving forward.

Therefore, the Ring card casting a shadow over the Sun and Anchor signifies a stalemate or fixed position; it is a refusal to rest, not allowing the sun to go down, not allowing the anchor to drop. The advice here is to harness the willpower of the Sun and halting power of the Anchor, granting time to plot a new course so change can take place.

26. The Book: Knowledge
Shadow Word: Responsibility

It has been said that a little knowledge is a dangerous thing, such as in the myth of the Pierian Spring at Mount Olympus, a source of knowledge and inspiration, sacred to the Muses. The warning is in reference to how, when we first become familiar with a subject of interest and dip into it, it is like sipping the "shallow draughts" of the Pierian Spring. It can go to our heads and we can easily fool ourselves into believing we know more than we actually do. We all know a know-it-all like that.

The Book casting a shadow over the Rider and the Cross would be very much about someone with a messiah complex. You are advised not to allow yourself to get carried away with your newly found belief or knowledge, resisting the urge to tell everyone about it. There is a need to pull back and take a deep breath. Think deeply but keep these ideas to yourself. Remember that not everyone will appreciate your enthusiasm! So, a little learning *can* be a dangerous thing!

… drink deep, or taste not the Pierian spring:
there shallow draughts intoxicate the brain,
and drinking largely sobers us again.
—Alexander Pope, "An Essay on Criticism"

27. The Letter: Sentiment
    Shadow Word: Regression

    Consider old-fashioned letter writing to our nearest and dearest, the care invested in a more pensive approach to communicating our thoughts and feelings. Such letters can be kept and treasured in a sentimental manner, and it would not be quite the same to keep our laptop or iPad under our pillow! However, the downside to letter communications is that in reality, it is time consuming and very slow on all levels.

28. The Gentleman: Analytical
    Shadow Word: Cynical

    Here we have a male figure in your circle who is prone to being a little bit cynical. It is almost guaranteed that if you believe in something truly, he will want to disprove it. There could be an argument waiting in the wings.

    The Gentleman card casting a shadow over the Sun and Anchor could spell out a period of unrest and agitation. If the sitter is asking about a relationship issue, this could mean the sitter is in for a very rocky ride or that they just aren't going anywhere in the relationship; the two energies just feed off each other.

29. The Lady: Intuitive
    Shadow Word: Nervousness

    Just as a little knowledge can be a dangerous thing, as seen in the Book's shadow entry, the ability to tune into the energies around us can also be detrimental. If not kept grounded, this way of being can leave us open to exhaustion. There are times when we need to be able to withdraw, and conserve and consolidate our energy on all levels, emotional and physical. We cannot be all things to all people all the time.

    The Lady card casting a shadow over the Fish and the Owl/Birds card brings in a swarm of nervous energy; this combination showing up for the sitter in regards to a home/money/security situation would warn of not responding to the situation with a knee-jerk reaction. The person needs to look at areas in life where general resources and personal energy resources are being drained. The sitter need to ask who in his or her life acts out the role of psychic vampire, and then take necessary actions of self-protection.

30. The Lily: Purity
    Shadow Word: Reservation

    A man who loves with purity considers
    not the gift of the lover, but the love of the giver.
    —Thomas à Kempis

    This shadow is about holding back and not giving. There is an air of reservation or being reserved when the Lily card casts its shadow over the Heart and Key. If these combinations materialise in the session, the sitter needs to delve deep into their heart and ask what they are holding back from expressing to another in their life, or who is holding back from them.

    You give little when you give of your possessions;
    it is when you give truly of yourself that you truly give.
    —Kahlil Gibran

31. The Sun: Will
    Shadow Word: Obsession

    When we get the bit between our teeth and let ourselves get carried away with the buzz of creating, it's hard to take a break. The urge of completion compulsion kicks right in, and you keep on at it until you are satisfied. This state of being ends up being the shadow of the Sun card, casting its shadow of obsession on the Anchor card and Heart card. The situation recalls to mind the movie *Groundhog Day*, an endless repetition of the same old thing over and over again. In a reading on relationships, well, you can imagine what that implies…Visualise the Anchor and the Heart being one entity, thrown overboard constantly. Just as you settle down, the heart (stability) gets tugged up again. This sort of relationship is in a state of constant flux—something has got to give.

32. The Moon: Dreams
    Shadow Word: Fantasy

    Some dreams are beautiful, and some can turn into nightmares literally overnight. This is especially so if we lose our grasp on reality, which is never good. We may find ourselves trying to live out those fantastical dreams in our daylight hours, and in the stark daylight there is no grounding or reality to them at all.

    The Moon card casting a shadow over the Cross and Clover cautions against taking a gamble or speculation gone too far. The sitter may be fooling themselves that a situation they are embroiled in is going to change for the better. They may need to reassess and think about pulling out.

33. The Key: Access
    Shadow Word: Control

    The Key can be a tool for release, or it can used to lock something away. In certain circumstances this can promote oppression and control. The

Key card casting a shadow (control) over the Ship and Whip cards during a sitting speaks of a life not being lived, opportunities being missed. This could be a career situation where a promotion is not forthcoming, and there is a feeling of not being valued for the hard work and dedication shown. It can also be about a relationship that has become hard work and is not moving forward; there is a feeling of being all washed up.

34. The Fish: Resources
    Shadow Word: Need

    The Fish card can be all about resources and making the most of your abilities in order to obtain these precious resources. We carry on working to achieve this result. The downside is that we may find ourselves driven by need alone. We may end up compromising what we really want in life to satisfy this need. Thus the shadow of the Fish card is need. If this card casts a shadow over the Book and Rider during a sitting, it could indicate that the sitter is not following a route in life true to their purpose. Perhaps they need to undergo a period of learning or training to fulfil their true purpose in life rather than to keep the proverbial wolf from the door.

35. The Anchor: Standstill
    Shadow Words: Burden, obsolescence

    The appearance of the Anchor as a symbol in the Lenormand draws attention to an aspect of the sitter's life that needs to become grounded in some way. There has been too much movement in their life, and the Anchor speaks of a need to settle down and stop seeking. In addition to being about a situation, it could also be about a person to whom the sitter is close. The Anchor casting a shadow across the Dog and Fox is about male energy out of control.

36. The Cross: Faith
    Shadow Word: Hope

    The Cross's shadow is about a false sense of reality, wishing on a star, and/or things that may be beyond one's reach. The Cross card casting a shadow upon the House and the Ways suggests that there is an important choice to be made, and a bad decision based on pie-in-the-sky dreams could bring the situation instability. The sitter may need to take a more realistic approach to the situation, and perhaps accept that they may be deceiving themselves.

NINE

Card Layouts and Sample Readings

We very satisfactorily have received the Tarot cards which you sent us: I have divided them according to their numbers... You alone could reinstate the ancient Tarot cards in their true and primeval splendour, Thanks to you, the study will become easier and more interesting since the hieroglyphs are now much more significant and, therefore, more intelligible.
—Eliphas Levi to Alliette (Etteilla) 14 March 1789, quoted in
A Wicked Pack of Cards, Decker, DePaulis & Dummett

Here we start with single card layouts and progress to a four-card layout. We will take you through each layout in order to demonstrate how cards might be read.

One-Card Readings
Love & Relationships/Relating
The sitter asks the question: Can I trust David?

- The Stork is a positive card to draw, unlike say the Fox. The Stork is looked on favourably. He generally delivers what he promises, and his behaviour is very reliable. He is the type of person who can make himself very much at home wherever he goes. However, being a Stork, he will bring something into your life that will require long-term commitment. This card indicates that David can be trusted.

The question: What do I need to know regarding my romantic relationship with Carlos?

- The Star is drawn. The outlook is a "starry" one, and it tells of a hopeful one. However, it may be advising that there are many stars in the sky; that is, there are many men to choose from romantically. The sitter should look carefully at the future or what the stars have in store before committing too soon. It may be sensible to consult an astrologer for a compatibility reading. Just remember, do not get too "starry-eyed" too soon!

Two-Card Readings

Finances/Money

A sitter wants to know: Will I come into money?

- Bouquet with the Sun: The Bouquet is a selection of flowers artistically arranged, bound together with a ribbon or other finery, and often given as a gift to someone we love or value to demonstrate our appreciation. This card showing up for the enquirer suggests that he or she will receive a show of appreciation from someone who values them; it could perhaps be in the form of a bonus.

- Sun: The Sun's appearance is very encouraging. Combined with the Bouquet, the Sun is symbolic of growth and regeneration, and is vital to the creation of the flowers of the Bouquet; the indication is that money will be abundant for the enquirer.

All in all, it is very likely that the enquirer may be receiving some good fortune.

Three-Card Readings

The sitter asks: My job situation is uncertain at the moment. What action should I take to prepare myself if I am made redundant? Could it happen soon?

We carry out a three-card reading using the first card as the present, the second as action required, and the third as to the timing aspect.

- Present situation: The Snake. The appearance of the Snake confirms the enquirer's present state: unsure and threatened by their work situation. Be wary of somebody conspiring against you.

- Action needed: The Heart. This card is saying that the enquirer should take heart and summon the courage to take the action needed. The Heart can be said to be about union, which could be the action the card is recommending. The sitter should speak with his or her work union or anybody representing worker rights to discuss various options. It's important the sitter learn his or her employment rights—forewarned is forearmed.

- Timing: The Lily. The Lily can be symbolic of death, so this is indicative that the redundancy is going to happen very soon. On a positive note, the Lily is also symbolic of fertility and rebirth, so something new will be born from the redundancy.

EXERCISE: LENORMAND KEYING METHOD

In this method we "key" three cards to represent our question—and this is where the art comes into the practice. In our experience, we've found that any question can be represented by three cards. It must be done in as literal a fashion as possible. The Lenormand readers we've met or read always agree that in this style of reading the question is very important (perhaps even more so than in tarot), even for a vague "what will happen today?" We'll incorporate it here, and perhaps you'll find it as accurate as we do.

Take a very literal and practical question requiring an equally practical answer. Select out three cards to represent your question. These should be in the order of the words and meanings in the question.

Here's a recent and real question we asked:

Where will we find a bigger venue for next year's convention if the Theatre is not available?

Select three cards for the three most important or meaningful concepts in your question, such as:

- Where = The Ways (Crossroads), i.e., direction
- Convention = The Garden (Park), i.e., social meeting space
- Theatre = The Child (the "Play") i.e., a literal pun

Take these three cards out of the deck, and lay them face-up left to right in front of you.

Whilst looking at the three key cards representing the question, shuffle the remaining cards, split into three (with the left hand), and restack. Take the top three cards, and place them face-up on top of the three question cards.

In effect, the three question key cards now function as the "house" or context of the three answer cards. So, for this example we receive the following three cards:

- On top of the Ways, we get and place the Tree.
- On top of the Garden, we get and place the Whip.
- On top of the Child, we get and place the Ring.
- We then look at the bottom card of the remaining deck as a clarification card, and we get the Book.

We first read these cards as literally as possible. We find it best to say this bit out loud as if we were talking to a young child or as if we were first learning to read: "The Tree is in the place of the Ways. The Whip is in the Garden. The Child holds the Ring."

This means that it is unlikely the Theatre will be the venue again, as each of the pairs seems constrained—the Tree should not be in the way of a crossroads, the whip has no place in a garden, and a child should not be let out to play with expensive jewelry. What does it mean? Where should we look for a venue?

The Book gives our first clue: a place of learning, a library, or close to a library or bookshop…perhaps even a school, although the Tower would probably be better for that.

Then we look at the actual cards. The Tree is in the position representing the "where" of the question. That is the answer, then—a tree! Should we hold our convention in a tree? Obviously not, so perhaps a tree is a symbol. Wherever we should look, it will be called "the Trees" or "the Pines" or perhaps have a symbol of a tree associated with it…perhaps a hotel called "the Birches" near a bookshop?

Actually, the answer turns out to be even more literal. We know the venues where we live, although we haven't looked at all of them. One is near the school—in fact, it is between the school and the bookshop! Not only that—and here's where these cards get spooky and clever—it is called Crossthwaite Centre. The word *thwaite* means "paddock": a forested area cleared for something. The Cross(roads) and the Tree!

The cards have literally spelt out the answer, plain as day. This is a real reading with a real, practical answer. You may notice it is somewhat similar to the way Lyra reads the Alethiometer in the His Dark Materials trilogy, by "setting" three of the dials to symbols and then reading from the other three that come about through the divination.

Let's look at the other two pairs. The Whip is in the Garden, meaning that it is unlikely to provide the social meeting place for the event, as the whip often means bad words or trouble. The indication here is that we'll likely have to ensure we will provide another venue for socialising if we go for this place; otherwise there will be negative vibes. This is not something we would have considered in advance—the Lenormand can give us literal warnings in advance, too.

Finally, the Ring (contract) is in the place of our Child, representing the Theatre.

This suggests that we should contact them first and see if they will commit to an early contract, and not delay or "play around." We should literally force them to *play* their *hand* (ring, finger) as early as possible.

I hope the above gives you an idea of how what we call "literal Lenormand" works. In selecting the three cards for the question, we actually key a literal question one level down into symbols. This makes the three answer cards even easier to read and more accurate (relevant) to the question, because they are answering the literal bits of the question. This method is one that works for Lenormand but not as well for tarot, for various reasons of symbolic analysis we won't bother with here. There's also a spooky mystery in it all—it gives you goosebumps when you see how accurate it can be, and for those lost in years of tarot's complex symbolic interpretation, it can rekindle the cards' magic.

Let the cards lead you again and they can show you all sorts of hidden wonders.

Four-Card Readings

A sitter asks: Where is my current job heading? Are things going to be successful or unsuccessful?

We draw four cards: the Moon, the Anchor, the Bouquet, and the Bear.

- The Moon: The Moon speaks of creativity in abundance and tapping into one's deep imagination. The sitter may be called upon to conjure and integrate new ideas in his or her work.

- The Anchor: This period of abundant creativity offers a safe period of stability and security; the person will be able to rest awhile and work out where he or she wants to go in the future.

- The Bouquet: This card is expressing appreciation and rewards for good work; the indication is one of success.

- The Bear: That being said, the sitter will have to stand firm and fight off competitors. The Bear can indicate financial success, if one speculates wisely.

Five-Card Readings

In an example reading for a male sitter's self-development, we draw five cards.

The question: What do I have to do to regain the self-confidence I used to have?

- The Garden: Get out there more, and mix with people who share your interests. Have you been out of social circulation for a while? Have you found yourself avoiding accepting invitations to social events? The cards are saying to stop doing this and socialise.

- The Lady: Spend time perfecting your image; adopt a certain style; take pride in your appearance. You may meet the woman of your dreams in this meeting place.

- The Book: Take a course and expand your knowledge. Doing so will increase your self-esteem; the more knowledge you have, the more confident you will be in the company of others. Such self-improvement leads to less chance of an awkward silence.

- The Ring: Make a pledge to do something you have always wanted to do but have put off. You need to be true to your own needs and desires. Think about doing something you have never planned on doing. Be spontaneous.

- The Ship: This card indicates that it may be a good idea to travel and broaden your horizons. There is a whole new world out there. It is good to get out of our old comfort zones, and into exciting new ones.

EXERCISE: THE FORTUNETELLING DAY SPREAD

In this method, you will practice developing accuracy in your fortunetelling by reading pairs of cards for nine aspects of your day. If you perform this reading in the morning, you can compare it with your day to see how accurate you are with your cards.

Take your deck and shuffle it. Place it face down on the table.

Lay out the top nine cards in a row face-down from left to right.

Lay out the next nine cards one at a time on top of each of the laid-out cards, making nine piles of two cards.

Starting from the left, each pair is then read together as a divination for the following aspects:

1. Someone you will meet, and what comes out of that meeting.

2. Someone you care about, what that person will do.

3. Someone who annoys you, what that person will do.

4. Something that will happen to console you.

5. Something that awaits you.

6. Something that will help you.

7. Something that will happen that is a surprise to you.

8. Something that you desire, whether it will happen or not.

9. Something nice.

In this practice method, which can be uncannily accurate, it is important to keep a journal and read the cards as pairs, merging their meanings together with each card having equal weight. As you experience the day, you may see that one card in the pair carries the event and the other card carries the manner of the event. This will teach you the cards in your own experience and which way of reading them is best for you personally.

One example might be for the "Something Nice" position, you receive the Book + the Star. The most literal meaning of this might be a book on astronomy or astrology. However, in the "nice" position, it is also likely to predict that you will gain some knowledge, probably in the written word, that will give you hope. If you read on the Internet that day something nice that gave you something to look forward to later in the week, this would be it!

Fixed Positional Spreads

You may like to explore a few positional spreads with your cards and discover how they work in this manner. Spreads with fixed positions are not used in Lenormand readings as much as in tarot, although some German traditions have a fixed meaning for every position in the GT.

Here is a standard pattern with a little twist.

Decision Assister (Simple Three-Card Reading)

- Card 1: What to do

- Card 2: What is needed to be revealed

- Card 3: What *not* to do

First, shuffle all thirty-six cards and then deal them face-down into three equal piles of twelve cards. Turn up the first card in each pile and read them as a simple three-card "spread." Then, if you wish to tweak it, you can turn over the next three cards, lay them underneath the first three, and read them in continuation. This method allows you to build up your confidence, so you can start with just the first three cards, and work up to doing, in effect, a 3 x 12 tableau reading.

Other Readings

Three-Card "My Day Ahead" Reading

Three cards for the day—morning, afternoon, and evening—is good to perform each morning to help guide you through the day. Look on it as guidance from a good friend, the person whom you trust to point you in the right direction. You will find the cards have a special voice to communicate to you. Let your intuitive voice free-wheel, trust your inner voice. These are your own personal Lenormand fortunes for the day. Doing these minis reading each day will improve your overall oracular voice. Write them out in your oracular journal, and see how you get on in the day. Combine them all, and they tell a story.

Here are some examples from real life. In journaling, we simply write out the numbers of the cards as shorthand.

- Monday: 9, 25, 20

    The day will begin well with the Bouquet (9), a show of appreciation. It may be for you or it may suggest you appreciate someone in your life.

    The afternoon will bring a Ring (25); this symbolises an act of commitment coming your way. Or, is there something you have been delaying, or some commitment you have not fulfilled?

    By the evening an event will arise from this, with the Garden (20) for example—a gathering of like-minded people. Accept an invitation that comes your way; you do not want to miss out on an opportunity to meet new people.

- Tuesday: 32, 35, 34

    The morning will bring a lot of emotion with the sensitive energy of the Moon (32); you may hear news of something you have dreamed of doing for a long time finally materialising. It is a good time for being intuitive—a good time to do a Lenormand reading.

The afternoon will bring with it stability and the grounding energy of the Anchor (35).

The Evening will bring news of money and resources coming your way with the energy of the Fish (34). It is a good time to make an investment of time or energy.

- **Wednesday: 18, 15, 22**

The morning may be a good time to get in touch with an old friend: the Dog (18) with whom you have not been in touch with for a while, or you may be surprised with a call from an old friend.

In the afternoon, the Bear (15) making an appearance may find you coming head to head with an overbearing person who may want to pick a fight, perhaps a difficult boss or workmate. You may feel a bit intimidated; don't let anyone bully you. If possible, go around this person—avoid and stay clear!

The evening with the presence of the Ways (22) could mean you finally make your mind up about whether you should carry on in that workplace, perhaps you need to go a new direction in life.

Five-Card Spread Mirror Readings

In the following, I perform this five-card reading, which I call the Mirror spread, for a client who asks, "What happens if I take this course of action?" I charge his significator card (the Gentleman), place it face-down, shuffle the rest of the deck, and select four cards. I place the first two to the left of the Gentleman and the remaining two to the right. Here are the cards:

- The Anchor (35), Ring (25), Significator (Gentleman [28]), Lady (29), Fox (14)

The two cards to the left of the significator (Gentleman) represent the past, and those to the right represent the future. The Anchor speaks of stability and the Ring of a pledge, and that in the past the sitter had opted for a position in life of stable commitment. However, in the future cards, this has changed to a life with the Lady—one of cunning and who has patience to wait for an opportune time to act. What came out of the discussion with the sitter after the reading is that the Lenormand has a tendency to tell sitters what they need to know rather than what they *want* to know.

The Lenormand has the ability to see what is really going on within and on the outside and beyond. It is in some ways like a deck of your own hopes, fears, and dreams waiting to take form just for your asking.

When I finish a reading, I like to thank the cards for letting me access their wisdom.

Another Mirror Spread

A client asks about an opportunity for an overseas trip and wants to know if there's anything to fear about taking up the offer.

I use the Mirror spread. I shuffle the cards, and in my mind create a dialogue with the cards. I ask them if they will help me again with this reading.

I charge the significator card for the female sitter (the Lady). I then shuffle the rest of the deck, take four cards out, and place the first two to the left of the Lady and the second two to the right. Here are the cards I received:

- The Scythe (10), Rider (1), Significator (Lady [29]), Fox (14), House (4)

The two cards to the left of the significator (Lady) represent the sitter's past and the two to the right represent the future. The Scythe in the past is about any work that has been done, from which something good has been reaped. The Rider has passed this on to our sitter, who in the spread is looking forward to her travel, but there are lingering fears in the form of the Fox, which represents the dangers that lurk in the world, and in travel. However, all will be fine with the presence of the House, which ensures a secure outcome. The House is the haven from the Fox.

Speaking with the sitter afterward, we deduced that the cards at play represented the work she has done and how she feels she deserves some good to come of it in the form of the opportunity to travel. The fear she felt was allayed by the security of the House card.

A Simple Nine-Card Lenormand Spread

In this traditional cartomantic method, we lay out a nine-card 3 x 3 square to divine the fortune of any domestic situation. It is useful for practice, as it provides a smaller reading than the Grand Tableau.

To do it, take your deck and shuffle whilst thinking about the situation. Place it face-down when you are ready, and cut it about two-thirds of the way down with your left hand. Place this larger cut of cards to the left, creating a second pile on the left of the first. Then cut it again in the same way from the second pile, creating a third pile on the left.

Take the top three cards, still face-down, from the left stack and place them in a row on your table from left to right. Then take the top three cards from the middle stack and place them in a row beneath the first row. Finally, take the top three cards from the right stack and make a third row below the other two, creating a 3 x 3 square. Move away the three remaining stacks and turn all the cards in the square face-up.

The first row of three cards signifies the sitter. The second row of three cards shows their domestic environment. The third row shows the fortune of the situation, its most likely outcome, and any advice.

The cards are read as a sequence creating an oracular sentence; each card to the right modifies the preceding cards like a story being developed to the end. Imagine the cards are the storyboard of a movie in three frames: what would you say about the movie when you left the cinema?

The Four Fans Spread

Deriving from an early and classic cartomantic tradition, this four-part spread is effective at parties and gatherings for presenting in an authentic salon style.

Shuffle the deck, ask the sitter to do likewise, and split it with your left hand into three piles. Restack the piles into one deck face-down, and then lay out the cards into four piles of eight cards each in a square with plenty of room between the four piles. Set the remaining four cards to one side. Then turn the four piles face-up and fan them out, whilst saying out loud the appropriate line from the verse below.

- Fan 1: That you will gain

- Fan 2: That you will lose

- Fan 3: That you may have

- Fan 4: That you would choose

Read the lines in each fan as separate readings. The final four cards present a verdict or overall summary of the reading, and are read as a straight line or blend of four cards.

To clarify: the first fan of eight cards shows what is coming to you or your sitter, the second fan shows what will be lost in its attainment. The third fan shows the choices and opportunities ahead, and the fourth fan what is best chosen out of those. We have found it very effective and atmospheric to intone the rhyme for the four fans whilst actually fanning the four piles out in a dramatic fashion.

A Grand Tableau Reading

In this example, we will look at a full Grand Tableau reading from real life, and demonstrate how much information can be gained from the layout, and the numerous ways of approaching a reading. Whilst different readers will have their own methods, we hope to present here a wide range of the methods we have covered in this book to help you pull them together in a reading.

The sitter is a married woman who has lived with her husband in the same house since their daughter left home to live in her own apartment. She has a job but it no longer provides a challenge. She has been thinking about moving house and perhaps changing career for a long time; however, this has become a constant thought for the last few months. Her husband works as a musician and can technically work from any location, although he has many friends in their current town. Her question is: "If I work toward changing where I live, what success will I attain in my own career?" We leave the other elements of the situation out of the question, which needs to be specific—it is often that other elements will be discovered in the tableau, as we'll see. This example is a real reading; nothing has been invented or created for it, despite its uncanny accuracy.

We lay out the tableau as illustrated:

Figure 89. A Grand Tableau Reading

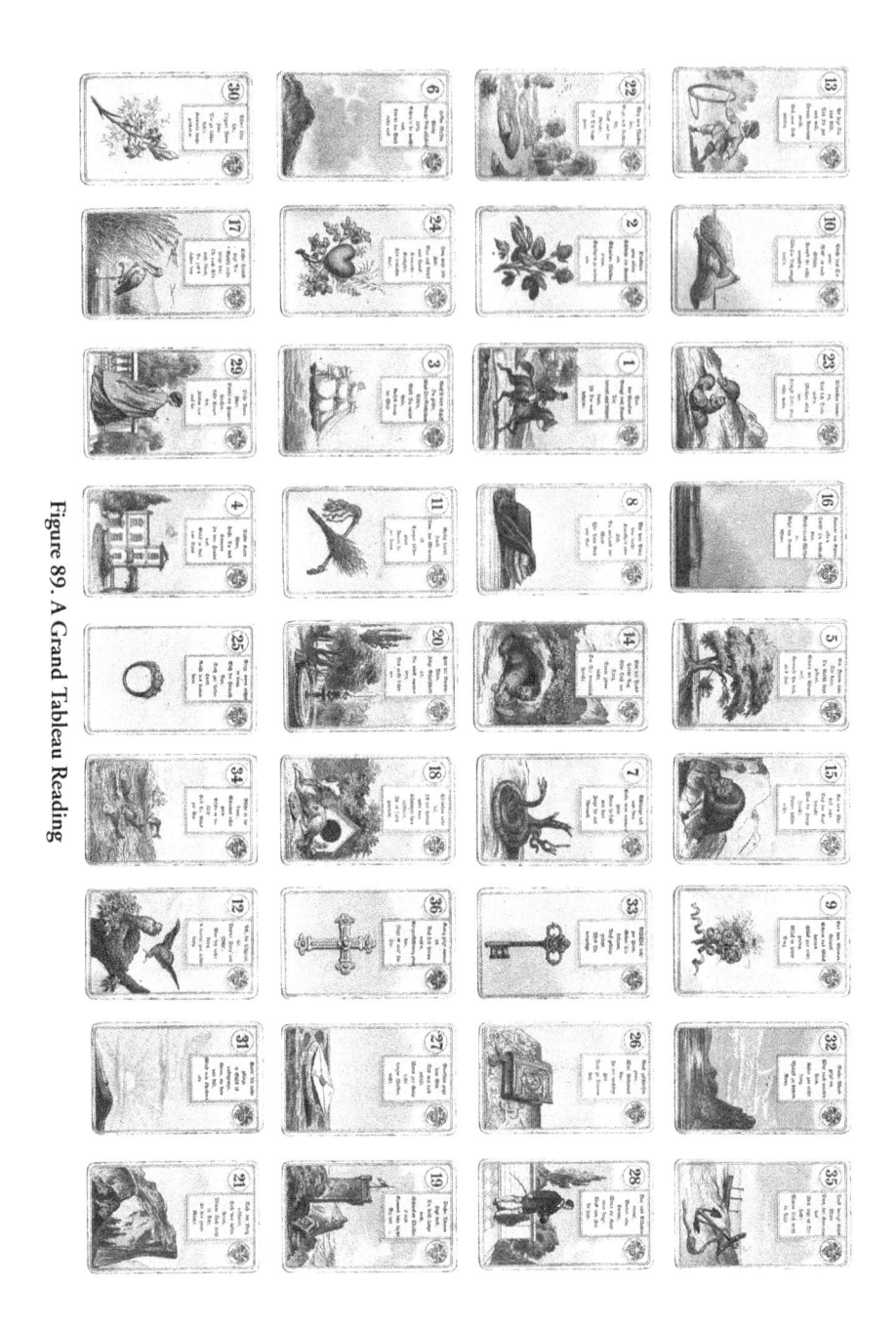

We first look and find the Lady card, as it represents the sitter. We immediately see it is in the bottom line of the tableau, facing the House card. This surprises the sitter with its immediate representation of her thoughts! We therefore decide to continue to quickly read this line as past and future—behind and ahead of the Lady card. Behind her we see the Lily and Stork, the cards of sexuality and delivery, and a literal return to the nest. We tell the sitter that her passion and the passage of her daughter through life is now behind her; however, it directly leads to her present thoughts.

We tend not to put too psychological gloss onto a Lenormand reading, although it may be apparent that the sitter has feelings about her daughter's newly found freedom. If we were to go this route, we can likely tell from these two cards alone that the daughter has just started a passionate relationship, prompting the mother's thoughts. A quick glimpse at the Snake card representing "the other woman" (here the daughter in the situation) shows this to be the case—in fact, that card is between the Bear above and the Dog below, showing a relationship with a strong and loyal man—but we do not have to raise this unless it seems relevant.[25]

We then look along the line to the future, seeing the House, Ring, Fish, Birds, Sun, and Mountain. This last card is of course in the last position of the tableau, so it represents doubly a "conclusion" of the reading.

In our fortunetelling style, then, we would read this line as "you will stay at your present location (the House represents the current home unless in the context of other "moving" cards such as the Ship) and make a commitment to doing so (House + Ring). Your resources will grow by networking (Fish + Birds) and your luck will improve despite the obstacle to movement (Sun + Mountain). The Mountain at the end of this line—and of the whole tableau—really tells us there is no movement."

This would be quickly read in the first moments of the reading, in effect answering the entire question and opening up new lines of questioning.

Let us quickly take a look at the husband in this situation, the Gentleman card. We immediately see him positioned at the far right of the second line down. He does not really look ahead to the future—and when we say this, the sitter agrees, saying he is a "typical musician, just living for the now." However, we also see quickly something else—the Snake is in the "past" of the Gentleman. As we have read this as the daughter, we can see that between the husband and the daughter cards are the Key and Book. We feel the need

CARD LAYOUTS AND SAMPLE READINGS • 235

to raise this, and say, "Your husband wanted your daughter to unlock her knowledge, her education, but he has put this behind him now." The sitter actually gasps and begins to cry, as this indeed has been a major issue in the family—the husband wished the daughter to go to university, but she did not. Actually, we understand why, although again we may not say it out loud—the Snake is in the house of the Bear, the symbol of strong force; she has inherited her father's stubbornness, leading to lack of ambition.

All of this is apparent in the first few moments of scanning the reading, and is made possible by following literal and simple rules—concentrate on the Lady and Gentleman cards, see how the House card fits between them, then follow the investigation of the Snake as here it represents the daughter who is quickly revealed to be still present in an influential sense.

If we were to now look at other options for the sitter, who perhaps was hoping the cards would say she was going to move to an exotic location and change career overnight, we might want to try knighting from her card (again, the Lady). This, in our approach, allows us to look outside of the box, still within the layout of the situation, but with wiggle room to make the most of it.

If we knight (count two cards one direction, then one card another; see the previous section on knighting) from the Lady, our first knighting takes us through the House, to the Ring, then to the Garden. This tells us that the sitter can make new friends in her current area, the Garden being the card of society. However she will have to tread somewhat carefully, as the Garden is bordered by the Whip and the Dog on either side, meaning troublesome speech on one hand, and loyal friends on the other.

Another knighting takes us upwards through the Ship and the Rider to either the Clover or the Coffin, depending on which of either direction we moved last in the knighting. The indication here is of possible travel whilst staying in the same house. This will lead to new experiences (Rider) and through those both good luck (Clover) and endings (Coffin) in equal measure.

Interestingly, the knighting that takes us back into her past, through the Stork and the Lily, leads to nothing but confusion—the Clouds, particularly bordered by the Heart and Ways. There is no point in looking back, a sentiment with which the sitter agrees. She does like the new ideas of extending her social network and travelling, however.

Looking a little deeper now into the overall context of the reading, we can use the houses to see that the Lady card is in the house of the Lily, i.e., the thirtieth position of the tableau. This is the card of passion and sexuality, so there is perhaps a deeper current to this domestic dissatisfaction. We look to the Lily card itself, which has already been read, and find it in the House of the Gentleman (position 28). This is really no surprise, but opens up new emotions in the sitter, who reveals her husband has not been active in this regard for some time. So we move quickly to the Gentleman card and find he is in the House of the Dog, literally, "in the dog house." (It sometimes becomes hard to believe the Lenormand cards can be so literal!) However, this is also the position of loyalty, so all is well in this context. We can then follow this chaining to find the Dog card, which is in the House of the Heart (position 24)—another positive position. The loyalty is deeply felt.

Whilst there are many other lines of reading we can explore, if we were to summarise thus far, we would reflect on the four corner cards to frame the reading, saying that whilst there is potential for a new childlike beginning and innocence, with the Child card commencing the whole tableau, there is no movement likely with the Mountain card concluding the layout. The frame is to work within the long-term development (Anchor, in the top-right corner) of passion (Lily in the bottom-left) for the benefit of both parties.

A Full Grand Tableau for a Pet

The following is an account of a personal GT reading Tali performed for Rufy, her dog who was unwell. It shows how the most mundane but meaningful events can be read with the Lenormand.

My five-year-old dog has recently been diagnosed with a kidney condition the vet has advised can be managed by feeding him a special kidney-friendly prescription diet. I am understandably concerned about my dog's future health.

The first thing I do is create a personal space and choose a suitable time for divination, a place where I will not be distracted by external factors. My chosen time was in the morning, not long after having woken; I find this is a good time to connect to the oracle energies at play, as we are more open after having been one with dream imagery and the astral realm through the night.

I use the space where I meditate to perform the reading.

I looked through the deck in order to pick out the charged card, which for this reading was the Dog. I focused on the issue at hand, my dog's health—the need to know more, perhaps clarification on managing the condition. I then slipped the card back into the deck and shuffled. Next I laid out all the Lenormand cards in a Grand Tableau.

Looking at the GT before me, I found where the Dog card was placed amongst the thirty-six houses. On the next page is the Grand Tableau for my reading, which I will take you through step by step.

The brilliant thing about reading the Grand Tableau is that once you have pinpointed your charged card, you have the key to opening up the reading. The charged card does as it promises: it charges you forward through the reading, acting as a triangulation point to aid in navigating the tableau. So let's discover where the Dog card is and where it wants to take us.

My Dog card is in the House of the Lily, position 30. Now this is very interesting because the Lily card is symbolic of purity. Taking into account that my dog has a kidney disorder, I see this as meaning his kidneys are not as effective as they should be at purifying his system. I know from this point that the cards are aligned with the question. This house placement is stressing the importance of "purity" for my dog. I know we are doing something right, as the prescription food is very pure and will put less stress on Rufy's kidneys.

Figure 90. GT for a Pet

Knowing that, where do I go from here? Well, we can look into the future at the card next along on the right. The Fish is placed in the House of the Sun. Sylvie Steinbach alludes to this in her book, that the body connections for the Fish card are the kidneys and bladder. Again this confirming the reading is on the right track, and it offers reassurance in that the cards are aligned to the question. The Sun offers a future of positive growth, contentment—and combined with the next card in the line, the Coffin—transformation through making changes.

Moving backwards in the cards about the past, the card to the left of my significator is the Tower. This card is very much the watchtower of the Lenormand, the card of caution.

CARD LAYOUTS AND SAMPLE READINGS • 239

It can relate to vision, surveying, and the need to know what is going on around us; the presence of this card indicates looking beyond, an outward projection. It is the all-seeing eye, the card of scaling great heights of awareness and being alert, on lookout. This to me very much summed up the role of the diagnostic blood screening that alerted me to my dog's condition. To be forewarned is to be forearmed. In the House of the Lady, it can be about putting emphasis on female intuition.

Preceding this period of caution and worry about the dog's health we have the past cards: the Bouquet combined with the Ring and the Lady. The Bouquet speaks of a gift that was unexpected from a lady (my sister) who entrusted us to look after her dog. We have made a pledge to care for him (the Ring).

The card directly above the Dog is the House, placed in the House of the Ways, whose context is one of choice, making decisions, and weighing the best action to protect my dog's well-being. Below the Dog we have the House of the Cross, where the Bear is placed. The Bear is known to correspond to diet and nutrition; placed in the House of the Cross, it may speak of keeping faith along the way.

A Question about a Work Project

The question regards a work project coming about successfully or not; money is involved.

The significator represents a man who is important to the project. I charge this card and put it back into the deck. I then shuffle and lay out all thirty-six cards into the GT. I read the cards framing the Gentleman in order to focus. The Gentleman is placed in the House of the Bear, a house whose context is money. The underlying energies of this house are related to primal survival, strength, authority, and power.

The Gentleman pictured in the Piatnik card is standing reading a letter, and in his right hand he holds his cane—he very much looks like a man about his business. In the immediate future, the card to the right of him is the Garden, where an event will take place.

In his immediate past to the left of him, we have a pledge in the form of the Ring; the Gentleman has made a pledge or commitment. If we read the cards together in a line from left to right, it reads, "A pledge made by a businessman for an event to come."

To know more about the Gentleman and his intentions, we look at the card directly beneath him, the Moon. Here we have dreamy aspirations, perhaps a wish for fame and recognition. The card above him is the Mice, representing surface-level activity in the practical world, the world of motivation and decision making. This is the energy of the mice doing things in bite-size pieces, working gradually to get things done for sheer survival.

To the left of the Mice we have the Fish, the card of resources and money. To the right of the Mice we have the Book: a source of knowledge and magic, it is a powerful tool one may use for self-mastery.

Knighting in the Reading

If we knight from the Gentleman to the Ring, then to the Fish, it speaks of a man making a pledge of money or resources.

Knighting from the Gentleman to the Moon, and then to the Clouds, the message is that the gentleman is emotionally changeable. The card to the left of him, the Clouds, signals uncertainty in the air, particularly if the darker edge of the clouds is closer to him.

Afterword: Lenormand for Tarot Readers

The Lenormand system has run parallel—mainly separated by language alone—to tarot for over two centuries. Whilst there are crossovers, starting with Etteilla and Mlle. Lenormand's claims to read "Tharot," to more modern versions such as the *Lenormand Tarot* (Lo Scarabeo, 2006), the two systems have remained separate. Perhaps there has been a bit of snobbery when referring to Lenormand as an inauthentic "gypsy"-connected deck with no pedigree, unlike tarot, which has had a long time to accumulate complexity and perceived history. Similarly, when mass media has reached for a symbol of the occult, they have usually picked a tarot deck from their stock shelves, rather than a Lenormand deck.

A surprising aspect of the Lenormand revival is that for those who have learnt the Opening of the Key method of reading tarot taught by the Golden Dawn from the turn of the last century (long felt by many to be Kabbalistic and complex), the reading of Lenormand, in sequence and by counting methods, has felt quite obvious. This is because the originators of the Golden Dawn method were utilising early cartomantic methods, glossing them with correspondences from other systems in a synthetic manner. We have now gone full-circle with the return to the more simple roots of cartomancy.

However, for the many tarot readers discovering Lenormand for the first time who are inexperienced with the Opening of the Key, the temptation is to apply their tarot experience to Lenormand, and this simply cannot work—it is a case of using a walnut to crack a hammer. It is far better to learn to "switch headsets" between one system and another, getting the best of both worlds, and bringing the best of one system, where appropriate, into the other. A tarot reading can benefit from many of the story-weaving skills required in Lenormand, and a Lenormand reading can benefit from many of the pinpointing and bridging methods required for tarot.[26]

Those who have been used to changing headsets, such as when switching from rune reading to I-Ching, to tarot, to astrology (or other oracle cards), will also be at an advantage in appreciating how different systems can take the stage for different purposes.

Here is a run-down of some of the primary differences, noting there may be exceptions to any given rule:

- The Lenormand has thirty-six cards (in general); tarot has seventy-eight.
- The Lenormand has simple and singular symbols (similes), whereas tarot usually has complex constellations of symbols on each card (metaphors).
- The tarot has a suit structure and three distinct sections (courts, majors, minors), whereas the Lenormand has no such structure.
- The Lenormand is usually read without a "layout," using only a sequential line or matrix method such as the Grand Tableau. Tarot often has fixed-position spreads where each position has a context.
- The Lenormand is read often as a keyword-driven language, where combinations often have traditional or semi-fixed meanings; the tarot is most often read from its symbol library.
- There is little variation between Lenormand decks, compared to the wide variations amongst tarot decks, which incorporate cultures as diverse as ancient Egyptian, to West African, to Native American, to science fiction.
- The Lenormand is more strongly associated with playing cards used in cartomantic methods than the tarot, which has been layered with many other associative systems.

In many ways, comparing tarot and Lenormand is like comparing the board games of chess and Go as discussed in chapter 8. The former has a fair set of rules to be learnt (symbols), and is played through standard openings and mid- and end-game sequences (spreads), whilst the second is based on a very simple rule, played on a wider board (tableau) with an endless variety of patterns (combinations).

Both systems—and different decks within each—have their own voice, and it is likely you will have to experiment with alternate Lenormand decks as you did with tarot before finding the one that's right for you. We would recommend trying at least one contemporary deck (such as the Steampunk Fairy Oracle) and one historical reproduction deck (The Original Lenormand) at the same time to calibrate which end of the scale you wish to explore first. Similarly, try one that is more pictorial (Mystical Lenormand) with one that is starker (Lenormand Arlo).

The Literal Lenormand

Whilst learning Lenormand, ensure that you keep going back to the core and literal meanings of the cards without your T-space head. Say the cards' names out loud, and keep them literal, objective, and grounded to real situations. Doing so may seem somewhat scary to those who provide very "psychological" tarot readings, but the result is often psychological insight through a different path. One reading we recall for someone led to a quite transformational and profound experience through the simple and literal statement: "the man is in the House of the Child under the Lady (mother)."

There has been some discussion with regard to "intuitive" reading versus "rule-based" reading, although we consider this a bit of a red herring. You can only "intuit" something from your existing knowledge, whether it is rule-based or experiential…otherwise it's just guessing. We recommend students study the available literature on the subject, read widely, and practice whilst remaining open to experience through experimentation, journaling, and contemplation. At some point, one will begin to intuit patterns and combinations in the cards based on knowledge and experience. Later, as you become ready, inspiration will also take a role in your readings.

Similarly, the notion of "tradition" has also been discussed at length. Our general practice is to encourage (for example, when learning any system of correspondences, such as tarot, astrology, or Kabbalah) the learning of one recognisable system at the beginning. It does not matter which system it is, although those based on study and experience will also be better building blocks.

Once you have experimented with that system, you will soon find disparities and tweaks; for example, you may simply not find yourself able to read the Moon as "work," finding instead another card always seems to hold that meaning for you. Later, you may find that your own personal tweaks bring you straight in alignment with someone else's system or tradition—because they have discovered the same things as you. However, you cannot get to this stage by simply cutting and pasting from one system to another—if several cards mean "work," you will struggle with your readings or find yourself fitting the cards to the desired answer, which is obviously not encouraged.

You might also like to take a bridging course by learning the counting method of the Opening of the Key, which uses tarot and symbolism to perform linear and literal readings. The written records we have of these Golden Dawn readings show they were frequently used—despite it being seen as an "inner order" and spiritual method—for mundane fortunetelling, such as a theatre's success, a lover's feelings, the outcome of a court case, and so forth. This may make it easier to move to Lenormand if you are only comfortable with fixed-meaning spreads.

With regard to the meaning of individual cards, take a while to familiarise yourself with the cards of the Tower, Moon, Star, and Sun. These do not carry the same symbolic interpretations as in tarot, and you are advised to consider the simple functionality of a tower, or the most simple connections to the stellar bodies—the moon is a measure of time in agriculture, which at the time of the early Lenormand was the main industry, so hence could be a card of work, success, and fortune. The stars were used for navigation, getting you to your destination, and are thus images of literal destiny. The sun meant summer, good crops, growth, and longer days, hence it is simply "big luck" like an endless summer holiday. It is not the card of Ra the ancient Egyptian solar deity, as it appears in Crowley's Thoth Tarot, nor "consciousness in spirit" as Waite would term it; the Lenormand card of the Sun is everything the sun actually is, and it represents its function in life on earth. We can move up to the symbolic layers and correspondences (and thus to every other system), but in Lenormand this has little or no bearing.

There are other, perhaps deeper issues with the move to Lenormand reading, particularly if you decide to deliver your messages in a more literal and fortunetelling type of voice. In tarot there has been much of a move toward "empowering" the querent, by telling the person that the future is not written in stone and that the cards provide a mechanism for reviewing potential futures, and making the most informed decisions. In Lenormand, there has been a history of stricter fortunetelling, i.e., choosing three cards for the day and waiting for events to match those three cards as "predicted." Such an exercise can only sharpen one's ability to make accurate predictions.

We must begin to consider the philosophical differences between fortunetelling and divination, and also consider how "luck" plays into this view of the universe if we are reading one or two of the cards as signifying "luck." If you are able to make predictions, what role does the random, unpredictable nature of luck play in your readings? This topic is somewhat beyond the scope of this book, but it is worth raising into awareness. L-space has a different environment that brings considerations like this to mind for both Lenormand and tarot.

A more useful analogy may be to consider the difference between prediction and forecasting, as suggested by the tarot reader Mike Hernandez.[27] We can forecast far better than we can predict, and forecasting at least offers us means of preparing for the storm or the season.

A final suggestion is to always start by performing a Grand Tableau or linear eight-card reading, but do not fall into the trap of one-card readings for simplicity. The Lenormand cards are more like letters in an alphabet, and you need several of them to make a meaningful word, and several more to make a sentence. If you try learning the "card a day" way, you'll train your brain to think in smaller chunks than is ideal for intermediate and advanced reading styles, i.e., counting across lots of cards, reading them as you go into one coherent whole.

Above all, discover the voice of the cards. In divination, the voice of the system, deck, and even your personal deck, are paramount. The Lenormand has something to tell you. Listen carefully.

Appendix One:
The Game of Hope

The following is the first English translation of the instruction leaflet accompanying the "Game of Hope" cards held in the British Museum as *Das Spiel der Hofnung* [Reg. 1896, 0501.495]. These cards, authored by J. K. Hechtel, were published c. 1800 by G. P. J. Bieling of Nuremberg. The instructions offer game-playing rules and a simple story-telling means of fortunetelling.

Their connection as a prototype of all following "petit Lenormands" was first made in 1972 by Prof. Detlef Hoffmann and Erika Kroppenstedt in *Wahrsagekarten: Ein Beitrag zur Geschichte des Okkultismus* (quoted in Decker, Depaulis & Dummett, *A Wicked Pack of Cards*, 1996).

The cards exist in a number of museums, and Tarot Professionals recently paid for a high-quality photograph to be taken of the deck and made available on the British Museum website. Following our additional visits to the museum and notes, we are able to offer this full English translation of the instructions by Steph Myriel Es-Tragon.

The cards themselves have been licensed exclusively to Tarot Professionals for publication as a deck, the Original Lenormand, in a limited first edition of 250 copies, although there is a new edition now available.

We believe that the translation below gives some indication of how the cards would have been viewed at the time of their origination in terms of interpretation as an oracle. Whilst some of these interpretations may be readily obvious—the Fox represents cunning—others are perhaps revelatory, such as the Book actually being seen as a "hex" (spell) book.

It is also apparent that the cards are divided into favourable and unfavourable cards, and indifferent, where no particular forfeit or reward is taken. We also examine in the book the origins of this system in early games of morality and teaching. This is one area that can be further explored to develop Lenormand reading into more spiritual interpretations in addition to mundane fortunetelling, without layering it with esotericism or complexity.

We hope you enjoy this translation and you might even attempt to use the Original Lenormand cards to play the game as well as for divination and fortunetelling.

The Translation

The Game of Hope

With a new figure card in illuminated 36 sheets, 2nd improved edition.

This game can be played with as many people as want to take part, and every player puts 6 to 8 marks into a pot. The 36 illuminated sheets are laid out in a square, that is, in 6 rows of 6 sheets each according to the numbers on top of the cards, that is 1, 2, 3 and so on, up to 36.

After every player has taken up a mark or sign, each in turn casts two ordinary dice. Each player moves their mark the number of pips cast starting at the first card. For example, a player who has cast 4 and 1 moves to the fifth card. When it is the turn of this person for the second time, he moves the number of the pips starting from the 5th card and so on until the end of the game.

The order of the game can be determined by the dice, for example it may be agreed that the player with the highest number of pips will begin the game and the one with the lowest number will start last. If two people cast the same number of pips, they are equal and they have to throw again.

On each of the 36 sheets, when a player puts his mark down, he meets with a figure there, which is favourable or unfavourable or indifferent to him. I call those sheets indifferent which have no influence on the progress or regress of the game, but where the mark remains standing quietly until the next round.

The following sheets are favourable or unfavourable:

- No. 3: The one who throws 3 pips and thus gets to the Ship will be happily taken by this ship to the Canary Islands, where the well-known beautiful birds are at home, no. 12.
- No. 4: On entry in this House, two marks have to be given up to the doorkeeper.
- 6: The Thundercloud drives back to no. 2.
- 7: To stay safe from the bite of this dangerous Snake, 3 marks have to be paid.
- 8: The one who gets to this Coffin is deemed to be dead until another player comes to this sheet or until he casts a double, for when it is his turn to roll the dice he is not excluded.
- 11: So as not to be castigated by this Rod, one pays two marks. For this one can move forward two more sheets—to the Lad on No. 13.
- 14: The cunning Fox leads the player astray and he has to find refuge in the Wood at no. 5.
- 16: Arriving at the Star of good prospects, the player receives 6 marks.
- 19: To enjoy the pleasant vista from the Tower, one pays 2 marks.
- 21: On these steep Alps, the player has to remain until another arrives to release him or he has to cast a double.
- 22: Unnoticed, this path leads around the mountains right back to the Garden at no. 20.
- 24: Whoever wins this Heart will immediately offer it to the Youth at no. 28 or to the Girl at no. 29. That is to say, if the player arriving at the card 24 is a woman, she will move up to 28, if it is a man to 29.
- 25: Whoever finds this Ring gets 3 marks.

- 26: Whoever reads in this Grimoire will by a hex therein be forcefully returned to the Garden in No. 20.

- 27: Whoever receives this Letter has to pay a fee of 2 marks for the bearer.

- 28: This Youth leads on to the brilliant Sun of hope in no. 31. However for those who got here by way of the Heart, no. 24, this does not happen. They wait here for the next turn.

- 29: The Girl leads on to no. 32, unless one has come here through the Heart.

- 33: On reaching this Key, one receives 2 marks.

- 34: Reaching the Fish, one has to pay 2 marks.

- 35: This is the most important sheet of the whole game, insofar as the one, who comes to stay on this picture of Hope has won the game and draws the whole cash-box or deposit.

- 36: So near to the luckiest field, the player is cheated as against his will he has to advance one step too far to the figure of the Cross, where he has to remain until another player takes this burden off him or he throws a double.

If a player casts a number, which leads over the 36 cards, he has to count back as many numbers as he would move beyond the 36. For example, he stands on 32 and casts 8, therefore he has to go back 4 numbers, because these are in excess of 36 and comes to stay at 28.

Also, it is not possible to take the cash box by counting back an excess to 36 but only in the advance movement. For example, if someone stands at 29 and casts a 6, he arrives in orderly fashion at the Anchor of Hope and has won the whole game.

If players want to add more variety to the entertainment of the game, say, by working in riddles, forfeits etc., this is easily done and any party will be able to find sheets to which these can be added as rewards or penalties. For example, sheets nos. 2, 5, 9, 13, 15, 18, 23, 30, 32, 36 may be declared as forfeits, whenever they are reached in the orderly way, on 10, 12, 17, 20, 29, 35 it is required to sing songs of friendship and health-wishing, for which you can find any number of proposals in the book *Selection of the Most Excellent Songs of Friendship* published by the same publisher.

In order to play any conceivable card game with ordinary German and French playing cards with these 36 figure cards for further entertainment, the German and French card pictures have been included at the top of the cards. It is only sometimes necessary to leave the Sixes and the Sevens out of the game. Also, this makes it very easy to learn to compare the German and French cards.

With these same cards it is also possible to play an entertaining game of oracles by shuffling the 36 cards and then letting the person, for whom the oracle is meant, cut the cards, then laying out the cards in 5 rows with 4 rows at 8 cards each and the fifth row with the remaining 4 cards. If the person querying is a woman, one starts from sheet 29, spinning a jocular tale from the cards nearby around the figures on display. If it is for a man, the tale is started from sheet 28 and again makes use of the cards surrounding this one. This will bring much entertainment to any merry company.

[End of translation]

Appendix Two:
The Game of Picket (Piquet)

Principal Games on Cards

Before you begin the Game of Picket, you must throw out of the pack the Deuces, Trays, Fours, and Fives, and play with the rest of the Cards, which are in number Thirty and Six.

The Usual set is an Hundred, not but that you may make it more or less; the last card deals and the worst is the dealer's.

The Cards are all valued according to the number of Spots they bear, the Ace only excepted, which wins all other Cards, and goes for Eleven.

The Dealer Shuffles, and the others cuts, delivering what Number pleaseth at a time, for the he exceed not four nor deal under two, leaving twelve on the Table between them.

He that is the Elder, having Looked over his cards, and finding never a Court—Card among them, says I have a blank, and I intend to discard such a number of Cards, and that you may see mine, discard you as many as intend; this done, the eldest shows his Cards and reckons ten for the Blank, then taking up his Cards again he discards those which he judgeth most fit: here Note, he is always bound to that number which he first propounded. This being done, he takes in as many from the Stock as he laid out; and if it should chance to fall out that the other hath a Blank too, the youngers Blank shall bar the former and hinder his Picy and Repicy, though the Eldest hands Blank consists of the biggest Cards.

It is no small advantage to the Eldest to have the benefit of Discarding, because he may take in eight of the twelve in the Stock, discarding as many of his own for them, not but that if he find it more advantageous he may take in a less number; after this the Antagonist may take in what he thinks fit, acquitting his hand of the like number. Her note that let the Game be never so good, the Gamesters are both obliged to discard one Card at least. After the discarding you must consider the Ruff, that is how much you can make of one suit; the eldest first, and if the youngest makes no more the Ruff is good, and sets up one for every Ten he can produce; as for example, for thirty reckon Three, for forty Four, and so onward; withal take notice you are to count as many for thirty five as for forty, and as much for forty five as for fifty, and so of the rest; but from thirty five to thirty nine yu muast count nom more than for thirty five, and so from thirty to thirty four count no more than for thirty; and this Rule is to be observed in all other higher numbers.

Ad for sequences and their value after the Ruff is played, the Elder acquaints you with his Sequences (if he have them) and they are Tierces, Quarts, Quints, Sixiesms, Septiesms, Huictuefsms abd Neufiesms, as thus; Six, Seven, and Eight, Nine, Ten, and Knave; Queen, King, and Ace; which last is called a Tierce Major, because it is the highest. A quart is a Sequence of four cards, a Quint of five, a Sixism of Six, et cetera. These Sequences take their Denomination from the highest Card in the sequence. It is a Tierce Major, aor a Tierce of an Ace when there is Queen when there is neither King, nor Ace, and so you come to the lowest Tierce, which is a Tierce of an Eight. You must reckon for every Tierce three, for Quart four, but for Quint fifteen, for a Quart four, but for a Quint fifteen, for a Sixism Sixteen, and so upward; now for whatever you can make of all you must add to your Blank, and count the whole together.

Here not that the biggest Tierce, Quart, or other Sequence, although there be but one of them, makes all the others less Sequences useless unto him be they never so many, and he that hath the biggest Sequences by virtue there of reckons all his less Sequences, though his Adversaries Sequences be greater, and other wise would have drowned them.

Further observe, that a Quart drowns a Tierce, and a Quint a Quart, and so of the rest, so that he who hath a Sixiefsm may reckon on his Tierces, Quarts, or Qunits, though the other may happen to have Tierce, Quart, et cetera of higher value than the others are that hath the Sixiesm; trace the fame Method in all the other like Sequences.

After you have manifested your Sequences, you come to reckon your three Aces, three Kings, three Queens, three Knaves, or three Tens, as for Nines, Eights, Sevens, and Sixes, they have no place int this Account, for every Ternary you count Three, and they are in value as it is in Sequences. Aces the highest the Knaves, and last of all the Tens. The Higher drowns the lover here, as in Sequences.

He that have three Aces may reckon three Queens, Knaves, or Tens, if he have them, though the other have three Kings; and this is done by reason of his higher Ternary. Now he that have four Aces, four Kings, four Queens, Four Knaves, or four Tens, for each reckons fourteen, which is the reason they are called Quatorzes.

You must show your Point, Quint, or Quart before you Play, or else the other may reckon his, tho Inferior, upon showing em.

Now they begin to Play the Cards, the Elder begins and the Younger follows in Suit as at Whisk, and for every Ace, King, Queen, Knave, or Ten, he reckons one.

A Card once Play'd must not be recall'd, unless he have a Card of the same Suit in his hand, if the elder Hand plays an Ace, King Queen, or Ten, for every such Card he is to reckon one, which he adds to the number of his Game before, and if the other be able to Play upon it a higher Card of the same Suit, he wins the Trick, and reckons one for his Card as well as the other. Whoforever wins the last Trick the last Trick reckons two for it, if he win it with a Ten, but if with any Card under, he reckons but one, then they tell their Cards, and he that hath the most is to reckon Ten for them.

After this each person sets up his Game with Counters, and if the Set be not up, deal again; now a Set is won after this manner, admit that each Party is so forward in his Game that he wants but four or five to be up, if it so happens that any of the two have a blank, he wins the Set, because the Blanks are always first reckoned; but if no Blanks, then comes the Ruff, next your Sequences, then your Aces, Kings, Queens, Knaves, and Tens, next what Cards are reckoned in play, and last of all the Cards you have Won. If any of the Gamesters can reckon, either in Blanks, Ruffs, Sequences, Aces, et cetera up to thirty in his own hand without playing a Card, and before the other can reckon any thing, instead of thirty he shall reckon any thing, instead of thirty he shall reckon ninety, and as many as he reckons, after above his thirty, Adding them to his ninety; this is known by the name of a Repicy.

Moreover he that can make in like manner, what by Blank, Ruff, Sequences, et cetera up to the said number, before the other hath play'd a Card, or reckoned any thing, instead of their thirty he reckons sixty, and this is called Picy. Here, note, that if you can but remember to call for your Picy, or Repicy before you deal again, you shall lose neither of them, otherwise you must.

He that wins more than his own cards reckons ten, but he that wins all the Cards reckons Forty, and this is called a Capet.

The Rules belonging to this Game are these: If the Dealer give more Cards than are due, whether through mistake or otherwise, it lieth in the choice of the elder hand whether he shall deal again or no, or whether it shall be played out.

He that forges to reckon his Blank, Ruff, Sequences, Aces. Kings and the like; and hath begun to play his Cards cannot recall them. So it is with him that showeth not his Ruff before he play his first Card, losing absolutely all the advantage thereof.

He that misreckons anything, and he play'd one of his Cards, and his Adversary finds at the beginning, middle, or end of the Game, that he had not what he reckoned, for his punishment he shall be debarred from reckoning anything he really hath, and his Adversary shall reckon all hath, yet the other shall make all he can in play. He that takes in more Cards than he discardeth is liable to the same Penalty.

He that throw up his Cards imagining he hath lost the Game, mingling them with other Cards on the Table though afterward he perceive his mistake, yet he is not allowed to take up his Cards and play them out.

No man is permitted to discard twice in one dealing.

He that hath a Blank, his Blank shall hinder the other Picy and Recipy, although he hath nothing to show but his Blank.

He that have Four Aces, Kings, Queens, et cetera dealt him and after he hath discarded one of the four reckons the other three, and the other say to him it is good; he is bound to tell the other, if he ask him what Ace, King, Queen, et cetera he wants.

If after the cards are cleanly cut, either of the Gamesters know the upper Card by the backside. Notwithstanding this the Cards must not be shuffled again. In like manner, if the Dealer perceive the other hath cut himself an Ace, and would therefore shuffle again, this not permitted; and if a Card be found faced, it shall be nor argument to deal again, but must deal on; but if two be found faced then may he shuffle again.

Lastly, Whosover is found changing or taking back again any of his Cards, he shall lose the Game, and be accounted a Foul Player.

To conclude with a small but pleasant addition, it is not amiss to insert an Ingenious Song of Mr. D'Urfeys, Famous at Court on this Subject.

> Within an Abor of delight,
> As Sweet as Bowers Elizian
> Where Famous Sidney us'd to write
> I Lately had vison:
> Methought beneath a Golden State,
> The turns of chance obeying;
> Six of the Worlds most noted great,
> At Piquet were a playing.
> The first Two were the Brave Eugene
> With Vendosme battle Waging
> The next a Nymph that to be Queen,
> He Monsieur was Engaging;
> The Fleur de Lis Old Maintenon
> With Fancified Careo
> And next above the Scarlet Don,
> Queen Ann with Gallick Nero
> The Game between the Martial Braves
> Was held in different caftes;
> The French—man got Quatorze of Knaves,
> But Prince Eugene Four Aces;
> And tho' the tothers elsest hand
> Gave hopes to make a jest on't
> Yet now the Point who soonest gain'd
> Could only get the best on't

From them I turn'd mine Eyes to see
The Church—man and the Lady,
And found her pleas'd to high degree,
Her fortune had been steady,
The Saints that cram'd the Spanish purse
She hop'd would soon oblige her,
For he had been a little Terse
When she produced Quint—Major.
And now between the King and Queen
An Empire was depending;
Within whose mighty games were seen
The Art of State contending;
The Mounsieur had Three Kings to win't
And was o'ev Europe roaming
But her full Point Quatorze and Quint
Won all and left him foaming.

Further Resources

This list will be also found updated on Tali's blog, the Tarot Speakeasy, located at www.tarotspeakeasy.com. This is not a comprehensive list; the first sites listed will take you to more sites across the Internet with a diverse range of Lenormand voices.

Websites

Learning Lenormand Online Course
A ten-lesson Lenormand course you can take in your own time, with authors Marcus Katz and Tali Goodwin. It is a series of ten one-hour videos that brings the information in this book to life with many additional spreads, methods, and insights.

- www.learninglenormand.com

Tarot-Town
The social networking site for Tarot Professionals worldwide, this site contains courses and information on tarot and Lenormand reading by Tali Goodwin. You can also become a member to discover more intermediate and advanced courses beyond this present work.

- www.tarot-town.com

The Lenormand Museum
A vast online collection of historical and some contemporary Lenormand decks, with profuse illustrations of the decks. The site has a searchable database by publisher, year, country, and even city of origin, as well as the number of cards in the decks.

- http://www.lenormand-museum.com/

Iris Treppner (in German, some content available in English)
Iris Treppner's course is seen as a fundamental teaching of the German tradition. She offers workshops and books in German, and some online teaching material in English.
- http://www.iristreppner.com

Britta Kienle (German, materials in English)
Britta's online course and materials are partially available in English, and augmented by several self-test sections, which are very useful. Britta also has a Lenormand deck that is available from her site.
- http://www.fortune-telling-lenormand.com/

Mary K. Greer's Blog
Mary's site features a wealth of invaluable research and insight into cartomantic tradition and development.
- http://marygreer.wordpress.com/2008/04/01/origins-of-divination-with-playing-cards/

Trionfi.com
A comprehensive site of tarot and cartomancy history, with an active forum of discussion between tarot researchers and historians.
- http://www.trionfi.com

Claire Seifert
Claire's accessible and straightforward explanations of the cards and reading ideas are wonderful viewing. At the time of writing, she is looking to translate more of her work into English.
- http://www.hexe-claire.de/english-pages.html
- YouTube videos at http://www.youtube.com/user/HexeClaire

Beyond Worlds Lenormand Podcasts
Donnaleigh de LaRose has established a wide range of tutorial videos on the Lenormand system and her podcasts as "Beyond Worlds" feature a growing number of Lenormand readers, teachers, and authors.
- http://www.divinewhispers.net/lenormandlessons.htm

Books

In English

A Wicked Pack of Cards. Ronald Decker, Thierry Depaulis, and Michael Dummett. New York: St. Martin's Press, 1996.

The Playing Card: An Illustrated History. Detlef Hoffmann. Leipzig, Germany: Edition Leipzig, 1973.

The Game of Destiny. Mario Dos Ventos. lulu.com: self-published, 2007.

Fortune-Telling with Playing Cards. Jonathan Dee. New York: Sterling, 2004.

Easy to Learn Fortune-Telling: Using the Cards of Madam Lenormand. Britta Kienle. lulu.com: self-published, 2001.

The Secrets of the Lenormand Oracle. Sylvie Steinbach. Charleston, SC: Booksurge, Publishing, 2007.

A Dictionary of Symbols. J. E. Cirlot. London: Routledge & Kegan Paul, 1985.

In German

Die Sibylle der Salons. Iris Treppner. Munich: Wilhelm Heyne, 2010.

Wahrsagen Mit Karten. Bernd A. Mertz. Munich: Sudwest, 2004.

Lenormand-Lernbuch. Halina Kamm. Hamburg: Corona, 2005.

Wahrsagekarten. Detleff Hoffmann and Erika Kroppenstedt. Bielefeld, Germany: Heinz Beier, 1972.

Judith Bärtschi Lenormand. Judith Bärtschi and Harald Josten. Krummwisch, Germany: Konigsfurt-Urania, 2007.

Kartenlegen mit Madame Lenormand. Erna Droesbeke. Neue Erde GmbH, Germany: Auflage, 2006.

Magazine Articles

Tarosophist International Lenormand Special. 2012. http://www.lulu.com/shop/marcus-katz/tarosophist-international-v1iss15-print/paperback/product-20159993.html

Lenormand Decks

We provide here a brief selection of Lenormand decks. You may wish to keep up-to-date with our Learning Lenormand Facebook group, where we showcase antique and new decks as they are published: http://www.facebook.com/groups/298383766946724/?fref=ts.

Original/European/Antique Decks

We first list a few essential decks which are amongst the earliest and most popular in Europe. These include the Original Lenormand, the "Blue Owl," Piatnik, Dondorf, and the Mertz decks.

The Original Lenormand (Game of Hope), Marcus Katz, Tali Goodwin, art direction by Ciro Marchetti. Keswick, UK: Tarot Professionals, 2012. A reproduction deck of the original Game of Hope, with thirty-six cards, with German and Italian playing card inserts. Comes with translation of game booklet as also given in this book. Courtesy of the Trustees of the British Museum, produced under license. It comes with the first English translation of the game instructions, provided by Steph Myriel Es-Tragon.

- www.originallenormand.com

French Cartomancy. Laura Tuan, Torino, Italy: Lo Scarabeo, 2005. Playing card inserts. A version of the German Dondorf deck.

Blaue Eule (Blue Owl). Krummwisch, Germany: Konigsfurt-Urania, 1993. There are a number of versions of this deck with playing card inserts or verses.

No. 194115 Mlle Lenormand Wahrsagekarten Cartomancy Deck. Piatnik: Austria, 1986. The Piatnik deck is a favourite of many for its nostalgic images.

Cartomancia Lenormand. Da Afamada Cartomante De Paris. F.O.L. A Portuguese Brazilian deck with playing card inserts.

Contemporary Decks

In this section we list a selection of contemporary Lenormand decks, which are growing rapidly in number, due to an interest in this system of cartomancy. We personally recommend the Gilded Reverie (for which Tali cowrote the accompanying text and assisted with some design and extra cards) and the stylish Lenormand Revolution deck.

Gilded Reverie Lenormand. Ciro Marchetti. Self-published, 2012. This comes with extra cards with names such as "Time," "Dice," "Masque," and "Bridge." They were derived from the Game of Hope from which we get our standard Lenormand. The playing card correspondences are given in small inserts, allowing the main image to take precedence. There is also an iApp available for the deck.

- http://www.ciromarchetti.com/Lenormand.html

The Lenormand Revolution. Carrie Paris and Roz Foster. Self-published, 2012. Using themes and images from the French and American Revolutions, this deck is also available as an iApp.

- http://www.lenormandrevolution.com/

Alice in Wonderland Vintage Lenormand. Pepi Valderrama. Self-published, 2011. A collage deck with no playing card inserts.

- http://mystic.depepi.com/decks/

Mystique d'Epoque Petit Lenormand. Pepi Valderrama. Self-published, 2012. A collage deck with playing card references. (See URL from previous entry).

Palimpset Lenormand. Bertrand Saint-Guillain. Self-published, 2012. A cartomantic-centric deck where the playing card and Lenormand image are merged together.
- http://www.tarotparis.com/

Melissa Lenormand. Melissa Hill. Self-published, 2011. A montage deck with no playing card inserts.
- http://sassysibyl.com/oracledeck/

Steam Punk Fairy Oracle. Mary Hoy. Self-published, 2011. A new take on the Lenormand, depicts steampunk fairies and sprites from another dimension.
- http://www.etsy.com/shop/cageddreams

Mystical Lenormand. Urban Trosch. Nehausen, Switzerland: AGM Mueller, 2005. Archway frames with astrological symbols, no playing card inserts. The cards contain additional symbology not found in most Lenormand decks, such as the inclusion of the Garden of Eden, a Lion and a Lamb, and other such symbols on the Heart card.

Lenormand Oracle Cards. Torino, Italy: Lo Scarabeo, 2003. A straightforward and clear version of the images inside green borders. No inserts.

Les Vieux Jours Lenormand. A collaged deck, anonymously published, no inserts.
- http://www.lesvieuxjours.com/lenormand.html

Chronata's Minute Lenormand. Robyn Tich Hollister. Self-published, 2012. A hand-drawn Lenormand with no playing card inserts.

LeNormand Arlo. Self-published, 2009. Handmade with playing card inserts, square-cut.
- http://www.etsy.com/shop/Lavengro

The Victorian Lenormand. Willis Briggs. Self-published, 2012. A nicely laid out deck with the card given in all four corners.
- http://www.thevictorianlenormand.info/

Under the Roses Lenormand. Kendra Hurteau and Katrina Hill. Self-published, 2012. Available with and without keywords, as well as a mini-size.

- http://www.undertheroseslenormand.com

Lilac Twilight Lenormand. Anna Simonova. Self-published, 2012. A Russian deck with small icons for the playing card correspondences. Very purple, and very popular.

Mysteries of the Old Castle Lenormand. Anna Simonova. Self-published, 2012. As above, a Gothic-themed deck.

- http://yarasvera.ru/modules/catalog/cards.php?ItemId=342

Vintage Lenormand. Andi (Rootweaver) Graf. Self-published, 2013. A collage deck, no inserts.

- www.tarottaxi.com/

Other Decks (Non-Lenormand)

We here list several decks that may be confused with the 36-card "standard" Lenormand images. These various "oracle," "fortunetelling." and "Gypsy" decks contain variations of cards. The basic rules and methods presented here in Learning Lenormand can be applied to parts of these decks, however, you may require the Little White Book with the deck to decipher variant cards. There are also "Kipper" cards and the "Grand Jeu" type of decks, which are not the same as the Lenormand; they are listed here for completeness.

Original Kipper Wahrsage Karten. Altenburg, Germany: ASS. Fortune-Telling Cards with Astrological Symbols. These are Kipper cards, not Lenormand cards.

Petit Lenormand/Small Lenormand. St. Max: Grimaud. These are a version of the "Grand Jeu" type of "Lenormand" cards, with scenes of myth and flowers on each card, playing card inserts, and wording. They are not the Lenormand cards covered in this book. Whilst fascinating, if the box has Hercules wrestling a lion on the front of it, "these are not the cards you are looking for."

Le Jeu du Destin Antique. Vienna, Austria: Piatnik, 1944. Another version of fortunetelling cards. With playing card inserts.

Madame Le Normand's Fortune Telling System. Anon, Atglen, PA: Schiffer, 2008. A reproduction of the *Unerring Fortune Teller* book from 1866, with a pack of playing cards and dice. Not a Lenormand deck or system.

Gypsy Witch Fortune Telling Playing Cards. Stamford, CT: US Games System, 2012. Cards with playing card inserts and a helpful hint on every card. Not Lenormand cards.

Glossary

Blue Owl, White Owl, Red Owl: The colour of the owl refers to a title given to various Lenormand decks. Whilst these can be inconsistent, different versions have poems, German, French, and English versions, and/or plain card inserts. There may also be differences in art or colouring.

Cartomancy: The art of fortunetelling by divination using cards.

Charged Card (also known as Key Card): A card that has been mentally infused with intent, such as on an issue or objective.

Counting: A method of counting from one card to another to create a sequence of cards that is read in a linear fashion.

Facing Card: A card wherein the direction of its image gives more indication of its significance in the context of the cards either side of it.

Gipsy Fortunetelling Deck: Any generic title of fortunetelling cards can be over thirty-six cards in number.

Grand Tableau (GT): The layout or matrix often used for the reading of the Lenormand. The GT uses all thirty-six cards. It can also be used to denote the house in which a card falls.

House: In a Grand Tableau reading, all thirty-six positions are given a house based on the corresponding card number in sequence. The first position of the Grand Tableau is therefore the House of the Rider (1) and the final position is the House of the Cross (36). A house provides a context for the card placed within it.

Insert Playing Card: In some Lenormand decks, a corresponding playing card is depicted, which can be used with traditional cartomantic methods. There is sometimes a disparity between the playing card meaning in different tradions and the meaning of the Lenormand card in different traditions.

Kipper Deck: German Kipper cards, originally devised by Susanne Kipper of Berlin, Germany. There are thirty-six Kipper cards to the deck, although the images are not of the Lenormand symbols. To give some idea of the images and title, number 29 is the prison "Gefangnis." The prison is a sturdy grey four-turreted tower, with a brown tiled roof, surrounded by a crocodile-infested moat. Beyond the Prison is thick green forest, and a large bird of prey flies over head. The card has a green ornate picture frame inlay, and a green border around the outside of the card. The back of the card has lilac flocked wallpaper print and a vertical green almond shape containing a grey crouching monkey holding a crystal ball.

Knighting: The direction that you read the card in the style of knighting used in the game of chess. The move forms an L-shape, counting two in one direction and one in another.

L-Space: A term coined by Tali Goodwin for the "headset" or mental attitude for Lenormand reading, usually as distinct from T-space for the tarot mindset.

Lenormand Deck: The deck of thirty-six fortunetelling cards named after the celebrated sibyl Mlle. Marie-Anne Lenormand and based upon the design of "The Game of Hope" by J. K. Hechtel.

Literal Lenormand: A term coined for the reading method of the Lenormand, where an object literally stands for itself. Reading the cards out loud aids this approach, such as saying, "The Child is under the Sun and in the House of the Garden," from which arises a literal picture that is then applied to the divination.

Piquet (Picket): An early-sixteenth-century thirty-two-card deck and game for two players. This card game adds to the melting pot of cartomancy and first originated in Spain and France, and then migrated to Germany during the Thirty Years' War. It was considered a fashionable game to play and is still played by some today. It first became popular in England after the marriage of Mary I of England to King Phillip of Spain; back then it was known as "Cent" after the Spanish game Cientos. It later took on the French name of Piquet when King Charles I married Henrietta Maria of France in 1625.

Salon: The working environment for the art of fortunetelling.

Shadow: We use this term to denote how a card might overshadow cards closest to it. This entirely optional way of reading the Lenormand is a variation on tarot's reversals. Lenormand cards are not read reversed.

Sibyl: The Greek word for a prophetess, used by Marie-Anne Lenormand to mean the reader or fortuneteller.

Sitter: The person receiving a reading.

Wahrsagekarten: German for fortunetelling cards.

Zone: A nontraditional term we use for different areas of the Grand Tableau.

Bibliography

Anon. *Fortune-Telling by Cards by Madame Camille Le Normand.* New York: Robert M. De Witt, 1872.

Anon. *The Complete Book of Fortune.* Kensington: Associated Newspapers Ltd, 1936

Bärtschi, Judith. *Judith Bärtschi Lenormand.* Krummwisch, Germany: Konigsfurt-Urania, 2007.

Cirlot, J. E. *A Dictionary of Symbols.* London: Routledge & Kegan Paul, 1985.

Decker, Ronald, Thierry Depaulis, and Michael Dummett. *A Wicked Pack of Cards.* New York: St. Martins Press, 1996.

Dee, Jonathan. *Fortune-Telling with Playing Cards.* New York: Sterling/Zambezi, 2004.

Dos Ventos, Mario. *The Game of Destiny: Fortune-Telling with Lenormand Cards.* Self-published: 2007.

Droesbeke, Erna. *Kartenlegen mit Madam Lenormand.* Amsterdam, Netherlands: Iris, n.d.

Flamstead and Partridge. *New Fortune Book.* London: Printed for A. Bettesworth and C. Hinch, at the Red Lyon, Paternoster Row, 1710.

Foli, P. R. S. *Fortune-Telling by Cards.* London: C. Arthur Pearson Ltd., 1903.

Hasbrouck, Muriel Bruce. *Pursuit of Destiny*. London: John Gifford Ltd., 1949.

Hoffman, Detlef, and Erika Kroppenstedt. *Wahrsagekarten*. Frankfurt, Germany: The Historical Museum, 1972.

Hoffman, Detlef. *The Playing Card*. London: George Prior, 1973.

Kamm, Halina. *Lenormand Lernbook*. Hamburg, Germany: Corona, 2005.

Kent, Cicely. *Telling Fortunes by Cards*. London: Herbert Jenkins Ltd., n.d.

Kienle, Britta. *Easy to Learn Fortune Telling*. Esslingen, Germany: B. Kielne BriKa Verlag, 2001.

Mertz, Bernd A. *Wahrsagen Mit Karten der Madame Lenormand*. Munchen, Germany: Sudwest Verlag, 2004.

Morley, H. T. *Old and Curious Playing Cards*. London: Bracken Books, 1989.

Platt, Charles. *Card Fortune Telling*. London: W. Foulsham & Co., n.d.

Pullman, Philip. *The Northern Lights*. London: Scholastic, 1997.

Renner, Christiane. *Arbiten mit den Wahrsagekarten von Mademoiselle Lenormand*. Saarbruchen, Germany: Iris, 2007.

Silvestre, Colette. *Le Petit Lenormand*. Montpellier, France: Gange Editions, 2003.

Treppner, Iris. *Die Sybylle der Salons*. Munchen: Wilhelme Heyne Verlag Munchen, 2010.

Waite, Arthur Edward. *The Pictoral Key to the Tarot*. London: Rider, 1974.

Will, Georg Andreas. *Nürnbergisches Gelehrten-Lexicon oder Beschreibung aller Nürnbergischen Gelehrten beyderley Geschlechtes nach Ihrem Leben, Verdiensten und Schrifften…* Leipzig, Germany: Nopitsch, 1805.

Wilson, Robert Anton. *Quatum Psychology*. Phoenix: New Falcon, 1990.

Endnotes

1. Philip Pullman, *Northern Lights* (London: Scholastic, 2007), p. 79.

2. His Dark Materials Wiki: A list of the symbols of the Compass: http://www.randomhouse.com/features/pullman/materials/definitions.php [last accessed 10 September 2012].

3. *Northern Lights*, p. 173.

4. Ronald Decker, Thierry Depaulis, and Michael Dummett, *A Wicked Pack of Cards* (New York: St. Martin's Press, 1996), pp. 116–142.

5. Detlef Hoffmann and Erika Kroppenstedt, *Wahrsagekarten* (Bielefeld, Germany: Heinz Beier, 1972), p. 17, items 50–63.

6. *A Wicked Pack of Cards,* p. 124.

7. The British Museum Online Collection: A full set of photographs of the original Lenormand commissioned by Tarot Professionals. http://www.britishmuseum.org/research/search_the_collection_database/search_object_details.aspx?objectid=3145089&partid=1&searchText=Das+Spiel+der+Hofnung&fromADBC=ad&toADBC=ad&numpages=10&orig=%2fresearch%2fsearch_the_collection_database.aspx&currentPage=1

8. Georg Andreas Will, *Nürnbergisches Gelehrten-Lexicon oder Beschreibung aller Nürnbergischen Gelehrten beyderley Geschlechtes nach Ihrem Leben, Verdiensten und Schrifften…*, Leipzig, 1805. [brief biography of Hechtel].

9. Copies of the deck can be purchased at www.originallenormand.com.

10. See H. T. Morley's *Old and Curious Playing Cards* (London: Bracken Books, 1989), p. 64.

11. The Word of Playing Cards: A selection of biblical morality cards of the day: http://www.wopc.co.uk/germany/geistliche.html

12. The Wellcome Library: An article on early games: http://wellcomelibrary.blogspot.co.uk/2011_08_01_archive.html

13. W. L. Braekman, "Fortune-telling by the casting of dice," *Studia Neophilologica*, vol. 52, iss. 1, 1980.
George B. Parks, "The Genesis of Tudor Interest in Italian" *Publications of the Modern Language Association of America*, vol. 77, no. 5 (Dec. 1962), pp. 529-535.

14. The Original Lenormand site. A site dedicated to the reproduction of the Game of Hope by J. K. Hechtel: www.originallenormand.com

15. Gidget London's site. The home of the Stick-Peeps Lenormand deck: www.gidgetlondon.com

16. The Carrie Paris site, home of the Lenormand Revolution deck: www.carrieparis.com

17. Helen Farley, *A Cultural History of Tarot*, (London: I. B. Tauris & Co., 2009), pp. 84–88.

18. Arthur Edward Waite, *The Pictorial Key to the Tarot* (London: Rider, 1974), p. 134.

19. Jonathan Dee, *Fortune Telling with Playing Cards,* (New York: Sterling/Zambezi, 2004), p. 55.

20. Marcuz Katz and Tali Goodwin. *Around the Tarot in 78 Days,* (Woodbury, MN: Llewellyn, 2012).

21. Guess what? There was indeed a "Dog and Anchor" pub in Kidlington, England, in 1891.

22. Marcus Katz and Tali Goodwin, *Tarot Flip,* (Keswick, UK: Forge Press, 2011).

23. This is a Lenormand version of the formula of PRDS for reading tarot in Marcus Katz, *Tarosophy* (Chiang Mai: Salamander & Sons, 2011), pp. 110-11.

24. Another useful grouping of cards is into themes, such as the cards related to different types of relationship (Dog = friendship, Heart = love, Ring = Understanding and marriage, Sun = Happy marriage), for which see Colette Silvestre, *Le Petit Normand* (Montpellier, France: Gange Editions, 2003).

25. This was the case as it was discussed after the main reading had concluded.

26. See Marcus Katz and Tali Goodwin, *Around the Tarot in 78 Days,* (Woodbury, MN: Llewellyn, 2012); *Tarot Face to Face* (Woodbury, MN: Llewellyn, 2012).

27. Mike Hernandez, "Tarot and the Future: Predicting vs. Forecasting": http://mjhernandeztarot.wordpress.com/2010/08/07/tarot-and-the-future-predicting-vs-forecasting/

Art Credit List

1. Antique Lenormand cards containing a "butterfly" card, [unknown publisher (Katz & Goodwin Collection)

2. Antique Dondorf Lenormand, copyright 1840, in the public domain

3. A Portrait of Mlle. Lenormand from *L'Illustration*, 1843 (Katz & Goodwin Collection)

4. A Consultation with Mlle. Lenormand from *L'Illustration*, 1843 (Katz & Goodwin Collection)

5. Mlle. Lenormand prophesying for the Duchess of Berry, Princess Caroline, from *Dieux De L'Olympe*, 1833, published by Lenormand herself in Paris (Katz & Goodwin Collection)

6. Portrait of J. K. Hechtel, original print by Hessell & Schlemer, 1800 (Katz & Goodwin Collection)

7. Nuremberg Lottery Sheet, original manuscript, 1840 (Katz & Goodwin Collection)

8. The Woman card, Lilac Twilight Lenormand, used with permission of Anna Simonova

9. The Snake card, Vintage Lenormand, used with permission of Andi (Rootweaver) Graf

10. The Ship card, Minute Lenormand, used with permission of Robyn Tisch-Hollister

11. The Messenger card, Stick Figure Lenormand, used with permission of Gidget London

12. The Tree card, Lenormand Revolution, used with permission of Carrie Paris

13. The Tower card, The Original Lenormand, based on Das Spiel der Hoffnung, used under license, copyright Trustees of the British Museum

14. Medieval Tower of Nuremberg Castle and half-timbered buildings, Germany, 123rf.com/jenifoto, copyright 2011

15. Bouquet and Book cards, Antique Dondorf Lenormand

16. Lenormand Keyword Kaleidoscope 1, created by Llewellyn art department using Antique Dondorf Lenormand

17. Lenormand Keyword Kaleidoscope 2, created by Llewellyn art department, using Antique Dondorf Lenormand

18. The Rider from The Original Lenormand

19. The Clover from The Original Lenormand

20. The Ship from The Original Lenormand

21. The House from The Original Lenormand

22. The Tree from The Original Lenormand

23. The Clouds from The Original Lenormand

24. The Snake from The Original Lenormand

25. The Coffin from The Original Lenormand

26. The Bouquet from The Original Lenormand

27. The Scythe from The Original Lenormand

28. The Rod, Birch, Whip from The Original Lenormand

29. The Birds from The Original Lenormand

30. The Child from The Original Lenormand

31. The Fox from The Original Lenormand

32. The Bear from The Original Lenormand

33. The Stars from The Original Lenormand

34. The Stork from The Original Lenormand

35. The Dog from The Original Lenormand

36. The Tower from The Original Lenormand

37. The Garden from The Original Lenormand

38. The Mountain from The Original Lenormand

39. The Ways from The Original Lenormand

40. The Mice from The Original Lenormand

41. The Heart from The Original Lenormand

42. The Ring from The Original Lenormand

43. The Book from The Original Lenormand

44. The Letter from The Original Lenormand

45. The Gentleman from The Original Lenormand

46. The Lady from The Original Lenormand

47. The Lily from The Original Lenormand

48. The Sun from The Original Lenormand
49. The Moon from The Original Lenormand
50. The Key from The Original Lenormand
51. The Fish from The Original Lenormand
52. The Anchor from The Original Lenormand
53. The Cross from The Original Lenormand
54. Two Triads for Triplets, Antique Dondorf Lenormand
55. Three Cards for a Film, Antique Dondorf Lenormand
56. The Clover and The Fish, Antique Dondorf Lenormand
57. The Grand Tableau, Antique Dondorf Lenormand
58. Grand Tableaux 9 x 4, created by Katz & Goodwin
59. Grand Tableaux 8 x 4 + 4, created by Katz and Goodwin
60. Determining Past and Future, created by Llewellyn art department using Antique Dondorf Lenormand
61. The Gentleman and the Lady, created by Llewellyn art department using Antique Dondorf Lenormand
62. Cards in Relationship, created by Llewellyn art department using Antique Dondorf Lenormand
63. Career Three-Card Reading, Antique Dondorf Lenormand
64. Heart (Emotional) Nine-Card Layout, Antique Dondorf Lenormand
65. Ship (Travel) Nine-Card Layout, Antique Dondorf Lenormand
66. Book (Education) Nine-Card Layout, Antique Dondorf Lenormand
67. Book Layout Cross cards, Antique Dondorf Lenormand

68. Book Layout Diagonal cards, Antique Dondorf Lenormand

69. Bear (Health) Nine-Card Layout, Antique Dondorf Lenormand

70. Coffin (Spiritual Life) Nine-Card Layout, Antique Dondorf Lenormand

71. The Grand Tableau Master, Antique Dondorf Lenormand

72. The Foli Master Method, Antique Dondorf Lenormand

73. The Houses, Antique Dondorf Lenormand

74. The House Positions, created by Llewellyn art department

75. Work/Career in the House of the Owl, Antique Dondorf Lenormand

76. Love/Relationship in the House of the Owl, Antique Dondorf Lenormand

77. Diagonals on a GT, created by Llewellyn art department using Antique Dondorf Lenormand

78. Knighting in a GT, created by Llewellyn art department using Antique Dondorf Lenormand

79. Knighting in Chess, created by Llewellyn art department

80. Grand Tableau for Counting, created by Llewellyn art department using Antique Dondorf Lenormand

81. The Frame, created by Llewellyn art department

82. Past Frame and Future Frame, created by Llewellyn art department

83. Upper and Lower Frame, created by Llewellyn art department

84. Example of Above and Below Frame, Antique Dondorf Lenormand

85. The Four Pin Cards, created by Llewellyn art department

86. Label Cards, Antique Dondorf Lenormand

87. The Hidden Cross, Created by Llewellyn art department

88. The Key and The Coffin, Antique Dondorf Lenormand

89. A Grand Tableau Reading, Antique Dondorf Lenormand

90. GT for a Pet, Antique Dondorf Lenormand

GET MORE AT LLEWELLYN.COM

Visit us online to browse hundreds of our books and decks, plus sign up to receive our e-newsletters and exclusive online offers.

- Free tarot readings • Spell-a-Day • Moon phases
- Recipes, spells, and tips • Blogs • Encyclopedia
- Author interviews, articles, and upcoming events

GET SOCIAL WITH LLEWELLYN

Find us on **f**   🐦 @LlewellynBooks

www.Facebook.com/LlewellynBooks

GET BOOKS AT LLEWELLYN

LLEWELLYN ORDERING INFORMATION

Order online: Visit our website at www.llewellyn.com to select your books and place an order on our secure server.

Order by phone:
- Call toll free within the US at 1-877-NEW-WRLD (1-877-639-9753)
- We accept VISA, MasterCard, American Express, and Discover.

Order by mail:
Send the full price of your order (MN residents add 6.875% sales tax) in US funds plus postage and handling to: Llewellyn Worldwide, 2143 Wooddale Drive, Woodbury, MN 55125-2989

POSTAGE AND HANDLING

STANDARD (US): (Please allow 12 business days)
$30.00 and under, add $6.00.
$30.01 and over, FREE SHIPPING.

CANADA:
We cannot ship to Canada. Please shop your local bookstore or Amazon Canada.

INTERNATIONAL:
Customers pay the actual shipping cost to the final destination, which includes tracking information.

Visit us online for more shipping options. Prices subject to change.

FREE CATALOG!
To order, call 1-877-NEW-WRLD ext. 8236 or visit our website